THIS BOOK
IS
DEDICATED TO
OUR SIR
LATE PROFESSOR
DR. H.M. SRIVASTAVA

Preface

Book of Production & Operation has been designed as a basic text for students who have to study this book as a part of their commerce, management & engineering curriculum.

The orientation of Production & Operation Management as a practicing discipline has changed significantly world wide. The all important change pertains to the fact that the customer is now very much in the focus. All decisions have to be taken with the customer interest being the main or the only agenda. Production facilities, planning & control or production form the base of the subject, technique of method study & work measurement help in managing production more effectively. There are much nobler winds of change and corporate has come to realize that it has social responsibility. In fact all the production and manufacturing operation have to be perceived and perform as social actions.

A production plant is not only producing a physical product but also producing & providing a social good, a social service. In this competitive world, we are opening up our economy to the world. Quality considerations therefore have become all the more important. We have a detailed chapter on all aspect of quality in this book.

At last we have made an attempt to offer students a comprehensive book on production & operation management from the encouragement of our favorite teacher Former Director KNIT Sultanpur, Ex- Professor IIT- Bombay, Late Prof. (Dr.) H.M. Srivastava.

We shall welcome suggestions for improvement in the future edition of the book.

AUTHORS

Contents

Chapter 1

Introduction

1.1 Production Management

Production managers plan, direct, and coordinate the production behavior required to produce the measureless range of goods manufactured every year in any country. They formulate in nodoubt that production meets output and quality goals while remaining within resources. Depending on the size of the manufacturing plant, industrial production management may oversee the entire plant or just one area.

Industrial production management work out methods to use the plant's human resources and capital assets to best meet production goals. They may determine which machines will be used, whether new machinery need to be purchased, whether overtime or extra shifts are necessary, and what the series of manufacture will be. They monitor the production run to make sure that it stays on schedule and correct any problems that may arise.

Part of an industrial production manager's job is to come up with ways to make the production process more efficient. Traditional factory methods, such as mass assembly lines, have given way to "lean" production techniques, which give managers more flexibility. While in a traditional assembly line, each worker was responsible for only a small portion of the assembly, repeating that task on every product, lean production employs teams to build and assemble products in stations or cells, so rather than specializing in a specific task, workers are capable of performing all jobs within a team. Without the constraints of the traditional assembly line, industrial production managers can more easily change production levels and staffing on different product lines to minimize inventory levels and more quickly react to changing customer demands.

Industrial production managers also monitor product standards and implement quality control programs. They make sure the completed product meets a certain level of quality, and if not, they try to find out what the problem is and find a solution. While traditional quality control programs reacted only to problems that reached a certain significant level, newer management techniques and programs, such as ISO 9000, Total Quality Management (TQM), or Six Sigma, emphasize continuous quality improvement. If the problem relates to the quality of work performed in the plant, the manager may implement better training programs or reorganize the manufacturing process, often based upon the suggestions of employee teams. If the cause is substandard materials or parts from outside suppliers, the industrial production manager may work with the supplier to improve their quality.

Industrial production managers work directly with the other managers of the firm to implement the company's policies and goals. They also must work with the financial departments in order to come up with a budget and spending plan. They work the closest with the heads of sales, procurement and logistics. Sales managers relay the client's needs and the price the client is willing to pay to the production department, which must then fulfill the order. The logistics or distribution department handles the delivery of the goods, which often needs to be coordinated with the production department. The procurement department orders the supplies that the production department needs to make its products. It is also responsible for making sure that the inventories of supplies are maintained at proper levels so production precedes without break. A breakdown in communications between the production manager and the procurement department can cause slowdowns and a failure to meet production schedules. Just-in-time production techniques have reduced inventory levels, making constant communication among managers, suppliers, and procurement departments even more important.

In addition to management and financial skills, a production manager must have comprehensive knowledge of all production disciplines counting a systematic thoughtful of the interface of these disciplines during the production procedure. This may involve dealing with matters ranging from the procurement of staff, materials and services, to shipment, customs synchronization, telecommunications, labor relations, logistics, information technology, government liaison, venue booking, scheduling, operations management and workplace safety.

1.2 Operation Management

Operations management is an area of industry that is concerned with the production of good quality goods and services, and involves the answerability of ensuring that business operations are well-organized and resourceful. It is the management of resources, the allocation of goods and services to customers, and the analysis of queue systems.

APICS The Association for Operations Management also defines operations management as "the field of study that focuses on the effectively planning, scheduling, use and control of a built-up or service organization through the study of concepts from design engineering, industrial engineering, management information systems, quality management, production management, inventory management, accounting, and other functions as they affect the organization".

Additionally, the *Operations Management Body of Knowledge* (OMBOK) Framework defines the scope of operations management and the activities and techniques that are a part of the operations management profession.

An operation also refers to the production of goods and services, the set of value-added activities that convert inputs into many outputs. Basically, these value-adding creative activities should be associated with market opportunity for optimal enterprise presentation.

Production is crucial part between all functional areas of industrial organizations. It is a process by which raw materials and other inputs are converted into finished product.

Word 'Manufacturing' is understood to refer to the process of producing only tangible goods, whereas production includes creation of both tangible as well as services.

Nature of production is very easy to understand, if we see the manufacturing function from three angles.

1- Production as a system
2- Production as an organizational function
&
3- Decision making in production.

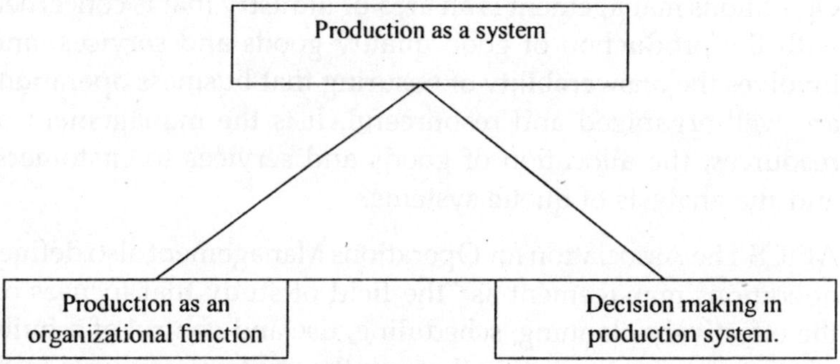

Fig: 1 Nature of Production

1.3 Production as a System

1.3.1 Production System Model:

A system means as whole which cannot work in parts. It must be studied as a whole, so production system is also the combination of three sub-systems:

1- Production System: A system, whose function is to convert a set of inputs into a set of desired outputs.
2- Conversion/ Process Sub-System: A sub System of the larger production system where, inputs are converted into outputs.
3- Control Sub-System: A sub-system of the larger production system where, a portion of the output is monitored for feedback signals to provide corrective action, if required.

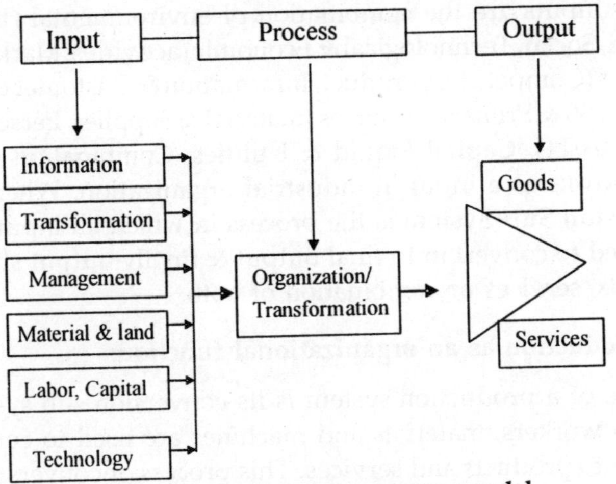

Fig: 2 - Production process system model

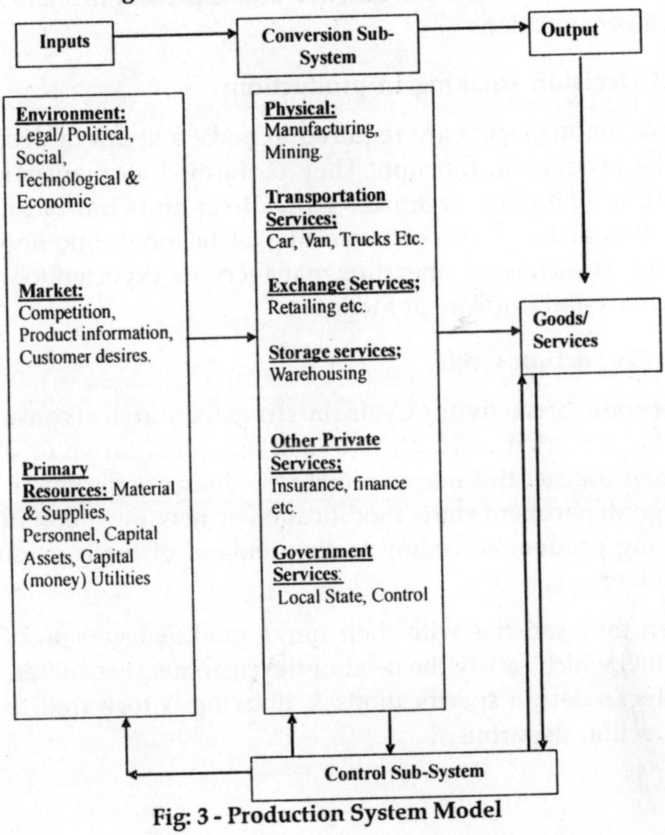

Fig: 3 - Production System Model

Inputs: Inputs are the combination of environmental (Legal, Political, Social, Technological & Economic) activities, Marketing activities (Competition, Product, Information & Customer desire & feedback) & Primary resources (material & Supplies, Personnel, Capital assets, Capital Liquid & Utilities. Combination of all above works as a input in industrial organization. Where as, **Conversion Sub-System** is the process in which all inputs are processed to convert in to final output & finally **output** should be goods/services or combination of both.

1.3.2 Production as an organizational function:

The core of a production system is its conversion sub system, wherein workers, materials and machines are used to convert inputs into products and services. This process of conversion is at the heart of production function and is present in some form in all organizations.

1.3.3 Decision –making in production:

Operation managers are required to make a series of decision in the production function. They performed all management function like plan, organize, staff, direct and control all the activities in the process of converting all the inputs into finished goods. At each level, operating managers are expected to make decisions and implement them too.

1.4 Production Cycle:

The production activity/ Cycle start from the search of consumer needs or market research. The marketing executive or other sources transfer this information to the design department. The design department starts modification or new invention in the existing product according to the demand of the consumer/ customer.

When they satisfies with their new/ modified version of his product which satisfy the need of the customer/consumer. The product's design specifications & drawing is forwarded to the production department.

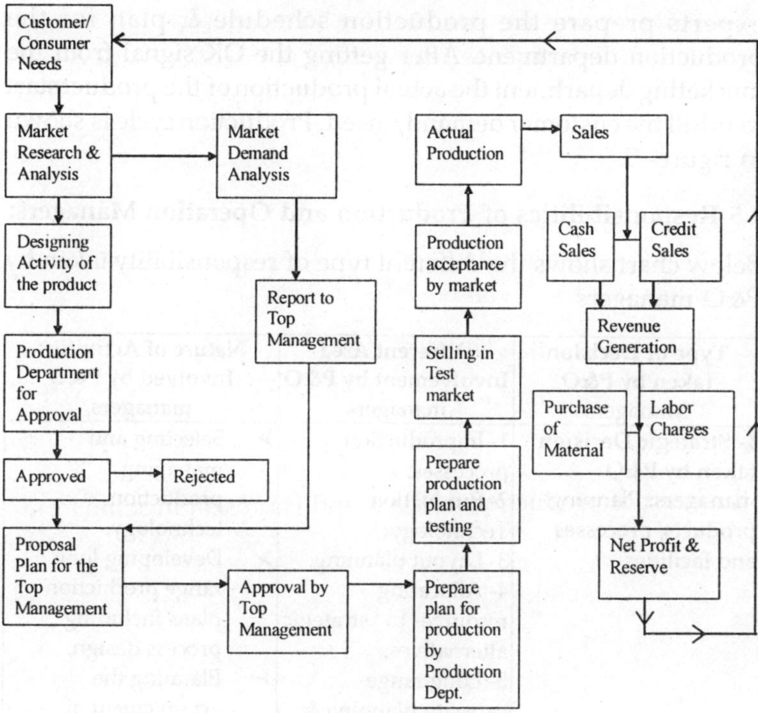

Fig: 5 Production Cycle

The production department verifies whether the product can be manufactured with the technology & skill available in the firm. If yes, it will give the acceptance otherwise the production manager, design engineer & marketing manager discuss together and make alteration in the product without sacrificing the customer needs. When the design of the product is approved by the entire design department, they conduct the market survey, verify the demand then submit its sales program to the higher management.

The top management, verifying the proposal through his experts and sanctions the budget & give OK signal for production. Production department produce a trial run and marketing department release the product in the test markets to get customer acceptance or feedback. In the mean time production experts prepare the production schedule & plan for the production department. After getting the OK signal from the marketing department the actual production of the product start to fulfill the customer demand/ need. Production cycle is shown in figure- 5.

1.5 Responsibilities of Production and Operation Managers:

Below chart shows the different type of responsibility taken by P&O managers.

Type of Decision taken by P&O Managers	Different Area Involvement by P&O managers	Nature of Activities Involved by P&O managers
1- Strategic Decision taken by P&O managers: Planning products, processes and facilities.	1- In production processes. 2- Production Technology. 3- Layout planning. 4- Allocating resources to strategic alternatives. 5- Long range capacity planning & facility location.	➢ Selecting and managing production technology. ➢ Developing long range production plans including process design. ➢ Planning the arrangement of facilities. ➢ Planning for the optimal distribution of scarce resources among product lines or business units. ➢ Answering the 'how much' and 'where' question about long range production capacity.
2- Operating Decisions taken by P&O managers: Planning production to meet demand	1- Production planning system. 2- Demand inventory system 3- Resource requirements system.	➢ Aggregate planning and master production scheduling. ➢ Planning and controlling finished goods inventories.

	4- Shop floor planning & control. 5- Material management.	➢ Short range decisions about what to produce and when to produce at each work centre. ➢ Managing all facts of materials system.
3- Control decision taken by P&O managers: Planning and controlling Operations.	1- Productivity and employees. 2- Total Quality control. 3- Project planning and control techniques. 4- Maintenance management and reliability.	➢ Planning for the effective and efficient use of human resources in operations. ➢ Planning and controlling the quality of products and services. ➢ Planning and controlling projects. ➢ Planning for maintaining the machines and facilities of production.

1.6 New Product Development:

A product is anything (tangible / or intangible) that is capable of satisfying desired need. Truly innovative, significantly & scientifically different from other existing product is called new products.

The development of a new product passes through eight distinct stages (See in figure.). The stages are: Idea generation, feasibility study, advanced design, detailed engineering design, production process design & development, product evaluation, product improvement, product use & support.

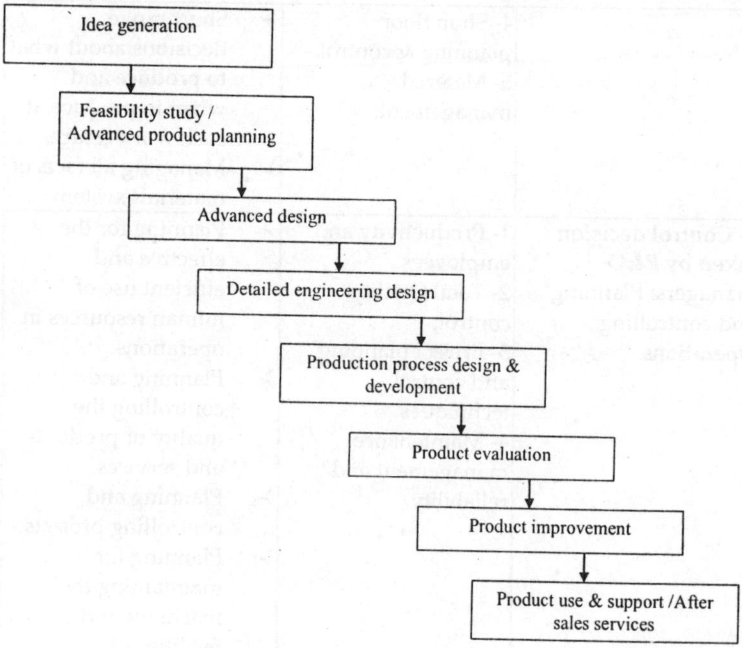

Fig: New product development

1.6.1 Idea generation: Idea generation comes after need identification. New product development process starts after identifying the need and idea gives the way to satisfy that need through new and unique product. Idea comes from customer, top management, staff of the marketing department, production department or from the R&D section.

Once the product idea comes on floor; it must be demonstrated that, the new product satisfy some customer need, & that existing products fail to satisfy the need.

1.6.2 Feasibility study: Feasibility study means advanced product planning includes preliminary market research, searching alternative concepts for the product; identifying operational requirements, establishing design criteria & their priorities; & estimating supply chain management system of the product in the market.

At this stage, conceptual design of the product shall emerge. The conceptual design for a mobile, for example, would articulate its length, weight, strength, shape, colours, technology, retail price & so on. Concept design is finalized by the production & operation management. Such joint effort would also help design and test new production processes early in the development process.

1.6.3 Advanced design: Now we further move to next step that is advanced design. In this step the main function are detailed through investigation by basic and applied researchers into technical feasibility and also identifying the trade offs in product design.

Promising design alternatives are evaluated according to critical parameters to determine whether design support such as analytical testing, experimentation, physical modeling & prototype testing will be required.

1.6.4 Detailed engineering design: This stage is important stage because it depends on all engineering activities. This stage involves a series of engineering activities to develop a standard definition of the product, including its system, sub-system, component, materials, size, length, strength, and so on.

The engineering process involve analysis, experimentation, & data collection, to find design. In this stage engineers ensure that product perform as per standard, consistently & at optimum cost. The product should be safe and cost should be optimal. They ensure that the design should be of optimal design.

1.6.5 Production process design & development: Armed with the detailed product design, engineers and manufacturing experts prepare plans for material acquisition; production; warehousing; transportation & distribution. This stage also involves planning for other supporting systems suchas controls information & human resources.

1.6.6 Product evaluation & improvement: After launching the product in the market the evaluation & improvement process plays a vital role. Field performance and failure data, technical breakthrough in materials & equipment & formal research are used to monitor; analysis if necessary; redesign and re- evaluate the product.

1.6.7 After sales services: In this stage professions try to give the answer of the customer's questions which comes in the mind of the consumers or customers like: how to run the product? About warranty & repair services, replacement of the parts and up-gradation of the product etc.

1.7 Classification of the operations:

Production system varies from factory to factory and from product to product. However, one of the most issues is production volume. The production systems can be classified as Job shop, Batch, mass, continuous production system.

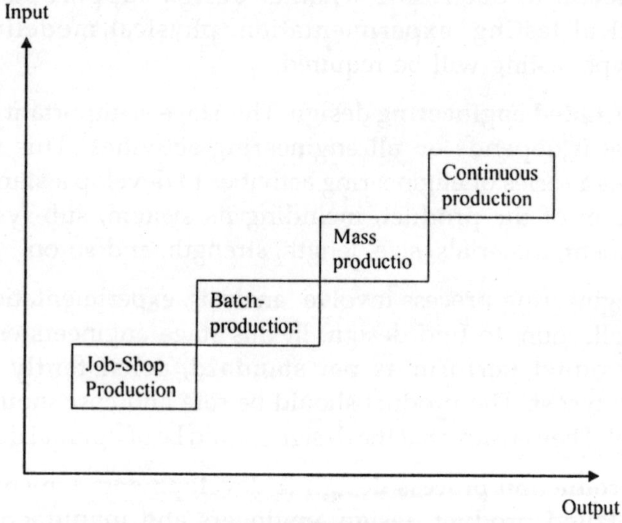

Fig: Classification of Production System

1.7.1 Job-shop production:

The job shop production system is characterized by the low production volume. A job shop comprises of general purpose machines arranged into different departments. Each and every job uses unique technological requirements, demand processing on machines in a certain sequence. It has following characteristics:

1- Commonly used to meet a particular customer need.
2- Production lot size is usually small.
3- Variety in product is usually very high.
4- Equipments used in production system are mostly general-purpose and flexible to meet specific customer order, which varies from time to time.
5- Highly skilled labor is needed to handle the equipments, as variety and product range are very high.

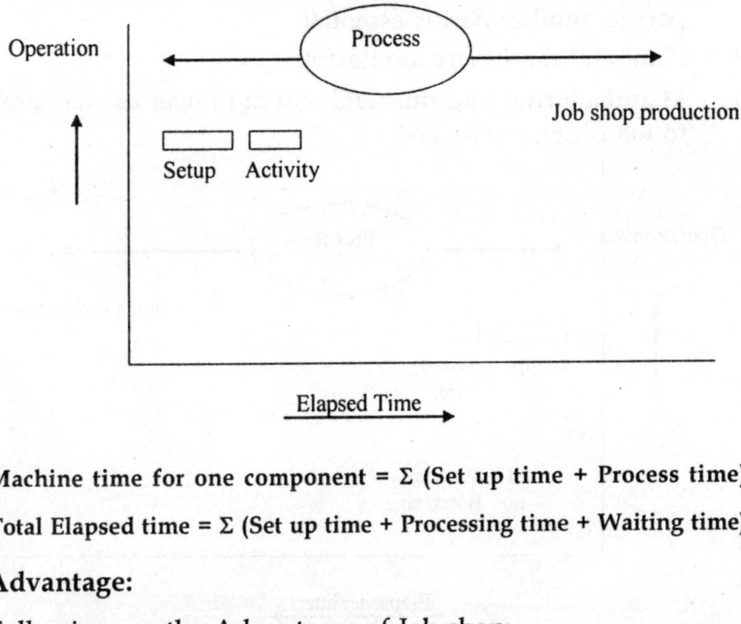

Machine time for one component = Σ (Set up time + Process time)

Total Elapsed time = Σ (Set up time + Processing time + Waiting time)

Advantage:

Following are the Advantages of Job shop:

1- General purpose machines and different facilities help to produce variety of products.
2- Operators will become more skilled and competent, as each job gives them learning opportunities.
3- Maximum potential of operator can be utilized.
4- Opportunity generates creative methods and innovative ideas.

1.7.2 Batch Production:

Batch production is suited for medium volume lot of same variety. It is characterized by the manufacture of limited number of products produced at regular intervals and stocks awaiting sales. The importance of batch production in current manufacturing scenario can be well realized, as according to a study, more than 75% parts manufactured worldwide are in batches of 50 or less. Batch production is characterized by:

1- Commonly used to meet repeated customer order.
2- Production lot size is medium and in batches. This may be despite continuous orders from the customer, as part variety is also medium and, therefore, switch over from one part to another part is essential.
3- Plant and machinery are flexible.
4- Manufacturing lead time and cost are lower as compared to job order production.

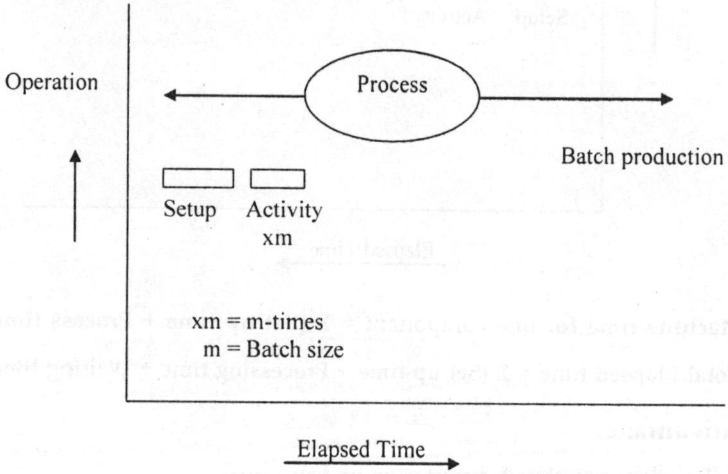

Fig: Activities Vs Time in batch production

Machine time for one component = ½ Σ (Setup time + Σ Processing time per part)

Total Elapsed time = Total Set-up time + n Σ Processing time per part

Advantages:

Following are the advantages of batch Production:

1- Better utilization of plant and machinery.

2- Cost per unit is lower as compared to job order production.

3- Promotes functional specialization.

4- Job satisfaction exists for operators.

1.7.3 Mass Production:

Mass production is suited for the manufacturing of continuous identical parts. Production rate is generally high. The machines are arranged in a line or product layout. Product and process standardization exists and all outputs follow the same path. It characterized by the followings:

1- Particularly suited for high demand items.

2- Production lot size is very high and production rate is continuous.

3- Product variety is very low, which may be one of its kinds.

4- Special purpose tools and equipments may be needed.

5- Lower in process inventory.

6- Material handling can be completely automatic.

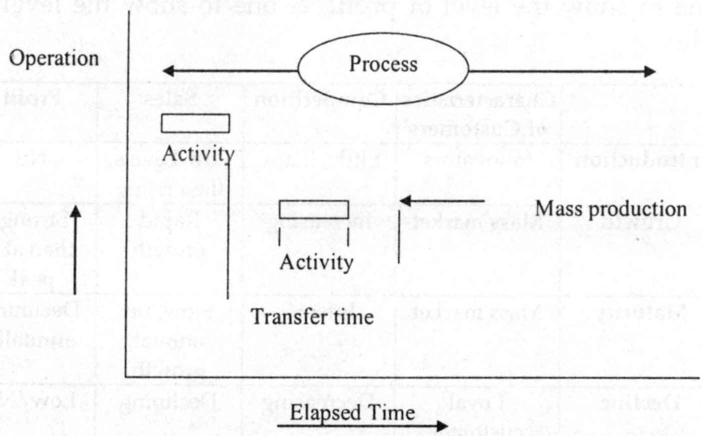

Fig: Activities Vs Time in Mass production

Machine time for one component = Processing time + Transfer time

Total Elapsed time = Processing time + Transfer time

1.7.4 Continuous Production: Continuous production is very common in food processing industry, drugs & chemical industry. This is a special type of production system. Production facilities are arranged as per the sequence of production operations from the first operation to the last operation. All such controls are generally automatic and computer controlled.

1.8 Product Life Cycle:

To be able to market its product properly, a firm must be aware of the product life cycle of its product. The standard product life cycle tends to have five phases: Development, Introduction, Growth, Maturity, & finally Decline.

The concept of product life applies to a generic category of a product and not to specific brands. A product life cycle consists of the aggregate demand over an extended period of time for all brands comprising a generic product category.

It can also be shown graphically. The graph often has two lines- One to show the level of profit, & one to show the level of sales.

	Characteristics of Customers	**Competition**	**Sales**	**Profit**
Introduction	Innovators	Little, if any	Low Levels, then rising	Nil
Growth	Mass market	Increasing	Rapid growth	Strong, then at a peak
Maturity	Mass market	Intense	Slow, no annual growth	Declining annually
Decline	Loyal customer	Decreasing	Declining	Low/Nil

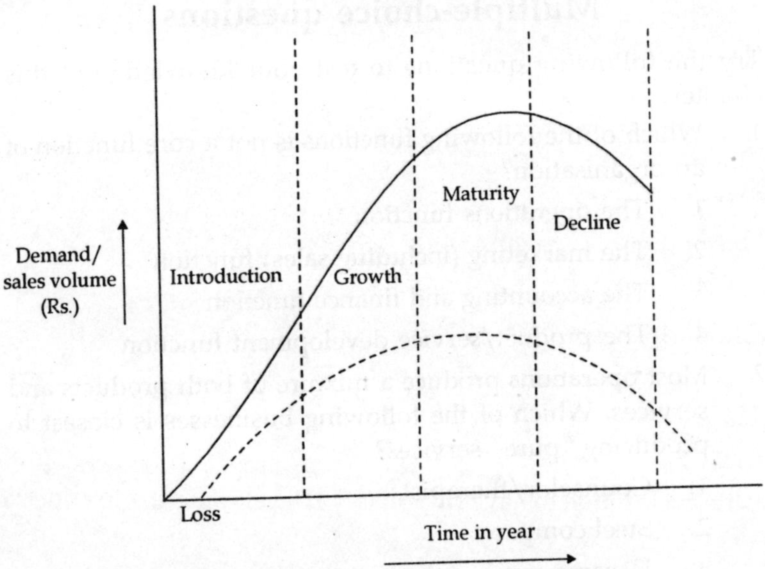

Fig: Product life cycle of a Product Category

Multiple-choice questions

Try the following questions to test your knowledge of this chapter.

1 Which of the following functions is not a core function of an organisation?

1. The operations function
2. The marketing (including sales) function
3. The accounting and finance function
4. The product/service development function

2 Most operations produce a mixture of both products and services. Which of the following businesses is closest to producing "pure" services?

1. Counselor/therapist
2. Steel company
3. IT company
4. A Restaurant

3 . Operations can be classified according to their volume and variety of production as well as the degree of variation and visibility. Which of the following operations would be classified as high volume, low variety?

1. A family doctor
2. A carpenter
3. A front office bank
4. A fast food restaurant

4. Which of the following activities is not a direct responsibility of operations management?

1. Determining the exact mix of products and services that customers will want
2. Designing the operation's products, services and processes
3. Planning and controlling the operation
4. Developing an operations strategy for the operation

5. Operations can be classified according to the degree of variation in demand and visibility of the operation as well as their volume and variety of production. Which of the following operations would be classified as high variation and high visibility?
   1. A family doctor
   2. A front office bank
   3. A fast food restaurant
   4. A carpenter
6. Which of the following would *not* normally be considered a general characteristic of a service?
   1. Many services involve both tangible and intangible outputs
   2. Low contact services can often be made more efficient than high contact services
   3. Production and consumption can always be spatially separated
   4. Production and sales cannot easily be separated functionally
   5. Production and consumption are simultaneous
7. Which of the following would *not* be normally considered as a key feature of Operations Management?
   1. World class Operations can give an organisation competitive advantage
   2. Most new technology is implemented in Operations areas
   3. Operations is the part of an organisation which creates wealth through the management of the transformation process
   4. Operations is the area of a business where most people work
   5. Operations researches mathematical techniques for optimising processes
8. Which of the following is the least likely decision to be

made by Operations Managers?

1. Selecting the location and layout of a facility
2. Designing and improving the jobs of the workforce
3. How much capacity is required to balance demand
4. Deciding which market areas to manufacture products for
5. How to use quality techniques to reduce waste

Discussion questions

1. The port of Vishakhapattnam is the largest port in India. It provides a vital link between sea-based transportation of cargo and inland transport into India such as rail, road and inland waterways. List the transformation processes which you think the port's operations managers have to run, and identify their inputs and outputs.
2. Describe the operations of the following organizations using the transformation model. Carefully identify the transforming resources, transformed resources, the type of transformation process and the outputs from the transformation process for:
   - An international airport
   - A supermarket
   - A high-volume car plant.
3. What mixture of goods and services is produced by the following operations?
   - Airbus Industries
   - The Channel Tunnel
   - Marks & Spencer
   - Federal Express parcel service
   - Volvo motor cars
   - Novotel hotels.
4. Why is operations management relevant to managers in other organization functions?
5. Explain the difference between micro and macro opera-

tions. Describe some of the micro operations in a university and discuss the relationships between their internal customers and suppliers.

6. Talk with an operations manager from a local organization and find out what he (or she) says or does and how he or she works with the organization's marketing, financial, personnel and purchasing functions.
7. Draw the hierarchy of operations for a small manufacturing company.
8. What are the main differences between internal and external customers?
9. Describe the relative volume, variety, variation and customer contact for the following organizations:
   - A theme park
   - A bread bakery
   - A dentist.
10. Explain the advantages and disadvantages to an operation of reducing its volume, variety and 'visibility'. How could a university change volume, variety and 'visibility' in order to reduce its costs?
11. What do you think would be the main design, planning and control and improvement activities in a large airport such as Indira Gandhi Airport?
12. Over recent years there has been a resurgence of interest in operations management in universities but especially in business. Why do you think this is?

Short Case (Case Study)

- A business trip to Delhi

My flight to Stockholm would be late landing. The pilot told us that we were in a 'stack' of planes circling above the snow clouds that were giving Delhi its first taste of winter. Air traffic control had closed the runways for a short period at dawn and the early morning flights from all around India were now being allocated new landing slots along with the long-haul jumbos from the Far East and the India. After a 20-minute delay, we descended bumpily through the clouds and landed on a recently cleared runway. Even then there was a further 'hold' on a taxiway; we were told that the de-icing of the apron was being completed so that planes could proceed to their allocated stands and air bridges. All around the airport I could see the scurrying flashing beacons of the snow-clearing vehicles, the catering suppliers' vans, the aviation fuel trucks, the baggage trailers, buses transporting crews and passengers, security police cars, and an assortment of other vehicles all going purposefully about their work. Indira Gandhi airport always looks busy, with over 10 million passengers a year, but this morning the complexity and scale of the operations were particularly evident.

Finally, about an hour late, we pulled up to the gate, the engines were turned off, and we disembarked into an icy-cold air bridge, leaving behind a particularly untidy plane strewn with litter from a full cabin of restless passengers. We passed the team of cleaners and maintenance staff waiting just outside. 'They will have a hard time this morning; more mess to clear and probably less time than usual to do it, as the airline will want a quick turnaround to get back on to schedule,' I commented to my colleagues. We could just hear the sounds of frantic activities going on below the plane: baggage and cargo being unloaded, catering vehicles arriving, fuel being loaded and technicians checking over the engines and control surfaces. Everyone trying to get their work completed quickly and correctly, not least so that they could get back indoors out of the biting cold wind!

From the air bridge we walked past the crowded seating areas, where plane-sized groups were gathering anxiously awaiting the signal from the gate staff to board their much delayed flights. Then on to the moving walkways, conveyed leisurely past other departure lounges, equally overfilled with passengers. Anxious to get ahead of the crowd, we took to a running pace past the rows of cafés, bars and shops, hoping to avoid the usual morning queue for Passport Control. I should have remembered the old saying 'more haste, less speed' because my next journey was to the First Aid room! I had apparently slipped on some spilt coffee that had not been cleaned up in the haste of the morning, and had fallen awkwardly, straining my ankle and breaking my duty-free brandy. 'At least they would clean the floor after that,' I thought, sadly.

Suitably patched up, I hobbled with my colleagues and joined the long queue for Passport Control, and eventually through to Baggage Reclaim. Even with the excellent new baggage-handling systems in Delhi, the passengers usually get there first, but the accident had changed all that! Scanning the video screens, we found no reference to our flight arrival; the remaining bags from our flight had apparently already been removed from the carousel and were stored in an adjacent office. After a simple signing ceremony, we were reunited with our belongings, and hastened (slowly in my case) to the taxi rank. Our hopes of a quick ride to the city were dispelled when we saw the long queue in the icy wind, so we made our way to the station below, where a dedicated 'City Express' train departs every 20 minutes for the *Noida* and *Greter Noida.* We just missed one!

After a busy and successful day at our Delhi office, a taxi was called, and we were back at the airport in the thick of the evening rush hour. The departures check-in area is the upper floor of a vast new terminal extension, and is very orderly and well equipped. Facing you on entry from the taxi drop-off point is a huge electronic display which lists all departures scheduled for the next few hours and showing the appropriate check-in desk number for each flight. The speed of the check-in systems has been improved dramatically, so there was no queue at our desk, and the three of us were issued with boarding passes in only a couple of minutes. Our baggage sped away on conveyors down to the new sorting hall two storeys below. Brochures explain that the new terminal extension was designed to make it possible to go from check-in to final boarding in only 20 minutes, which has involved investment in a state-of-the-art automated baggage-handling system. On my last visit, following traffic delays on the way to the airport, I found that this system works, but I doubt that it would if everyone arrived only 20 minutes before departure! It is no wonder that they advise checking in one hour before; it also gives passengers much more time to spend money in the duty-free shops, restaurants and bars!

By this time, my injured leg had swollen up and was throbbing painfully. This seemed to be a routine situation for the check-in staff, who arranged for a wheelchair and attendant to take me through Border Control and security checks. While my colleagues travelled down to the departures hall by escalator, I took the slower route by lift, meeting just outside the duty-free shops where the attendant left them to take care of me. We had some time to spare, so we replenished the brandy, bought some Coconut chocolates and headed for a café-bar. While Delhi is renowned for its excellent cuisine, we didn't expect to find high standards of food in the quick-service environment of an airport, but we were wrong! The delicious aromas of freshly prepared food attracted our custom, and we weren't disappointed. After a welcome glass of speciality raspberry-flavoured beer to round off the meal, we headed for the airline's executive lounge.

The view across the airfield was not promising! After a bright, crisp day, more snow-laden clouds had arrived and a chill wind cut across the tarmac. De-icing crews were working on the parked aircraft and others were treating the runways, taking quick action between the aircraft movements. Concerned that we might be delayed and miss our connection at Lucknow, we checked with the staff at the airline's flight information desk. After some phoning, they confirmed that, although there could be some delays, Lucknow had arranged to hold connecting flights, as many passengers originated from Delhi. Their professional and friendly advice made us feel much more at ease, and they even offered to allow us to send fax or phone messages to our destination. They couldn't have been more helpful.

Announcements of the minor delays were made over the speaker system, but it wasn't long before we were directed to the departure lounge and were preparing to board. Outside, around the aircraft in the gloom, the baggage trucks were pulling away and the giant push-off tractor was being connected up to the nose-wheel. Ten minutes later, we were at the end of the runway, ready for take-off.

'Today must have been a very busy one for everyone involved in keeping the airport open,' I thought, 'but perhaps every day has its own challenges in such a complex operation.'

Questions

1 Identify all the micro operations and their activities which are mentioned.

2 Classify them in accordance with their type.

3 Which of these micro operations were most affected by the severe weather?

4 Approximately how many different organizations are involved in delivering the goods and services described in this report? What are the implications of this?

Answer

A Business Trip to Delhi

1. Identify all the micro operations and their activities which are mentioned.

The micro operations are categorized in 'order of appearance'. In class this stage can be missed, going straight on to the analysis matrix. For assessed work both steps would probably be used.

2. Classify them in accordance with the structure.

Starting with the blank matrix, and filling it out on the board or overhead projector is a really good way of getting interaction with a big class early on a course. Everyone has an opinion, and there is a lot of debate about where each activity should fit. Often, of course, there are many places to put some activities, so we may decide to classify only dominant types of processing. In each case ask what is being processed (material, information, customers) and how is it being transformed to give value-added. The downside of this approach is the time it will take: allow at least half an hour for about 20 activities filled in.

3. Which of these micro operations were most affected by the severe weather?

The case study describes the effects of severe weather on the daily micro operations within the airport. All the micro operations listed in Question 1 have a challenge to meet due to the weather conditions, but in the majority of cases this is not caused directly by the weather. Rather, the severe weather affects some micro operations which in turn cause problems in other micro operations. This creates an operational 'chain reaction',

Air Traffic Control (ATC) reacts to the severe weather first by closing and later reopening the airfield. This micro operation then uses the limited flexibility of its operations by rescheduling aircraft take-off and landing slots. Meanwhile, on the airfield itself, runway clearance and de-icing operations commence as a direct consequence of the severe weather.

The ongoing rescheduling of the flights has consequences for information processing operations (general flight information, inter-airport communications and customer announcements) and operations involved in aircraft turnaround. ATC cannot, however, break the safety rules for separation of aircraft, and often increases effective capacity by batching groups of landings and then of takeoffs. One may therefore assume that many flights have been compacted, shortening the time between them.

Consequently, many operations have to increase their speed and flexibility to meet this challenge.

The micro operations affected are inflight catering, aviation refuelling, baggage handling, cabin cleaning, servicing units, technical maintenance, passenger/crew transport, departure gate control, check-in desk, and push-off tractors.

Further consequences of ATC's rescheduling are flight delays. This means that capacity within the airport is stretched - more people are waiting in the airport for flights, so this area becomes a bottleneck.

A number of micro operations are affected by an increase in people (WIP). This can be a problem - for example, airport catering facilities need to increase the speed and flexibility of their operations to increase the volume of customers served. There may also be a shortage of seating in departure lounges. However, this situation can also be advantageous, as trade will increase for catering and retail facilities. Frustrated customers may complain more, taking scarce capacity away from more serving.

In this case, the micro operations affected are customer waiting areas, customer transportation, airport catering, shops, first aid, airport cleaning, border control, customs, left luggage, flight information desk and customer announcements.

Rescheduled flights and flight delays are not necessarily caused by the severe weather. Other causes could be ATC strikes or technical problems. Similarly, flight delays will increase the number of people waiting in the terminal, but this can also occur for other reasons, e.g. busy holiday periods.

Therefore, the micro operations which are most affected by the severe weather are those which are affected directly - Air Traffic Control, de-icing and runway clearance.

4. Approximately how many different organizations are involved in delivering the goods and services described in this report?

It appears that there is a different organization for each micro operation listed in question 1. The table below, although by no means exhaustive, lists the majority.

What are the implications of this?

a) The airport appears to operate as a co-operative between a numbers of different organizations which are located in the same area. The airport itself will have some overall management, but this will not be directly responsible for all the separate organizations. Consequently, co-operation between all the organizations is necessary to ensure the macro operation of the airport itself is effective.

b) Despite all of the organizations forming part of the airport macro operation, each organization has its own individual objective. These objectives may sometimes conflict. For example, the objective of the Air Traffic Control organization could be to ensure that all flights safely leave and land on time with minimal disruption to the crew, passengers and technical staff, and the objective of a gift shop would be to maximise profits. In the case study, Air Traffic Control has failed to meet its objectives because the weather has caused flight delays, yet the gift shop may have increased its sales for the day because the delay has resulted in more passengers waiting in the terminal.

c) The typical passenger may be unaware of the number of separate organizations involved in the airport macro operation, seeing each micro operation as an indication of the level of service in the airport itself. Therefore, if a particular organization fails to meet its objectives, this will reflect on the customer's perception of service in the airport as a whole. For example, the writer of the case study may identify the service at Delhi Airport in general as being careless because they slipped on spilt coffee, rather than associating the problem with just the cleaning company.

Footnote:

Although not specifically included in the questions, the tutor could use this case to discuss the Input-Transformation-Output model for each micro operation. When we teach it now at Warwick we also look at the key performance objectives of some different micro operations. For example (not a comprehensive list):

Speed (responsiveness) is critical:

- Fire service
- First aid
- De-icing services

Dependability is critical:

- Air Traffic Control
- Customer conveyors
- Baggage handling

Quality (conformance to process and specification) is critical:

- Check-ins
- Refuelling
- Inflight food preparation

Flexibility is critical (because of wide range of outputs required):

- Information desk
- Aircraft servicing
- Airport police

Cost is critical:

- Economy in-flight catering
- Certain retailers (newsagent, fast food)
- Cleaning services

Multiple Choice Questions

Try the following questions to test your knowledge of this chapter.

1. There are four perspectives on operations strategy. The term emergent strategy is most closely associated with which perspective?
    1. Operations resources perspective
    2. Top-down perspective
    3. Market requirements perspective
    4. Bottom-up perspective
2. There are four perspectives on operations strategy. The term core competency is most closely associated with which perspective?
    1. Market requirements perspective
    2. Top-down perspective

   3. Operations resources perspective
   4. Bottom-up perspective

3. An order-winning factor could be described as:
   1. A factor which directly and significantly contribute to winning business
   2. A factor which is at a higher level than the standard for the industry
   3. A factor which may be of significant in other parts of the organisation
   4. A factor which has to be above a particular level to be considered by the customer

4. In the growth stage of the product/service life cycle, the operation is likely to focus on which combination of performance objectives?
   1. Speed, Dependability and Cost
   2. Dependability, Quality and Cost
   3. Speed, Quality and Cost
   4. Speed, Dependability and Quality

5. A model for comparing the gap between market requirements and achieved performance is:
   1. The operations strategy matrix
   2. The Hill methodology
   3. The Operations resources perspective
   4. The Platts-Gregory procedure

6. A successful Operations Strategy would often address the following issues:
   1. Distinctive Capabilities, Performance Goals, Core Competencies
   2. Economic Order Quantities, Stock Replenishment, Route Planning
   3. Marketing Capability, Production Scheduling, Equipment Maintenance
   4. Sales Forecasts, Work Study, Method Study

5. Joint Ventures, Technology Transfer, Measures of Performance

Discussion questions

1. Explain the difference between corporate strategy, business strategy and functional strategy. Illustrate for the Disney Corporation.
2. Describe what you think is the business strategy for your university (you might like to have this confirmed). Describe what you think might be the strategies of some of the micro operations, such as the library, catering, student union and grounds maintenance. You might like to compare your views with those of the managers of some of these operations.
3. Illustrate how the four perspectives would operate in a 'not-for-profit' organization such as a charity which provides hostel accommodation and other welfare services to the homeless.
4. Explain how an individual branch of a large supermarket chain can:
   a) Contribute directly to the strategic aims of the whole company;
   b) Help other parts of the company to contribute.
5. Take the example of a prison and describe the specific needs of the different groups of customers (prisoners, society and the victims). For each customer, identify what you think will be the key operations performance objectives and discuss any conflicts between them.
6. Identify what you think might be the order-winning, qualifying and less important objectives for a music store selling compact discs. Discuss how the organization might go about changing its operation by focusing on the less important objectives to give itself an advantage in the marketplace.
7. Assuming that video cassette recorders (VCRs) are in the maturity stage of their life cycle, how might the main performance objectives of a VCR manufacturer have changed

over the life of the product type so far?

8. For organizations providing the following products or services, what do you think would be their order-winning factors and qualifying factors?
   - Estate agency services
   - School textbooks
   - Basic aluminum extrusions
   - Accountancy services
   - Industrial washing machines.
9. 'When a company is introducing a totally novel product or service, it is competing exclusively on the technical specification of that product or service. The operations function therefore has no significant role to play.' Discuss.
10. Many Japanese manufacturers have based their success on products which were regarded as well into their 'mature' stage, such as automobiles and televisions. How did they manage to revitalize the markets for these products and what part did operations management play in this?
11. 'A Rolls Royce motor car will always cost more than a Skoda.' Does this mean that manufacturing cost is unimportant to Rolls Royce?
12. Draw up a list of structural and infrastructural decisions for the following operations:
    - a TV rental company
    - a ship repair facility
    - Disneyland Paris
    - a national train network.

Chapter **2**

Plant Location

2.1 Introduction

Location of facilities is a problem associated with the planning stage of any factory. The selection of location is a key- decision as large investment is made in building plant and machinery. It is also advisable or not possible to change the location very often. So an improper location of plant may lead to waste of all the investments made in building and machinery equipment.

Location decisions are affected by many factors such as the capacity of production, the financial status of the factory, availability of the work force and also by economic, political & social conditions in the various locations.

The facilities location problem is concerned primarily with the best location depending on the appropriate criteria of effectiveness.

2.2 Factors affecting Plant Locations:

I

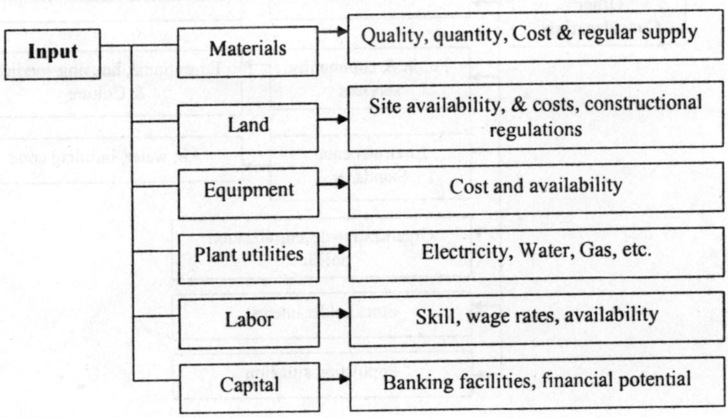

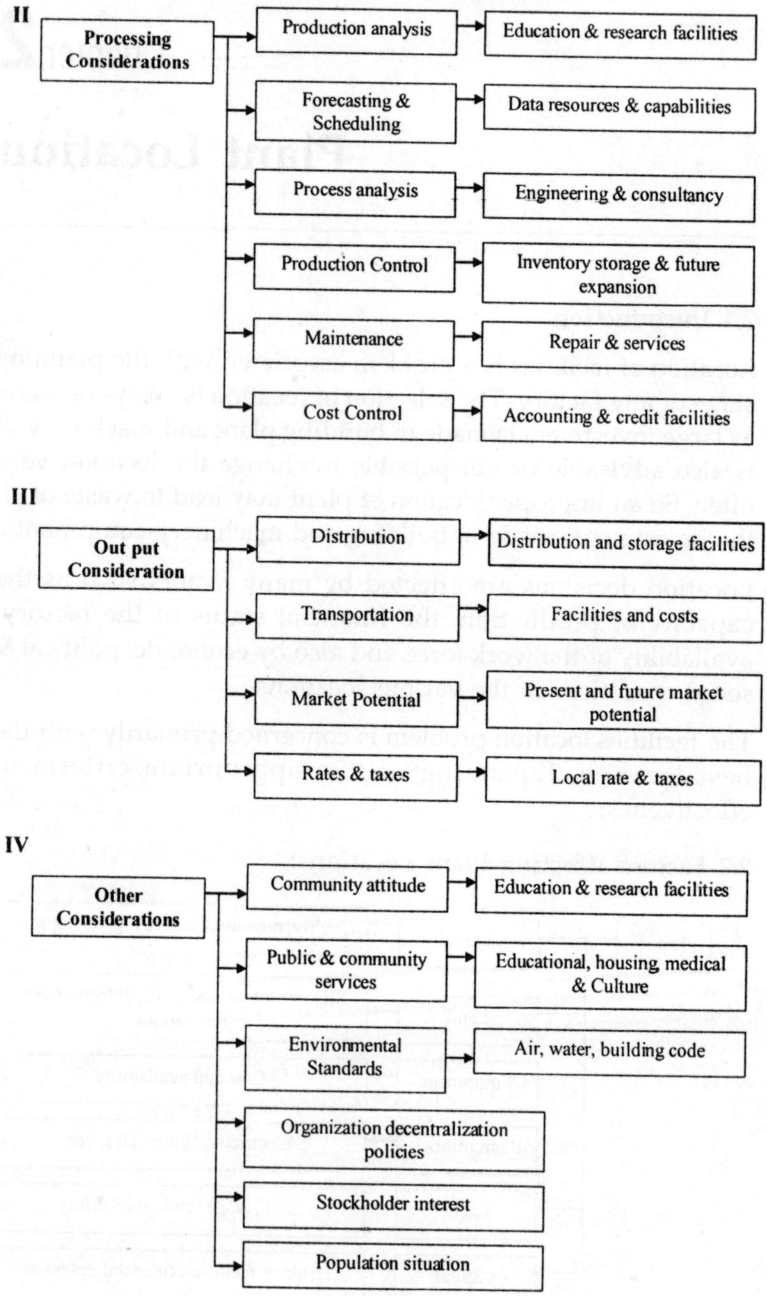
II
Processing Considerations
Production analysis
Education & research facilities
Forecasting & Scheduling
Data resources & capabilities
Process analysis
Engineering & consultancy
Production Control
Inventory storage & future expansion
Maintenance
Repair & services
Cost Control
Accounting & credit facilities
III
Out put Consideration
Distribution
Distribution and storage facilities
Transportation
Facilities and costs
Market Potential
Present and future market potential
Rates & taxes
Local rate & taxes
IV
Other Considerations
Community attitude
Education & research facilities
Public & community services
Educational, housing medical & Culture
Environmental Standards
Air, water, building code
Organization decentralization policies
Stockholder interest
Population situation

2.3 Steps in Location Study:

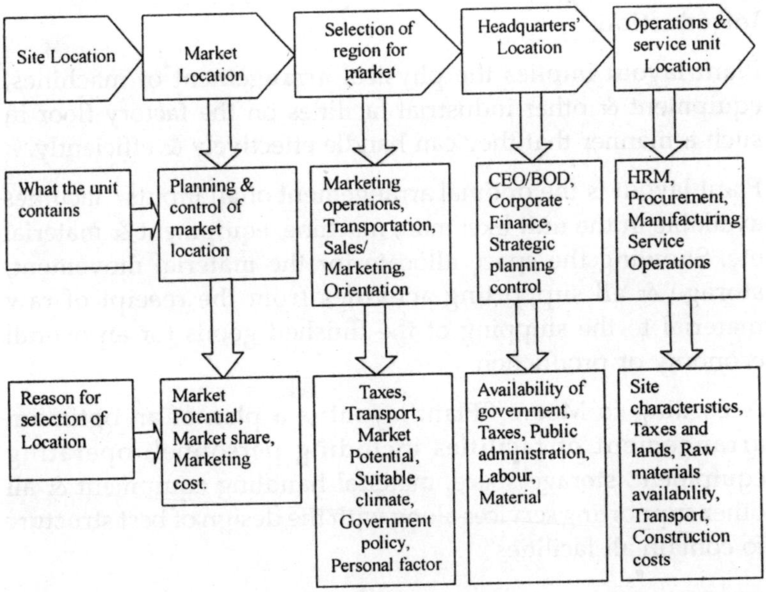

Fig: Location steps

A location decision arises due to the various reasons listed below:

1) - When starting a new organization.
2) - In some cases, the facility or plant operations & subsequent expansion are restricted by a poor site, thereby necessities the setting up of the facility at a new site.
3) - The growing volume of business makes it advisable to establish addition facilities in new territories.
4) - The original advantages of the plant have been overweighed due to new development.
5) - New economic, social, legal or political factors could suggest and change of location of the existing plant.

2.4 Plant Layout:

Introduction:

Plant layout implies the physical arrangement of machines, equipment & other industrial facilities on the factory floor in such a manner that they can handle effectively & efficiently.

Plant layout is the optimal arrangement of all inputs/ facilities available in the unit like: man, machine, equipment & material etc. Showing the space allocate for the material movement, storage & all supporting activities from the receipt of raw material to the shipping of the finished goods for an overall economy of production.

According to Moore "Plant layout is a plan of an optimum arrangement of facilities including personnel, operating equipment, storage space, material handling equipment & all other supporting services along with the design of best structure to contain all facilities".

2.5 Objective of Plant layout:

Some of important objectives of a good plant layout are as follows:

1- Simplified production process in terms of equipment utilization, reducing manufacturing time, reducing all delays & better arrangement for maintenance work.

2- Best possible utilization of men, machine, materials, money & other supporting activities.

3- Best possible location of floor space & effective space utilization, & less confusion.

4- Increased output & reduced inventories- in- process.

5- Effective supervision & control.

6- Provide excellent working environment and reduce accidents.

7- Maximum productivity & minimum waste.

8- Maintain flexibility of arrangement & operation.

9- Avoid unnecessary capital investment.

10- Worker convenience; improved morale & worker satisfaction.

2.6 Principles of Plant layout:

1- **Principle of overall integration of all inputs:** A good layout is one that integrates men, materials, machines and other supporting activities and others in order to get the optimum utilization of resources and maximum effectiveness.

2- **Principle of minimum distance to move by man & material:** This principle is concerned with the minimum travel of man & materials. The facilities should be arranged such that, the total distance traveled by the men & materials should be minimum and as far as possible straight line movement should be preferred.

3- **Principle of flow order of materials & other things:** A good layout is one that makes the materials to move in forward direction towards the completion stages.

4- **Principle of optimum use of cubic space:** The good layout is one that utilizes both horizontal and vertical space. It is not only enough if only the floor space is utilized optimally but the third dimension, i.e., the height is also to be utilized effectively.

5- **Principle of workers satisfaction & safety:** A good is one that gives due consideration to workers satisfaction & safety and also safeguards the plant and machinery against fire, theft etc.

6- **Principle flexibility:** The good layout is one that can be altered without much cost and time, i.e., future requirements should be taken into account while designing the present layout.

2.7 Classification of Layout:

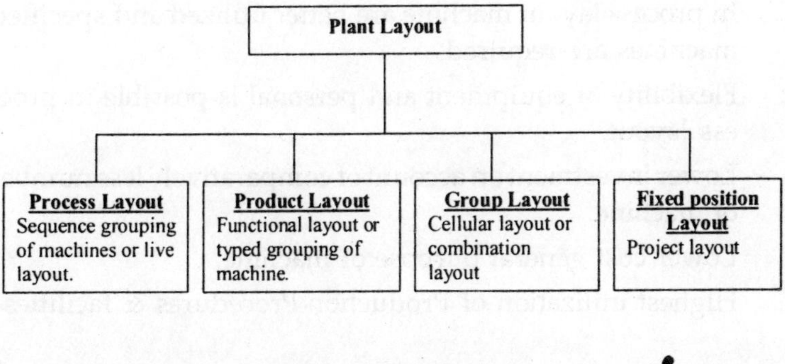

Classification of layout: -

Layout can be classified into the following four categories:-

1. Process Layout
2. Product Layout
3. Group Layout
4. Combination Layout
5. Fixed position layout

2.7.1 Process Layout: -

Process layout is suggested for batch production. All machines performing similar type of operations are grouped at one location in the process layout e.g. all lathes, milling machines, etc are grouped in a specified shop will be clustered in like groups.

Thus, in process layout the arrangement of facilities are grouped together according to their activities. A typical process layout is Sharon in fig. The flow paths of material through the facilities from one activity area to another are very from product to product. Or material based on activity.

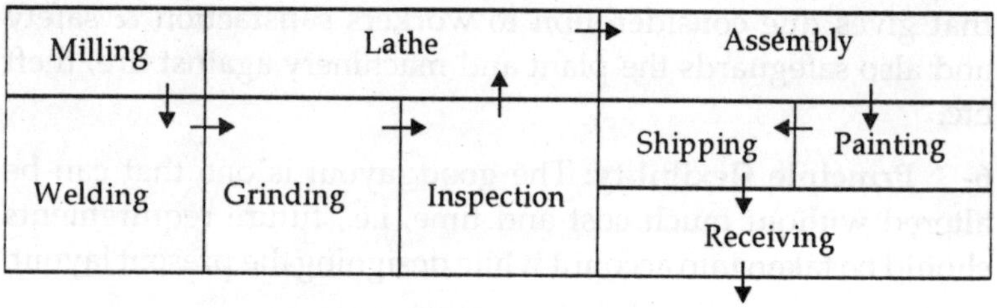

Advantage of process layout:-

1. In process layout machine are better utilized and specified machines are required.
2. Flexibility of equipment and personal is possible in process layout.
3. Lower investment on account of comparatively less number of machine.
4. Lower cost general purpose of machine.
5. Highest utilization of Production Procedures & facilities.

6. AA Highest degree of flexibility with regards to work distribution to machines & workers.
7. The diversity of task and variety of job makes the job challenging & interesting.
8. Supervisor will be of highest knowledge about the fuss under their departmental activities and performance.

Limitation of Process:

1. Back tracking and long movements may occur is the handling of materials thus, reducing material handling efficiency and effectiveness.
2. Material handling cannot be mechanized which adds to cost.
3. Process time is prolonged which reduce the inventory turnover and increases the in process inventory activity.
4. Lowered productivity due to number of activity.
5. Through put (tine gap between in & out in the process) time is longer.
6. Space & capital are tied up by work in process.

2.7.2 Product Layout: -

In this type of layout, machines & ancillary Service are located according to the processing sequence of the Product. If the volume of Production of one or more product is large, the facilities can be arranged to achieve efficient flow of material & lower cost/ unit. Special purpose machines are used to perform the required fuss quickly & reliably.

Limitations of Product Layout:-

1. A breakdown of one Machine is a product line may cause stoppages of machines in the downstream of the line.
2. A change in product design may require major alterations in the layout.
3. The line output is decided by the bottleneck machine.
4. Comparatively high investment is equipment is required.
5. Lacs of flexibility -A change in the product may require

the facility modification.

2.7.3 Combination Layout:-

This is also called the hybrid or mixed type of layout, usually; a process layout is combined with the product layout. ***For Example***: - Refrigerator manufacturing uses a combination layout. The process or functional layout is used to produce various operations like stumping, welding, heat treatment are carried out in different work centre as per the requirement. The final assembly of the product is done in a product type layout.

Thus for manufacturing various component parts process layout is used & for assembly product layout is used.

Fixed position layout: - This is also called the project type of layout. In this type of layout, the material, or major component remain in a fixed location & tools, machinery, men & other materials are brought to this location. This type of layout is suitable when one or a few pieces of identical heavy product are to be manufactured and when the assembly consists of large number of heavy parts, the cost of transportation of these parts in very high.

The product layout is selected when the volume of production of a product is high such that a separate production line to manufacture it can be justified. In a strict product layout, machines are not shared by different product.

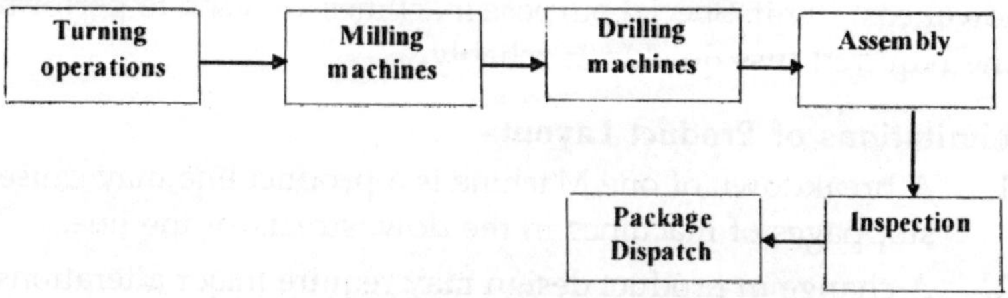

A typical product layout is shown in figure.

Advantage of Product Layout:-

1. The flow of Product will be smooth & logical in flow lines.

2. In process inventory is less.
3. Through put time is less.
4. Minimum material handling cost.
5. Simplified production, planning & control system are possible.
6. Less space is occupied & work transit & for temporary storage.
7. Reduced material handling cost due to merchandised handling system & straight flow.
8. Perfect line which eliminates bottlenecks & idle capacity.
9. Manufacturing cycle is short due to uninterrupted flow of materials.
10. Small amount of work in process inventory.
11. Unskilled workers can leave & manage the product.

Advantages:-

1. The major advantages of this types of layout are.
2. Helps in job enlargement & upgrades the skills of the operators.
3. The workers identify themselves with a product in which they take interst & pride in doing the hob.
4. Greater flexibility with this type of layout.
5. Layout capital investment is lower.

2.7.4 Group Layout:-

Group layout is a combination of the product layout & process layout. It combines the advantage of both layout systems. If there are manufacturer machines & production components, in group layout (Group Technology Layout), the manufacturer machines and production component will be divided into distinct number of machines components.

In group technology layout, The objective is to minimize the sum of the cost of transportation & the cost of equipments. So,

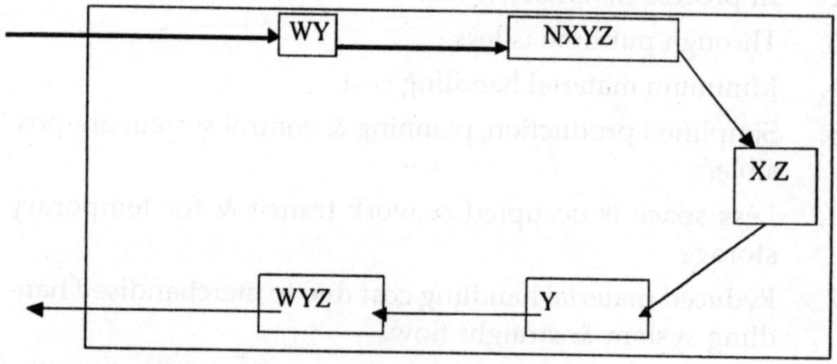

this is called as multi-objective layout.

Advantages of Group Technology layout:-

Group Technology layout will increase-

1. Component standardization and rationalization.
2. Reliability of estimates
3. Effective machines operations & productivity.
4. Customer Service.

2.8 Material Flow System:-

The raw materials move from one work station to another for the purpose of processing. The raw materials pass through various paths till they are converted into finished Products.

The pattern of material flow is an important considerate in the plan layout divided into two on the basis of the nature of the availability of floor space as under:

(1) Horizontal Flow (2) Vertical flow System

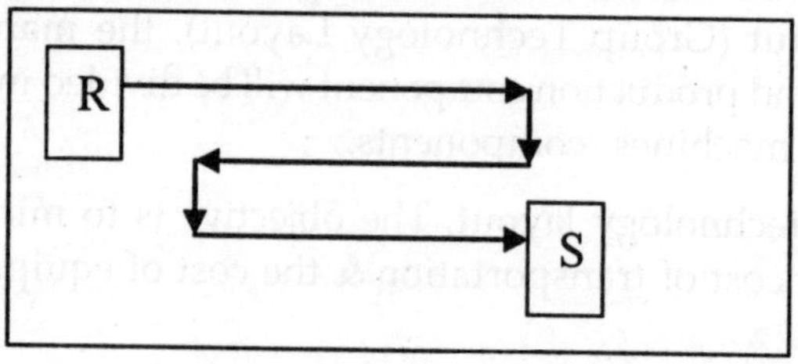

'S' or invented 'S' type flow

1. Required roads on both sides.
2. Absence of rushing of outside transportation
3. Required square like floor area.
4. Difficulty in returning empty containers.
5. Suitable for longer production lines

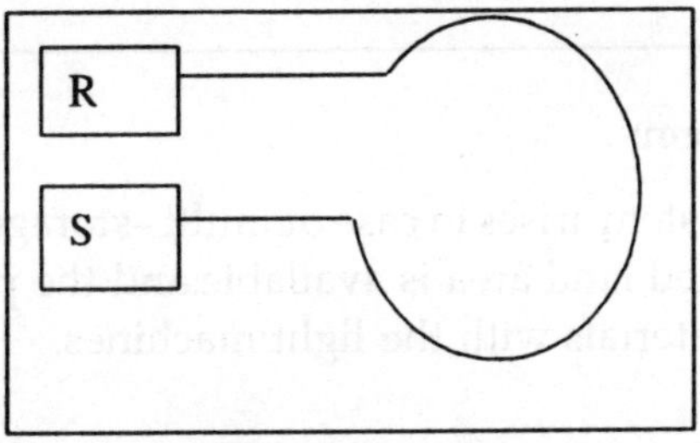

'O' type flow or Circular flow:-

1. One side road facility is required.
2. Heavy rush of transportation.
3. Ease in returning empty containers.
4. Requires square –lie floor area.
5. Suitable for longer production line.

Combination of 'I' & 'U' type :- (vii) Combination of 'I' & 'S'

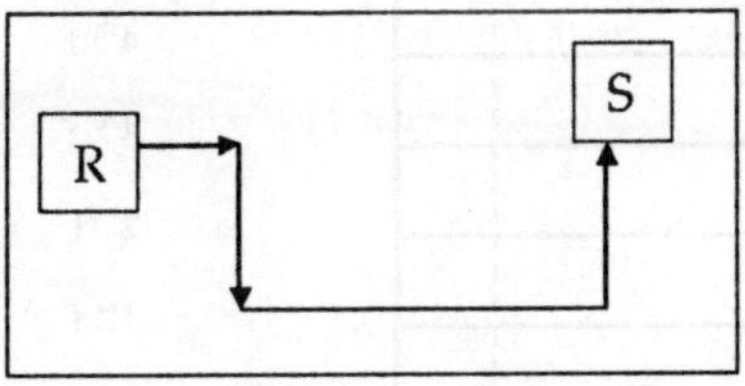

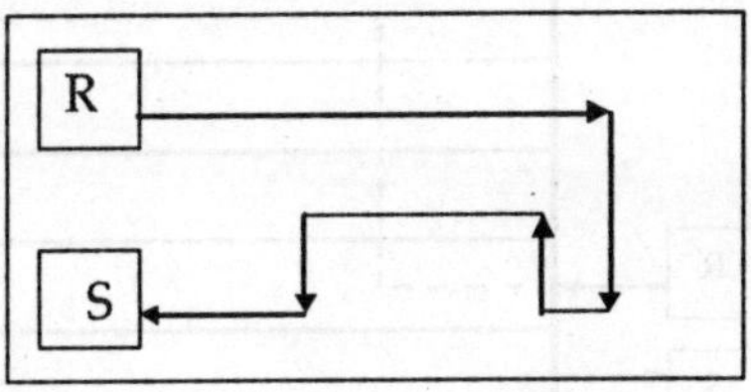

type flow:-

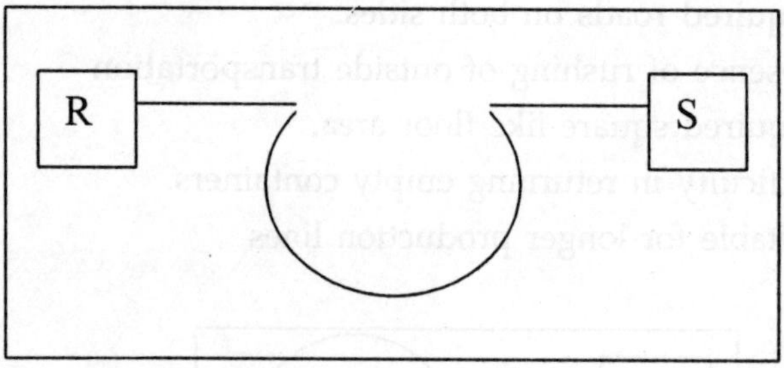

Vertical flow System:-

The vertical flow system arises in case of multi -storage building is used where limited land area is available and the processing is done on light materials with the light machines.

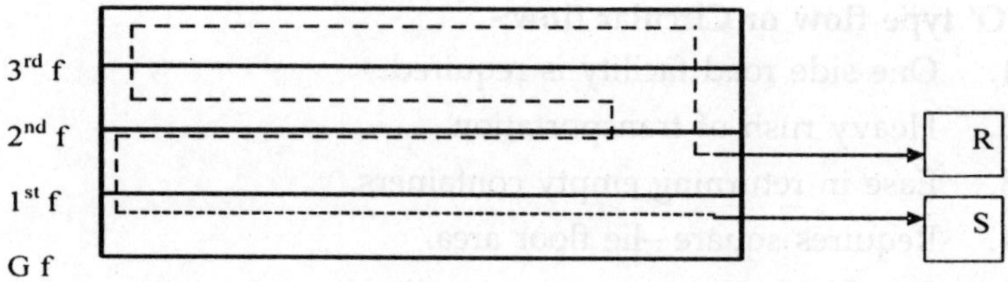

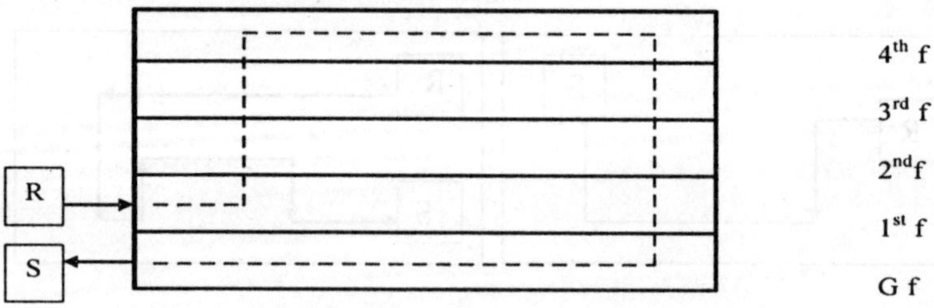

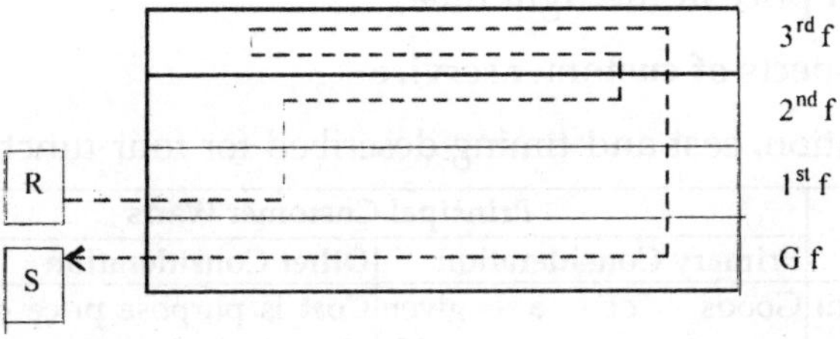

Symbol's of Activities:-

Operations ------ 

Transportation ------ 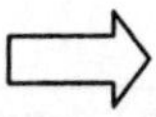

Inspection ------ 

Delays ------ 

Storages ------ 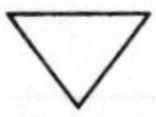

2.9 Objective of Operating Management –

Objectives of operations management can be categorized into

(1) Customer service

(2) Resource utilization.

Customer Service:-

The first objective of operating systems is the customer service to the satisfaction of customer warts. Therefore, Customer service is a key objective of operations managements. The operating system must provide something to a specification which can satisfy the customer in terms of cost and timing. Thus, primary objective can be satisfied by providing the 'right thing at a right price at the right time.'

These aspects of customer service –

Specification, cost and timing described for four functions

Function	Principal Customer Warts	
	Primary Consideration	**Other Consideration**
Manufacturer	Goods of a given requested or acceptable specification.	**Cost** is purpose price or cost of obtaining goods. **Timing** - delivery delay from order or request to receipt of goods.
Transport	Management of a given requested or acceptable specifications.	**Cost-** Is cost of movement. **Timing-** 1. duration or time to move. 2. Wait or delay from requesting to its commencement.
Supply	Goods of a given, requested or acceptable specifications.	**Cost-** Purpose price or cost of obtaining goods. **Timing-** delivery delay from order or request to receipt of goods.
Service	Treatment goods a given requested or acceptable specifications.	**Cost-** cost of movements. **Timing-** 1. duration or time requested for treatment. 2. Wait or delay from requesting treatment to its commencement.

They are the principle sources of customer satisfaction & must therefore be the Principle dimension of the customer service objective of operation managers.

Multiple choice questions

Try the following questions to test your knowledge of this chapter.

1 . The lay out where the equipment, machinery, plant and people move as necessary is known as:

1. Fixed-position layout
2. Process layout
3. Product layout
4. Cell layout

2 . A supermarket is usually positioned as:

1. Fixed-position layout
2. Process layout
3. Cell layout
4. Product layout

3 . A self-service cafeteria is usually positioned as:

1. Product layout
2. Process layout
3. Fixed-position layout
4. Cell layout

4 . A process with high variety and low volume is likely to have a:

1. Cell layout
2. Fixed-position layout
3. Process layout
4. Product layout

5 . Which of the following is not an advantage of a long-thin line?

1. Simple materials handling
2. Lower capital requirements
3. Higher mix flexibility
4. Controlled flow of materials or customers

6. Which of the following is usually considered a characteristic of a product or line layout?
   1. This layout can easily handle high volume but low variety
   2. Transforming resources are costly to maintain
   3. Transforming resources move to the work
   4. This layout tends to be very flexible
   5. This layout can easily handle high variety but low volume
7. A product layout:
   1. Groups transforming resources into dedicated cells
   2. Is appropriate for low volume operations
   3. Involves locating the transforming resources entirely for the convenience of the transformed resources
   4. Moves resources to the place where the operation is to be carried out
   5. Allows a wide variety of products to be manufactured on the same equipment
8. Cell layouts typically:
   1. Cost more to run than other types of process layout
   2. Are dominated by the transforming resources
   3. Involve all the operations on a product being located adjacent to each other
   4. Are the most efficient form of process layout
   5. Locate transforming resources entirely for the convenience of the transformed resources
9. Which of the following is <u>not</u> usually considered a characteristic of a fixed position layout?
   1. Transforming resources often move to the work
   2. Fixed position layouts are often used for large or delicate products or services
   3. Transforming resources are grouped in cells
   4. The recipient of the process or the work being undertaken remain in the same place

5. Fixed position layouts are able to offer high flexibility

Discussion questions

1. Identify the type of layout that might be adopted by the following organizations, explaining the reasoning behind your choice:
   1. a ski resort
   2. a dairy farm
   3. a tree surgeon
   4. a bakery
   5. a bank.

Discuss the implications of variety and volume on flow.

2. A tractor manufacturer, making a wide range of tractors to customer specification, is considering changing its layout from product to process. Discuss the implications of so doing.
3. Identify the main stages in the construction of a house from laying services and foundations to plastering and decorating. If each of these tasks were to be carried out by different sub-contractors, describe the potential layout problems.
4.
   a. Visit a supermarket in your area. Try to get an appointment to talk with the manager to discuss the layout design issues.
   b. Compare the design of your supermarket with that of the Delhaize store described in the box. List and tabulate the main similarities and differences, and try to understand the reasons for these differences.
   c. What do you think, therefore, are the main criteria considered in the design of a supermarket layout?
   d. What competitive or environmental changes may result in the need to change store layouts in the future? Will these apply to all supermarkets, or only certain ones, such as town centre stores?

Short Case

Layout of Big-Bazaar supermarket in Lucknow, India

The Future Group operates over 50 retail outlets in India, of which there are around 100 local big bazaar supermarkets. Big bazaar supermarkets compete both by choices of location, which are convenient for frequent shoppers and by the quality of the products and service. To remain profitable every big bazaar manager must maximize the revenue and contribution per square meter but must also minimize the costs of operating the store, in terms of material handling and checkout productivity, for example.

The Lucknow supermarket has a somewhat unusual layout, having two entry points and two exit points. In common with most supermarket designs, the checkouts are positioned near the outside wall, but during most of the day only a few are used. Newspapers are sold near the checkout queues, so that customers can catch up with the news while waiting. Checkout operators face into the store, towards the queue, to emphasize the need to work quickly when there is a queue. The store has 10 checkouts - a very large number for a store of only 1500 square meters. This is because there is a large peak of sales in the early evening, and long queues at the checkout would be unacceptable.

Big bazaar uses relatively wide aisles between the shelves, to ensure good flows of trolleys, but this has been at the expense of reduced shelf space which would allow a wider range of products to be stocked. The actual location of all the products is a critical decision, directly affecting the convenience to customers, their level of spontaneous purchases, and the costs of filling the shelves. The overall layout of the supermarket has separate, clearly marked self-service areas for packaged food, drinks, fruit and vegetables, and household items. The served delicatessen area (which sells products with above-average margins) is positioned centrally so that most shoppers must pass it. The displays of fruit and vegetables are located adjacent to the main entrance, as a signal of freshness and wholesomeness, providing an attractive and welcoming point of entry.

High-turnover, 'essential', known-value items such as rice, pasta, sugar and oil is positioned centrally and visibly, so that they are easy to find. Profitable, fast-moving items are displayed at eye level, both to help the customer and to make restocking easier for the employees. Conversely, low-margin and low-turnover items are placed low down. Bulky or heavy products, such as packs of beer, are located near the storage area to facilitate restocking. Frozen foods are located at the ends of aisles, near the checkouts, so that they can be purchased last. In some supermarkets, these positions are only used for promotions, as customers move slower around the ends of aisles and the goods on display can be seen from most directions.

Questions

1 What is the basic layout type used by this supermarket?

2 Are the objectives in designing a supermarket layout broadly similar to the objectives in designing a high-variety manufacturing operation? If not, what is the difference?

Answer

Layout of Big bazaar supermarket in Lucknow, India

1. What is the basic layout type used in this supermarket?

Predominantly the layout is process layouts in so much as all similar goods are grouped together. So, for example, all frozen food is stored using its specialist technology (freezers), canned food is stored using its specialist technology (shelves), etc. Customers with different needs will move along different paths through the supermarket 'assembling them' to whatever goods they wish to purchase.

2. Are the objectives in designing a supermarket layout broadly similar to the objectives in designing a high-variety manufacturing operation? If not, what is the difference?

In some ways the objectives are similar. Planning for the movement of materials in a high variety manufacturing operation, one would be concerned with ensuring that the quality of products was not affected in any way through damage, etc. Similarly, in the supermarket one is concerned that customers do not damage themselves by having to reach too high or stoop too low etc. However, the main objective of a supermarket layout is very different to that of a manufacturing operation. In fact it is the opposite. Whereas in a manufacturing operation one is usually trying to minimize the distanced traveled (to make the process more efficient), in a supermarket one is often trying to deliberately get the customer to walk past certain areas (in order to encourage them to buy certain products).

Chapter 3

Forecasting

3.1 Introduction:

Forecasting is the primary activity in the planning. It involves study of past data & present data. The main purpose of forecasting is to estimate the occurrence timing and magnitude of future activity. For example, the trend of past 10 years in the demand of electronic goods and corresponding purchasing power of the consumers may from a basis of forecasting the demand of electronic goods during next year. Once, the reliable forecast for the demand is available, a good planning of activities is needed to meet the future demand. Forecasting provides the input to the planning and scheduling process.

3.2 Benefits of forecasting:

Managers needed a good/ effective forecast of materials, labour and other resources for production and operations.

If goods projection of future demands is available; the management may take suitable action regarding inventory. Similarly, if production and operation activities are exactly forecasted, then balanced work load may be planned. Good employee relations may be established, as there would be lesser hiring and firing activities by the management with better manpower planning. Therefore, forecasting event is useful due to following benefits-

1. Effective handling of happing.
2. Better employee's interpersonal relations.
3. Minimizing the fluctuations of production.
4. Balance work load distribution.
5. Better material management.

6. Better utilization of production resources.
7. Better customer services.
8. Optimum utilization of capital and resources.
9. Better plant layout and better location distribution of production system.

Efforts in forecasting activities involve two types of costs. While more effort in forecasting causes increased cost due to data collection and analysis; lesser forecasting activity involves lost revenue, which may be due to unplanned labour, material and capital coat. Therefore, each organization should maintain a balance in its forecasting efforts and stick to a zone near to accuracy cost trade off.

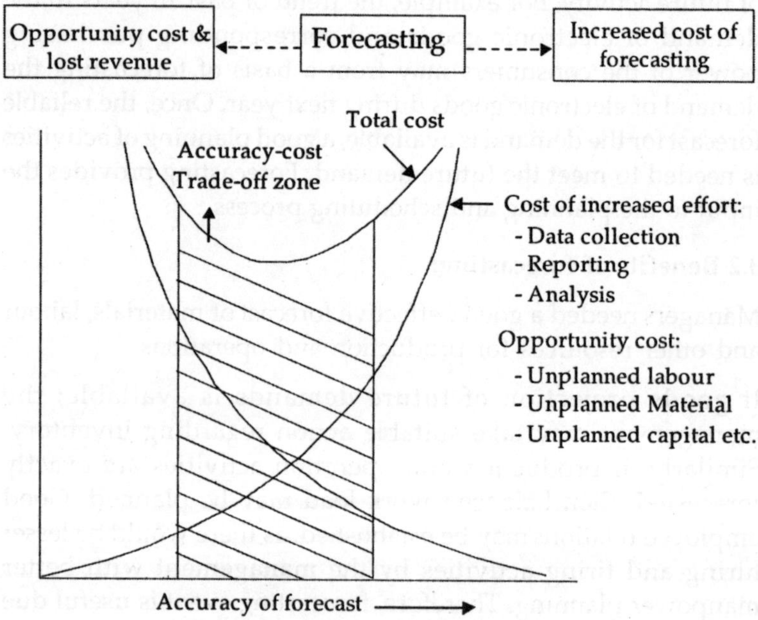

Fig. Balance of forecasting efforts

3.3 Types of forecasting:

The forecasting can be classified on the basis of timing span or range of forecast. The forecasting can be categories in three types.

1. Long range forecasting

2. Medium range forecasting
3. Short range forecasting

3.3.1 Long range forecasting:

Long range forecasting means time period should be more than 5 years. Normally, it is difficult to model and foresee events for more than 5 years. It is mainly due to economic uncertainty and variation in the behaviour of the interrelation processes.

Applications of long range forecasting :

Long range forecasting is useful in the following areas-

- Capital planning
- Plant location
- Plant layout or expansion
- New product planning
- Research and Development planning
- Technology management etc.

Method of Long range forecasting:

Long range planning is a difficult task. These forecasts are broad in natures and general type in characteristics. Mostly qualitative techniques are used. Acknowledgements to technological break through economic studies, marketing survey, demographic projections etc., are used to make judgmental estimate of the future event.

3.3.2 Medium range forecasting:

Medium forecasting range is in between 1 to 5 years. As the range of forecast shorts with in 1 to 5 years, the accuracy of forecast increases.

This is due to better calculation of future and relatively lesser uncertainty. This is a numerical based forecasting system. Estimation of reliability of forecasting can be useful in medium range forecast.

Application of medium range forecasting:

- Sales planning and sales force decision for the upcoming products.
- Production and operation planning.
- Capital and cash planning.
- Inventory planning.
- Admission system in the school etc.

Method of medium range forecasting:

Medium range forecasting needs judgment as well as a time series analysis, Regression analysis, correlation of different index and inflation, combination of collection opinion etc can be useful in forecasting.

3.3.3 Short range forecasting:

The range of short forecasting is in between one hour to one year. In most of the cases, is for one session, for months or few weeks.

The short range forecasting is needed at detailed level, such as demand of specific items. This forecast can affect the purchasing activity. There is less scope of judgment in short range forecast. Therefore past data are mainly projected into future.

Application of short range forecasting:

Short range forecasting is commonly used in immediate control of activities.- Some applications are-

- Purchasing.
- Over time decisions.
- Scheduling of job.
- Machine maintenance etc.

Method of Short range forecasting:

Short range forecasting is based on past data. The trend of data is projected in to future. For this type of forecasting exponential smoothing, graphical projections, past explosion in to product, family etc, are used.

3.4 Qualitative methods of forecasting: Qualitative methods are generally used in forecasting when data, necessary to use time series or causal model, are not available. For example past demand data are not available when a new product is to be launched in the market. Therefore, time series trend analysis is impractical qualitative techniques, which incorporate human judgment, expert opinion, management intuition, market research, grass root forecasting or historical analogy are useful in these cases.

Some useful approaches are as follows-

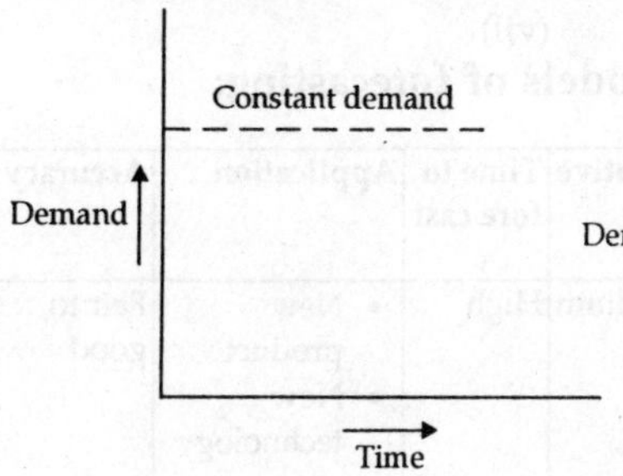

(i)

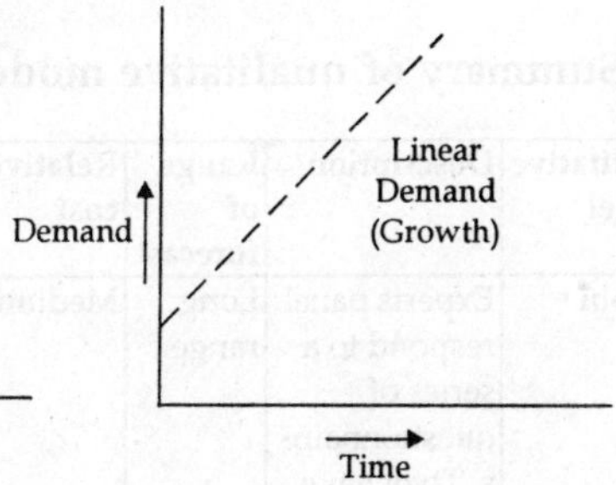

(ii)

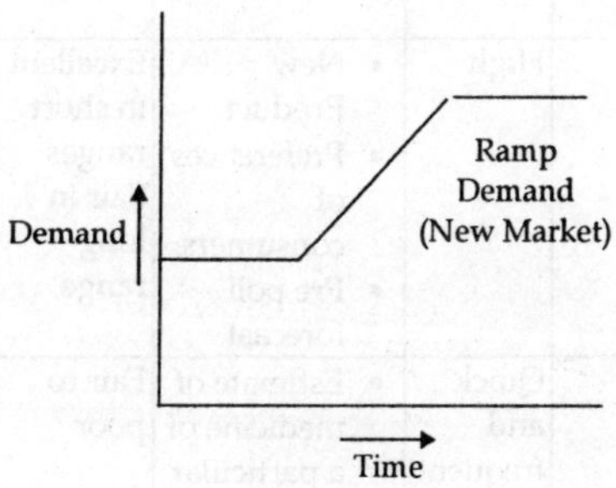

(iii)

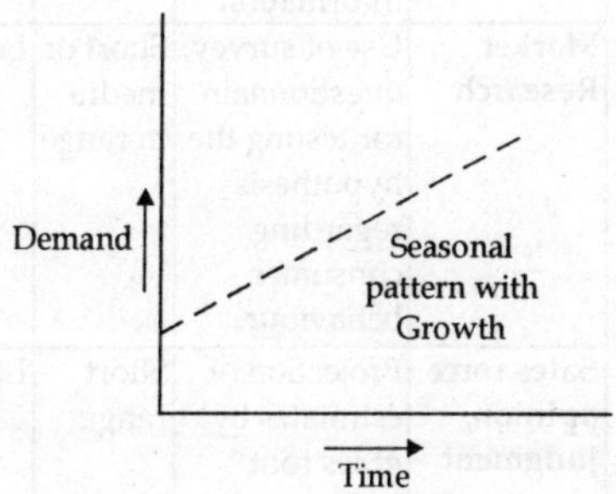

(iv)

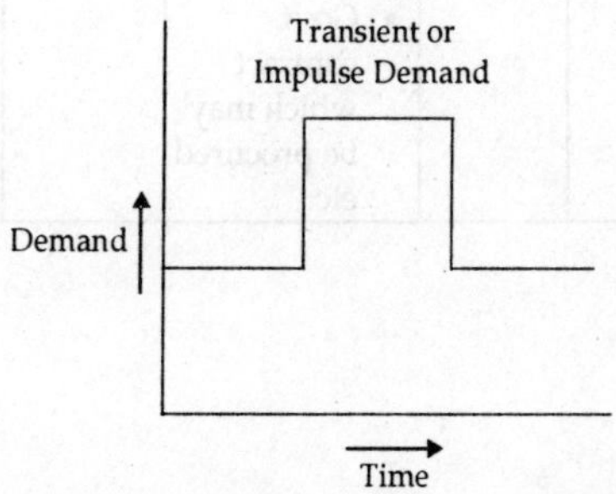

(v)

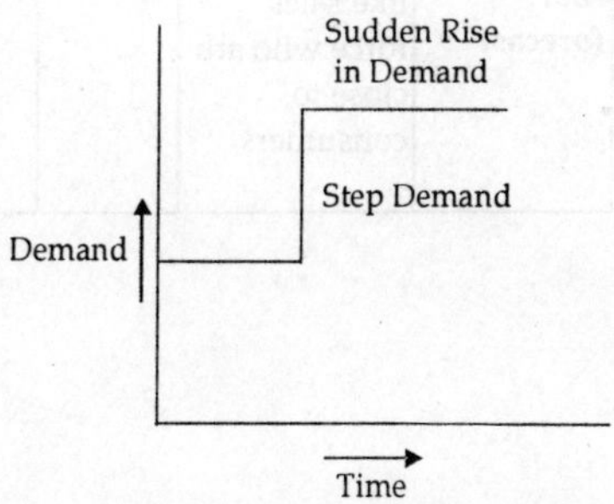

(vi)

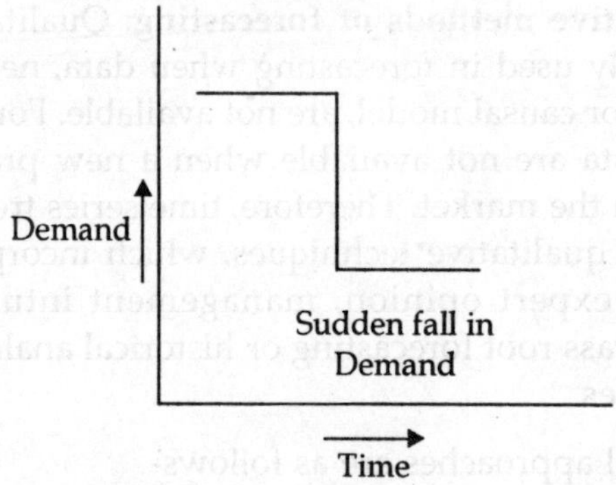

(vii)

3.5 Summary of qualitative models of forecasting:

Qualitative Model	Description	Range of forecast	Relative cost	Time to fore cast	Application	Accuracy
Delphi	Experts panel respond to a series of questionnaires. They have access to all information	Long range	Medium	High	• New product • New technology	Fair to good
Market Research	Use of survey, questionnaire for testing the hypothesis regarding consumer behaviour	Short or medium range	Low	High	• New Product • Preferences of consumers. • Pre poll forecast	Excellent in short ranges. Fair in long range.
Sales force opinion, judgment or grass root forecast	Projection of estimates by grass root level people like sales force who are close to consumers	Short range	Low	Quick and frequent	• Estimate of medicine of a particular type • Govt. contract which may be procured etc.	Fair to poor

Historical analogy	Life cycles of similar products or services are compared. Demand pattern for each stage of life cycle is assumed to be analogous for comparable products/ services.	Long range	Low to medium	Quick	• New product • New services	Poor to fair

Source: Page 57 Industrial engineering and management by Ravi Shankar

3.6 Accuracy of forecast:

For managers it is impossible to obtain an exact forecast all the time. This is due to many factors, which affect the trend in data. It is difficult to capture the exact position of these influencing factors. Therefore some errors can be supposed in every forecasting activity.

3.7 Measures of forecasting error:

1. Mean Absolute Deviation (MAD)

This is calculated as the average of absolute value of difference between actual and forecasted value. The negative sign in this differences is ignored as over estimate as well as under estimate are both off target and thus undesirable.

$$MAD = \Sigma^n_{t=1} \mid D_t - F_t \mid / n$$

Where,

D_t = Actual value of demand for period n.

F_t = Forecasted demand for period n.

n = Number of period considered for calculating the error.

2. Mean Sum of Square Error (MSE):

The average of square of all error in the forecast is termed as MSE.

$$MSE = \Sigma^n_{t=1} (D_t - F_t)^2 / n$$

3. BIAS

BIAS is measure of over estimation or under estimation. Positive BIAS indicates under estimation while a negative BIAS indicates over estimation.

$$BIAS = \Sigma^n_{t=1} (D_t - F_t) / n$$

4. Tracking Signal (TS)

It is used to identify those items, which do not keep pace with either positive or negative bias or trend.

$$TS = (BIAS)_n / (MAD)_n$$

3.8 Time Series analysis:

These are some models in forecasting which involve analysis of past data or happenings. These models are:

1. Simple moving average
2. Weighted moving average
3. Exponential smoothing
4. Double exponential smoothing.

3.8.1 Simple Moving Average:

Compute the mean of only a specified number of consecutive data which are most recent values in series. We can call it F_t. This F_t would be the forecast for next period of time.

In general, the forecast at end of t periods, the n period simple moving average forecast for (t+1)th period is given by

$$F_{t=1} = (1/n) \Sigma^t_{I = t+1-n} D_i$$

Where, D_i = the actual demand for the ith period.

n = the number of periods included in each average.

Example: Forecast for 3 month simple moving average.

Week	Demand for the week (units)	Cumulative demand for the past 3-week		3- week average demand
10	105			
11	110			
12	107			
13	118	322	÷ 3	107.33
14	120	335		111.67
15	101	345		115
16	106	339		113

3.8.2 Weighted Moving Average:

This principle is based on the principle that more weightage should be given to relatively newer data. The forecast is the weighted average of data.

$$F_{t+1} = \Sigma_{i=t+1-n} w_i D_i$$

Where, w_i = the relative weight of data for the ith period.

And $$\Sigma^{t}_{i=t+1-n} w_i = 1$$

Example:

Period	1	2	3
Actual Demand	105	108	112
Weightage	0.1	0.3	0.6

What is the forecast for the 4th period?

Solution: the weighted moving average forecast for the 4th period

$F_4 = (0.1 \times 105 + 0.3 \times 108 + 0.6 \times 112)$

$= 110.1$

In case of simple moving average,

$F_4 = \Sigma\ (105 + 108 + 112)$

$= 108.33$

In case that weightage is 0.6, 0.3 and 0.1 in the above problem,

$F_4 = (0.6 \times 105 + 0.3 \times 108 + 0.1 \times 112)$
$= 106.6$

It may be noted that when more weight is given to the recent values, the forecast is nearer to the likely trend.

3.8.3 Exponential Smoothing:

Exponential smoothing method is the method where the weight-age of the data diminishes exponentially as the data become older. In simple moving average approach, the only few past data are accounted and in exponential smoothing, all past data are accounted. The weight-age of every previous data decreases by (1- α) times, where á is called as exponential smoothing constant.

For example: Where α = 0.32, Weight-age of last period data = 0.32 & Weight-age of last to last period data = 0.32 (1- 0.32)

Period	Demand	Weight
1	101	$\alpha(1-\alpha)^2 = 0.32\,(1-0.32)^2 = 0.147$
2	105	$\alpha(1-\alpha) = 0.32\,(1-0.32) = 0.217$
3	110	$\alpha = 0.32$

Let, F_t = One period ahead forecast made at time t
D_t = Actual demand for period t
a = Smoothing constant

Then,

$$F_t = \alpha\, D_{t-1} + (1-\alpha)\, F_{t-1}$$

Finally we can say it,

$$F_t = \alpha\, D_{t-1} + \alpha\, (D_{t-1} - Ft_{-1})$$

Thus, forecast for the next period is the algebraic sum of forecast for the last period and α times error in forecast for the last period.

Now, since $F_t = \alpha\, D_{t-1} + (1-\alpha)\, F_{t-1}$
Therefore, $F_{t-1} = \alpha\, D_{t-2} + (1-\alpha)\, F_{t-2}$

Putting this in the previous equation, we get

$$F_t = \alpha D_{t-1} + (1-\alpha)[D_{t-2} + (1-\alpha) F_{t-2}]$$
$$= \alpha D_{t-1} + \alpha (1-\alpha) D_{t-2} + (1-\alpha)^2 F_{t-2}$$

Now, we observe the above expression. We know that the value of á is between 0 & 1. Therefore, weight-age to the past data decreases as the data becomes older. This is called double exponential smoothing.

3.9 The Box – Jenkins Method:

Forecasting has been done using tested stochastic or stochastic-dynamic time series models. The necessary grounds for this situation is that an appropriate class of stochastic models had not been identified as possessing the flexibility necessary to represent efficiently (i.e., using a reasonable number of parameters) the remarkable variety of characteristics of economic time series. This situation no longer holds, for Box and Jenkins have thoroughly investigated a class of models that prove to be quite satisfactory for both the stochastic and stochastic-dynamic situations. We shall first explain the purely stochastic models. Strictly, these models are called autoregressive integrated moving average (ARIMA) models or simply models Box – Jenkins for short. The Box – Jenkins models may be used to represent processes that are stationary or non-stationary. A stationary process is one whose numerical properties are the same over time; in exacting, such a time series fluctuates around a fixed mean value. Examples of no stationary time series include series which include changes in level, trends, changes in trends, or seasonal behavior.

1. The only stochastic Box – Jenkins model is remarkably simple in form. The present inspection is represented by a linear combination (weighted average) of previous observations, plus an error term associated with the current observation, plus a linear amalgamation of error terms associated with previous observations. The slip-up terms have zero mean, constant variance, and are uncorrelated with each other. The segment of the model involving the observations is called the *autoregressive* part of the model, and the segment involving the error terms is called the *moving average* part of the model.

The problem of building a stochastic Box – Jenkins model of a procedure in spirit involves influencing the number of terms in the autoregressive and moving standard parts of the model, and determination of values for the parameters associated with those parts. By statistical analysis of the time series data, it is possible to choose from the full class of autoregressive-integrated moving average models, subclasses of models having a specific structure appropriate to the particular time series under examination.

By determining such a realistic structure for the model, the number of parameters to be probable in the model can be considerably reduced. This parameter reduction is quite important, for "nonlinear" numerical estimation actions are generally required to fit a tentative Box – Jenkins model. And determination of values for the parameters associated with those parts. By statistical analysis of the time series data, it is possible to choose from the full class of autoregressive-integratedmoving average models, subclasses of models having a exact arrangement suitable to the particular time series under inspection. By determining such a reasonable structure for the model, the number of parameters to be estimated in the model can be significantly reduced. This parameter reduction is quite important, for "nonlinear" statistical estimation procedures are generally required to fit a tentative Box – Jenkins model.

After a tentative Box – Jenkins model has been fitted; it is subjected to various analytical checks to test its competency as a stochastic representation of the procedure under study. If the model is found to be insufficient, analysis of the model residuals suggests ways to transform the model structure to obtain a new tentative model which will likely do an enhanced job of representing the process. The basic statistic for assisting identification of a reasonable structure for a new tentative model is the autocorrelation function of the residuals of the current model. For testing model adequacy, the power band of the residuals can also be used as an alternative to the autocorrelation function. This process of fitting a tentative model, testing it, and determining a new tentative model, is repeated until a model is found which does an adequate job of representing the process.

2. Derivation of the Optimal Forecaster

After a model has been determined that, according to the various tests to which it is subjected, is considered to be an adequate demonstration of the time series under assessment, we are in a position to get a predictor for the time series. In order to determine an analyst from a model, it is necessary to specify a criterion which the predictor satisfies. Ideally, the criterion should take the "cost" associated with forecast errors into account. We would then like to derive the predictor for which the expected cost associated with forecast errors is minimized. If the cost function is not clear, a reasonable approach is to determine the (linear) predictor that has the least forecast error variance, or mean squared error of prediction. That is, for each specified time in the future we wish to determine the forecast that has minimum mean squared error at the point. The minimum mean squared error forecaster is usually referred to as the "optimal" forecaster. The optimal forecaster corresponding to a Box - Jenkins model turns out to be the expected (mean) value of the process, conditional on the past observations. For example, the best possible forecast one time period into the future is the expected value of the process at that point in time, given that the past values of the time series are as observed. Calculation of the optimal forecast is quite easy for a stochastic Box - Jenkins model.

To calculate the lead-one forecast, for example, we simply substitute, into the formula defining the model, the observed (past) values and the optimal estimates of the past error terms. These errors terms can be estimated recursively: they are simply the past forecast errors. To compute the optimal forecast beyond lead one, we substitute forecasts for future observations and zeros for future error terms. Thus we see that the computational effort required forecasting using a Box - Jenkins model's on the same order as that required by the simple smoothing techniques. Calculation of tolerance (probability) limits around the forecasts is straightforward for a Box - Jenkins model. If we have a stationary procedure, the distance between these limits will gradually increase for forecasts further and further into future time, to a fixed value proportional to the variance of the process. For a non-stationary process, the variance of the process is undefined, and the tolerance interval grows substantially wider as we forecast further into the future. It is of interest to note that a forecaster derived from a stochastic model is an adaptive forecaster. Adaptively are, of course, very desirable possessions for a forecaster to acquire and a necessary one for a predictor of a non-stationary process. (The various smoothing methods — exponential smoothing, moving average — have been so widely used because, in addition to requiring few computations, they are adaptive in nature.)

A very important feature of the Box - Jenkins models is their ability to efficiently represent quite general non-stationary processes. By its very definition, a stochastic model embodies the changing environment of the process, and the corresponding predictor is in essence a explanation of how the future is likely to turn out, given the recent past performance of the process. Suppose, for example, that a process appears to have "trends" that change slope over time, or that it exhibits pseudo-periodic behavior with a stochastically varying phase and amplitude. If such a process is modeled using, for example, trends, trend adjustments, seasonal, and seasonal adjustments, then the parameters of the model will almost certainly have to be updated rather frequently; i.e., the predictor cannot get used to automatically to the changing situation, since the model does not represent the process well. The key point here is that we want an adaptive *predictor* rather than an adaptive *model*. We wish to derive a fixed model and to derive an adaptive forecaster from it. An adequately tested stochastic model of a process meets this requirement. By taking the essential stochastic characteristics of the process properly into account, it produces a forecaster that in essence tells *how to* take the changing features of the process into account.

3. Simulation Using a Stochastic Box – Jenkins Model

Although we are principally concerned with forecasting, a few words are in order regarding the use of the Box – Jenkins models for simulation. For example, we may be concerned in determining the effect of sales unpredictability on a new inventory policy, starting from the current sales position. In such a case, we need a model which exhibits the same numerical properties as the actual sales themselves. An econometric model would be difficult to use in such a situation because, as the model is pretend into the future, we need to substitute values for all of the variables of the model, and the econometric model does not specify the behavior of any of these variables other than the variable(s) of primary interest.

A Box – Jenkins model can readily be used in such a situation, for it is in fact a description of the statistical properties of each succeeding observation in terms of the previous explanation. Each simulated observation becomes input to the succeeding simulated observation. It should be remembered, however, that a Box – Jenkins model is concerned essentially with the local (short-term) behavior of a process, since it is through understanding the local behavior that we are able to predict the near future from the recent past. If a long-term simulation model is desired, then special care must be taken to make sure that the model reflects the longer-term properties of the process.

B. Stochastic-Dynamic Box – Jenkins Models

1. General Considerations

As we mentioned earlier, the Box – Jenkins method can be used to develop stochastic-dynamic models, in which the behavior of the variable of primary interest (the endogenous variable, or variable we wish to forecast) is related not only to its past behavior, but to the behavior of other (exogenous) variables, as well. The reason for including exogenous variables is obvious: since the model class is expanded, the precision of the forecast may be increased over thatcorresponding to the pure stochastic model.

If an exogenous variable is included in a model to be used for forecasting, however, then the values of that variable must be known or forecast over the forecasting period of interest. Typically, the behavior of the exogenous variable presages that of the variable of primary interest; that is, the current behavior of the variable of main interest is related to the past behavior of the exogenous variable. Such an exogenous variable is called a *leading indicator*. Apparently, if there is a strong lagged association between an exogenous variety and the variable of primary interest, the precision of the forecasts will be considerably enhanced. It is recalled that a stochastic-dynamic model is a mixture between a purely econometric model and a purely stochastic model. In it, the behavior of the variable of interest that cannot be explained in terms of the behavior of the exogenous variants is represented by a stochastic portion of the model. As we add additional exogenous variables to the model, the stochastic portion of the model becomes less and less detailed, and we may approach the "purely dynamic" model in which the stochastic segment of the model is simple uncorrelated random variation. (In a particular situation it may not be feasible to derive such a "purely dynamic" model; the practical limit may be a stochastic-dynamic model with a nontrivial stochastic component.) Note that once we have introduced an exogenous variety into a model, we might refer to such a stochastic-dynamic model as an econometric model. Rather than simply implying the inclusion of more than one economic variable, however, the term *econometric* usually indicates that the model has a special structure dictated by economic theory, rather than empirically determined. Usually, the stochastic part of such econometric models is quite simple in form, and the analytical power of the model arises out of the dynamic rather than the stochastic relationships. Hence, while an econometric model is certainly an example of a stochastic-dynamic model (in which the stochastic portion is usually simple in form), we shall generally use the term "stochastic-dynamic" to describe models in which the relationships between the variables are empirically determined.

A multivariable Box - Jenkins stochastic-dynamic model may include all of the relevant variables of a so-called econometric model. The Box - Jenkins stochastic-dynamic models just represent a particular class of empirical models that are capable of professionally representing a wide range of processes involving more than one variable. While the structure of these models is quite flexible, the economic nature of a process may suggest a special model structure which could be an even more efficient representation of the process. In a sense a Box – Jenkins stochastic-dynamic model could be viewed as an empirically-derived "econometric" model, in contrast to a causally-derived "econometric" model. To the extent possible, of course, mathematical model building should always take advantage of special features or understanding of the real-world process being modeled. Such understanding forms the original basis for selecting a particular class of models to represent a process. The performance of a predictor based on an econometric model is often compared to that of a predictor based on a simple stochastic model, such as a limited autoregressive scheme. The forecasting aptitude of the autoregressive predictor is frequently taken as a minimum usual of performance for an econometric model. Needless to say, a more reasonable assessment would be that of the econometric predictor to a predictor based on a tested stochastic model, rather than on an arbitrarily selected and probably inappropriate stochastic model.

2. Identification of Stochastic-Dynamic Model Structure

Often econometric models have been constructed using linear regression analysis. The term "linear" refers, of course, to the nature of the numerical estimation, rather than the functional form of the regression meaning, which may be extremely nonlinear. Computationally, about the most difficult problem that might arise with this move toward would be that the residuals (error terms) of the model may be auto correlated, but the standard regression methods can usually still be used for the analysis after suitable steps have been taken. There are essentially two reasons for such autocorrelation.

First, it may simply not be possible or practical to include a sufficient number of exogenous variables in the model so that the stochastic part of the model would be simple in form (not auto correlated). *Second,* the structure of the model can not be representing the relationship between the variables of the model in a very efficient style. By way of similarity, suppose that a one-parameter moving average process best described the stochastic behavior of a time series, but that an autoregressive model was fitted instead to the data. By allowing a sufficient number of parameters in the autoregressive model, a satisfactory fit could be obtained, with residuals having negligible autocorrelation. However, if we restrict the number of autoregressive parameters, we would have neither a very good fit nor negligible autocorrelation in the residuals.

Similarly, with the stochastic-dynamic model, it may be quite inefficient to insist that the variable of interest be explained solely in terms of linear combinations of other variables. A much more efficient structure for the model, allowing for a better fit with fewer parameters and less autocorrelation in the residuals, may be possible if we represent the process also in terms of a linear mixture of the variable of primary interest.

Thus we see that, if we are to determine stochastic-dynamic models which, in terms of the number of parameters used, are efficient representations of the processes, it is important to identify reasonable model structures to investigate. The practical question that arises is, of course, how to accomplish this identification, which can be rather difficult whenever both the variable of interest and the exogenous variables are auto correlated. It turns out that this identification is often facilitated through the use of stochastic models for the exogenous variables of the model.

Essentially what is done is to develop a stochastic model for an exogenous variable and then use this model as a "filter" to convert the exogenous variable to a "white noise" series. This same filter is also applied to the variable of primary interest. In electrical engineering terminology, the preceding process is known as "preheating." It then turns out that a certain statistic (the cross correlation function between the preheated variables) can be used to quickly recognize a sensible structure for the part of the model relating to the exogenous variable. Thus, just as the autocorrelation function assists identification of the structure of a stochastic model, the cross correlation function assists identification of the structure of a stochastic-dynamic model.

3. Process Control Applications

This article is primarily concerned with the forecasting applications of the Box-Jenkins method. As noted earlier, the models can be used for simulation as well. Another area of significant application is the field of process control. In control applications we can not only observe the behavior of the "explanatory" variables of the model (called control variables, rather than exogenous variables), but we can control them to produce changes in the variable of primary interest. To control the variable of primary interest in the desired style, we need a good statistical model of the process. As in forecasting applications, the Box-Jenkins models have adequate flexibility to efficiently model the behavior of a wide variety of physical processes.

In developing a model for control, a somewhat different position from the situation in forecasting, in that data can be collected corresponding to forced changes in the control variables. In economic situations we can in general only observe, not manipulate, the exogenous variables. The manner in which the data are collected has a basic effect on the use to which the developed model can be put. For example, we cannot use a model to predict what changes in a system will result from our manipulating a control variety, if the model was developed from data in which the system was merely observed, and not interfered with. The way in which the control variables are manipulated to produce the data from which the model is derived will depend on the application.

Chapter 4

Work Study

4.1 Introduction

Work study is defined as a technique that embraces (hold, square) method study and work measurement which are employed to ensure the best possible of human and material resources in carrying out the specified operations.

The principle objective of work study is to improve productivity of men, material & machines.

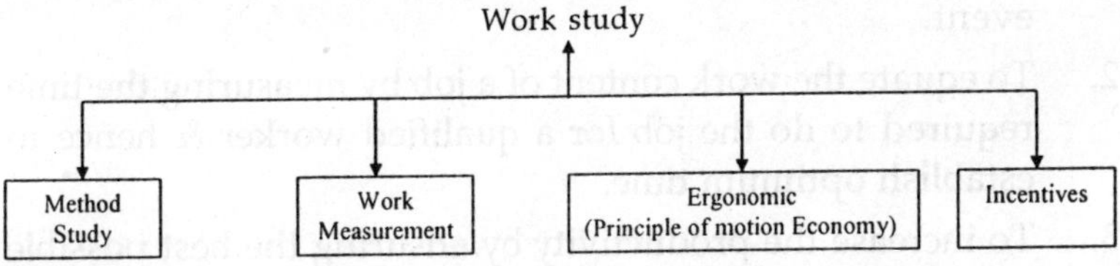

4.2 Method Study: - It is the systematic recording and critical examination of exiting & proposed ways of doing work so as to develop/ apply more effective methods and to reduce cost. It investigates how jobs are done and also how the procedure of doing them can be improved.

4.3 Work Measurement: - It is the application of procedure to establish the time for qualified workers to carry out a specified job at a definite level of performance. It tries to establish how long job should take once the method is decided.

4.4 Purpose of Work Study: - Basically it has three objectives:-

1. The most effective use of plant & equipment.
2. The most effective use of human effort.
3. The evaluation of human work.

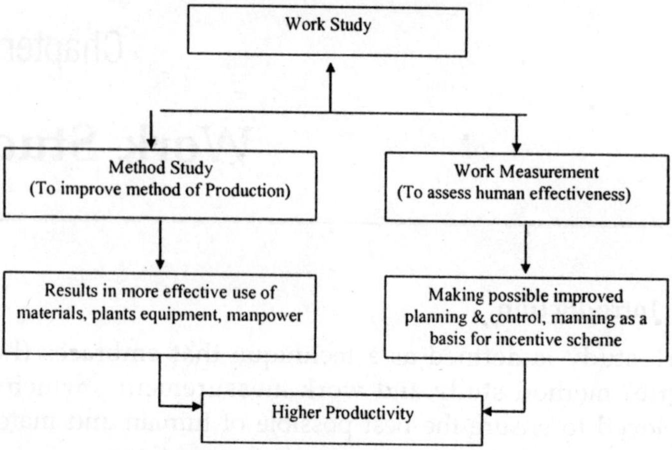

4.5 Objectives of study:-

1. To analyses the present method of doing a job, systematically in order to develop a new & better, producer of the event.
2. To equate the work content of a job by measuring the time required to do the job for a qualified worker & hence to establish optimum time.
3. To increase the productivity by ensuring the best possible utilization of human & material resources & to achieve best quality product/ service at minimum possible cost.
4. To improve operational efficiency & effectiveness.

4.6 Benefits of work study:-

1. Increased productivity & operational efficiency &effectiveness.
2. Reduced manufacturing costs.
3. Improved work place layout & techniques.
4. Better manpower planning & capacity planning.
5. Fair wages to employed& other agencies.
6. Better working atmosphere to employees.
7. Improved work flow.
8. Reduced material handling costs & other expenses.

4.7 FLOW DIAGRAM OF WORK STUDY

Steps involved in work study:-

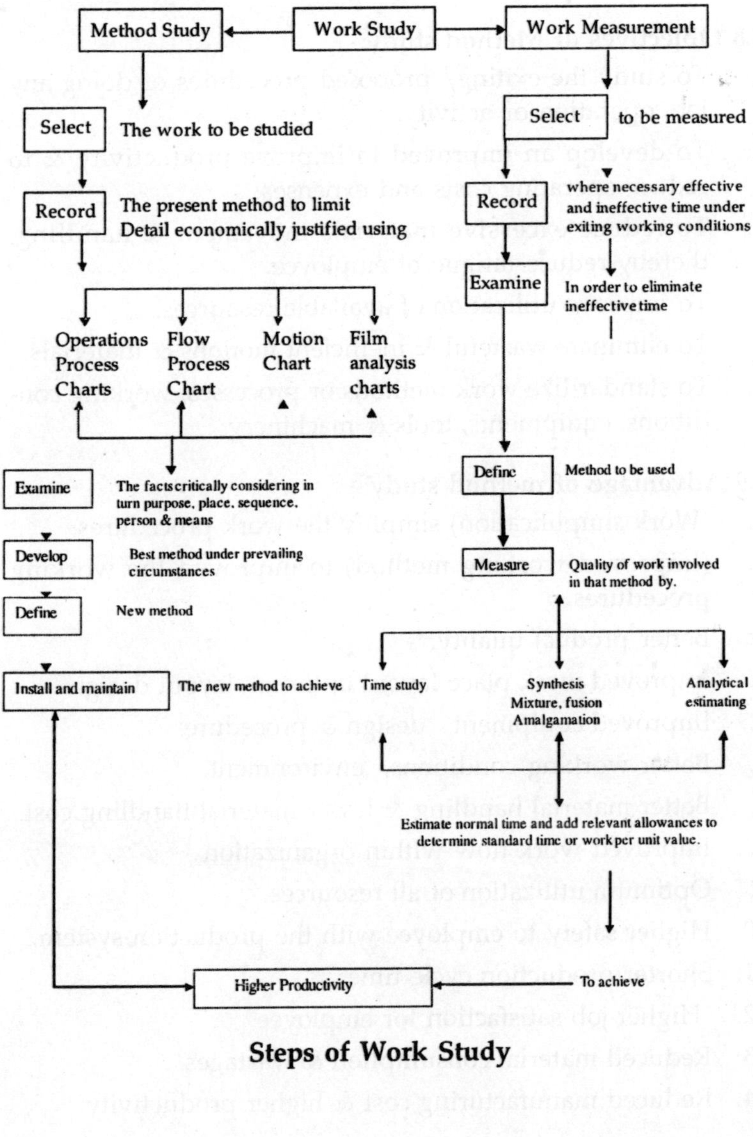

Steps of Work Study

9. Better industrial relations & employee morale.
10. Provides better job satisfaction to employees.
11. Reduce the employee turnover from the organization.

4.8 Objectives of Method study:-

1. To study the exiting/ proposed procedures of doing any job, operation or activity.
2. To develop an improved to improve productivity & to reduce operating costs and expenses.
3. To reduce excessive materials movement & handling, thereby reduce fatigue of employee.
4. To improve utilization of available resources.
5. To eliminate wasteful & inefficient motions & materials.
6. To standardize work methods or processes, working conditions, equipments, tools & machinery.

4.9 Advantage of method study:-

1. (Work simplification) simplify the work procedures.
2. (Improved working method) to improved the working procedures.
3. Better product quality.
4. Improved work place layout optimum layout design.
5. Improved equipment design & procedure.
6. Better working conditions/ environment.
7. Better material handling & lesser material handling cost.
8. Improved work flow within organization.
9. Optimum utilization of all resources.
10. Higher safety to employee with the production system.
11. Shorter production cycle time.
12. Higher job satisfaction for employee.
13. Reduced material consumption & wastages.
14. Reduced manufacturing cost & higher productivity.

4.10 Method Study Procedure: - The various steps involved in method study are:-

Select: The work or Job to be studied and define the objectives to be achieved by method study. The job selected to have maximum economics advantage, shall offer vast scope for work improvement through reduction of excessive materials handling & fatigue of workmen, often scope for improving the working conditions & improving the utilization of resources.

Record: All the relevant facts or information pertaining to the existing method using the recording techniques such as-

Process chart-

1. Outlines process chart.
2. Operation process chart.
3. Flow process chart- man/ machines/materials flow.
4. Man machine chart.
5. Multiple activity charts.
6. Simultaneous motion chart (SIMO chart).
7. Motion chat.

Diagrams:

1. Flow diagrams.
2. String diagram.
3. Cycle graph.

Examine: The recorded facts critically, challenging everything being clone& seeking alternatives, questioning the purpose (what is achieved) the measure how is it be achieved, sequence (when is it achieved), place (where is it achieved) & the person (who achieved it).

Develop: - The improved procedure of operation alternatives technique and select the best method. The factor to be considered while evaluating alternatives & selecting the best procedures are:-

(a) Cost of implementation.

(b) Expected savings in time & cost.

(c) Feasibility - economic flexibility.

(d) Productivity & operations.

(e) Acceptance to design, Production planning & control, quality control, production &sales departments.

(f) Reaction of employees to the new method or feedback of the employees.

(g) Short term or long term implication of the alternatives.

Installations of the procedures are divided in the improved/ new method in three phases planning arranging & of implementing phases. In the first two phrases, the programme of installation & schedule are planned & necessary requirements such as resources, equipments, tools operating instructions to workers are provided.

Maintain: - The new method by ensuring that the installed method is functioning well. This is done b periodic checks & verifications at regular intervals.

4.11 Work Measurement:-

Work measurement is defined as the application technique designed to establish the work content of a specified task by determining the time required for carrying out the task at defined standard of performance by a qualified workers.

Work measurement is also called by the name 'Time study'.

Time study has been defined by British standard institution as "The application of technique designed to establish the time for a qualified workers to carryout a specified job at a defined level of performance".

4.11.1 Objectives of work measurement: - The use of work measurement technique as a basis for incentives is only a very small part of its total activities.

1. Comparing alternative procedures.
2. Assessing the correct initial manning (manpower require-

ment planning).

3. Manning & control of the technique & procedures.
4. Realistic costing.
5. Financial incentive schemes.
6. Delivery date of goods or very accurate lead time.
7. Cost reduction & Cost control techniques.
8. Identifying substandard workers or target below standard employees.
9. Training development of new workers & employees.

4.11.2 Technique of work measurement: - For the purpose of work measurement, work can be regarded as

1. **Repetitive work: -** The type of work in which the main operations or group of activities repeat continuously during the time spent at the specific job. These apply to work cycle of extremely short duration.

2. **Non- repetitive work: -** It includes some type of maintenance and construction work, where the work cycle itself is hardly ever repeated identically.

Various Technique of work measurement is:-

1. Time study (stop watch technique) measurement.
2. Synthesis Technique.
3. Work sampling Techniques.
4. Predetermine motion & time study procedures.
5. Analytical estimating of Techniques.

Time study and work sampling involved direct observation & the remaining data based & analytical in nature.

4.11.3 Steps in making time study or work measurement:-

Stop watch time is the basic technique for determining accurate time standard. They are economical for repetitive type of work. Step are-

1. Select the work to be studied.
2. Obtain and record all the information available about the job, the operator and the working conditions likely to affect the time study work.
3. Break the operation into elements. An element is a initial part of a specified activity composed of one or more fundamental motions selected for convenience of observation and timing.
4. Measure the time by means of a stop watch taken by the operator to perform each element of the operation, either conditions method or snap back method timing could be used.
5. At the same time, assess the operator effective speed of work relative to the observer's concept of "Normal" speed this is called performance rating.
6. Adjust the observed time by rating factor to obtain normal time for each element.

$$\text{Normal} = \frac{\text{Observed time} \times \text{Rating}}{100}$$

7. Add the suitable allowances to compensate for fatigue, personal needs, contingencies etc, to give standard time for each element.
8. Compute allowed time for the entire job by adding elemental standard times considering frequency of ascendance of each element.
9. Make a detailed job description describing the method for which the standard time is established.
10. Test and review standards whenever necessary. The basis in the study are represented by a block diagram.

4.12 Step in Time study:

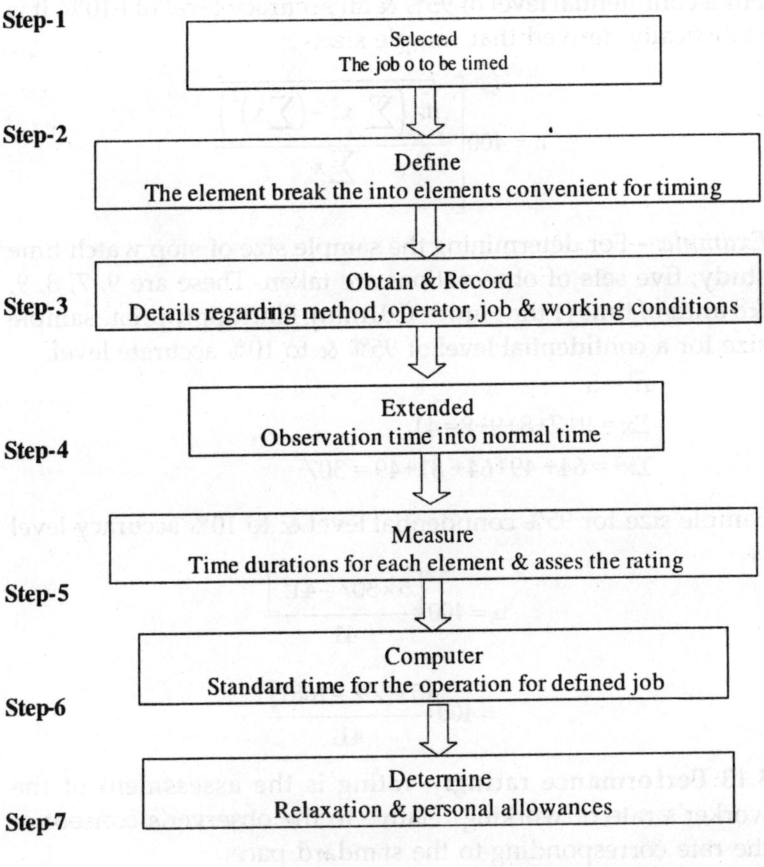

Fig: Flow chart steps in time study.

Flow to determine the sample size:-

Let:

N = number of cycle to be timed, i.e, preliminary reading first taken.

N = number of observation (or, sample size) required at a given confidence level.

Σx. = Sum of preliminary sat of individual observations(x).

Σx^2 = sum of square of preliminary observation (x)

For a confidential level of 95% & an accuracy level of I 10%, it is statistically derived that sample size:-

$$n = 400\left[\frac{\sqrt{n^1\left(\sum x^2-\left(\sum x\right)^2\right)}}{\sum x}\right.$$

Example: **-** For determining the sample size of stop watch time study; five sets of observations are taken. These are 9, 7, 8, 9, &8 units of time (1 time unit = 0.01min). Find appropriate sample size for a confidential level of 95% & to 10% accurate level.

$n^1 = 5$

$\Sigma x = 9+7+8+9+8= 41$

$\Sigma x^2 = 64+ 49+64+ 81+49 = 307$

Sample size for 95% confidential level & to 10% accuracy level is

$$n = 400\frac{\left[5\times 307 - 41^2\right]^2}{41}$$

$$= 400\frac{\left[5\times 307 - 1681\right]^2}{41}$$

4.13 Performance rating: - rating is the assessment of the worker's rate of working relative to the observer's concept of the rate corresponding to the standard pace.

Rating is always compared with the standard rating, which may be taken as 100.

$$\text{Then, Basic time} = \text{Observed time}\frac{\text{Rating}}{100}$$

Example: - If an operator is judged to be working faster (rating 125) & observed time is 0.25 min, then basic time =

$$= \frac{0.25\times 125}{100} = 0.3125 \text{ min}$$

Standard Time:-

Example: - In a time study for a job done by a worker whose rating is 90, the data are as follows;

Observed time = 20 min

Personal need allowance = 4%of basic time

Fatigue allowance = 2.5% of basic time

Contingency work allowance = 2% of basic time

Contingency delay allowance = 1%of basic time

Find: - 1) Basic time, 2) work content, 3) standard time.

Solution:-

1. $$\textbf{Basic time} = \frac{\textbf{observed time} \times \textbf{Rating factor}}{\textbf{Standard rating}} = \frac{15 \times 9.0}{100} = 13.5 \text{ min}$$

2. Allowances are-

a) $$\textbf{Personal need allowances} = \frac{4}{100 \times 13.5} = 0.54 \text{ min}$$

b) $$\textbf{Fatigue allowances} = \frac{2.5}{100 \times 13.5} = 0.3375 \text{ min}$$

c) $$\textbf{Contingency work allowances} = \frac{2.00}{100 \times 13.5} = 0.27 \text{ min}$$

d) $$\textbf{Contingency delay allowances} = \frac{1}{100 \times 13.5} = 0.135 \text{ min}$$

Hence,

Work content = Basic times + relaxation allowances + contingency work allowances.

= 13.5 + (0.54 +0.337) + 0.27 = 14.65

Standard time = work content + contingency delay allowances.

= 14.65 +0.135 = 14.65 min

= 14 min 0.78× 60 sec.

= 14 min 47 sec.

Example: - Assuming that total observed time for an operation of assembling an electric switch is 1.00 min. If the rating is 12% find normal time. If allowances of 10% are allowances for the operation, determine the standard time.

Solution observed time (ok) selected time = 1 .00 min

Rating =120%

Allowances =10%

Normal time = observation time× $\frac{\text{Rating \%}}{100}$

$$=1.00\times \frac{120}{100} = 1.20 \text{ min}$$

Standard time = normal time + allowances. = 1.20 + 0.12 + 1.32 min

4.14 Work sampling or Activity sampling Ration Delay Method:-

Work sampling is a work measurement technique that randomly samples the work of one or more employees at periodic intervals to determine the proportion of total operations that is accounted for in one particular activity.

These studies are frequently used to establish the percentage of time spent by the employees in unavoidable delays, repairing finished products from operations & supplying material to an operation.

Uses of work sampling Techniques:-

1) To estimate the percentage of a (protracted) time period consumed by various activity state of a resources such as equipment, machines or operators.
2) To determine the allowances for inclusion of standard times,
3) To indicate the nature of the distribution or work activity with in a gang operation.

4) To estimate the percentage of utilization of gang of similar machines or equipments.

5) To indicate how materials handling equipment are being used.

6) To provide a basis for indirect labour time standards.

7) To determine the productive and non productive utilization of clerical operations.

8) To determine the standard time for a repetitive operation as an alternative t\to the stop watch method.

Steps in work sampling: - the work sampling study consists of essentially the following steps:-

1. Determine the objective of the study, in including definitions of the states of activity to be observed.
2. Plan the sampling procedure including :-
   a) An establish of the percentage of time being devoted to each phase of the activity.
   b) An establish of the number of observation required.
   c) The selection of the length of the study period and the programming of the number of readings over this period.
   d) The establishment of the machines of making the observations, the route to follow and the recording of data.
3. Collected the data as planned.
4. Process the data present the result.

Advantages:-

1. Economical to use and usually costs considerably less than a continuous time study.
2. Can be used to measure much activity that is impractical to measure by time study.
3. Not necessary to use a trained work measurement analyst to make the observations.
4. Measurement of the utilization of people & equipment directly.

Chapter **5**

Production Planning and Control

5.1 Introduction

Production Planning Operations involves the organization of an overall manufacturing operating system to produce a product.

The various operations involved in production operation planning are designing the product, determining the equipment & capacity requirements, designing the layout of physical facilities & material handling system, determining the sequence of operations & the nature of the operations to be performed along with the requirements (standard time) & specifying certain production quantity & quality level.

Objective of Production Planning is to provide a physical system together with a set of operating guidelines for efficient conversion of raw materials, human skills and other inputs into finished products.

5.2 Need for Production Planning & Control:

The present techno-economic scenario of India focused on competitiveness in manufacturing industry. Indian industries have to streamline the production activities and attain the maximum utilization of firm's resources to enhance the productivity. Production planning & control serves as a useful tool to coordinate the operations of the Production system by proper planning and control system. Production system can be compared to the nervous system with PPC as a brain. Production Planning & Control is needed to achieve:

1. Elective utilization of firm's resources & Procedures.

2. To achieve the production objectives with respect to quality, quantity, cost & timeliness of delivery, optimum production system & techniques.
3. To obtain the production flow in order to meet customer's varied demand with respect to quality & committed delivery schedule.
4. To help the company to supply standard quality production to the customer on the continuous basis at competitive standard rates.

5.3 Objectives of Production Planning & Control:

Following are the objectives of Production Planning & Control:

1. Systematic Planning of Production activities to achieve the highest efficiency in Production of outputs.
2. To organize the Production facilities like machines, men etc., to achieve stated production objectives with respect to quantity, quality, time & cost.
3. Optimum arrangement of available resources.
4. Coordination with other departments relating to production to achieve regular balanced and continuous production flow.
5. To confirm the delivery commitments.
6. Materials Planning & Control of the Production Systems.
7. To be able to make adjustments due to changes in demand & rush orders for supply of the products.

5.4 Production Planning: Production planning procedures involves in the organization, an overall manufacturing / operating system to produce a final product.

The various activities like designing the product, determining the equipment & capacity requirements, designing the layout of physical facilities & material handling system, determining the sequence of operations & the nature of the operations to be performed along with time requirements are involved in production planning activities.

Objective of production planning in to provide a physical system together with a set of operating guidelines for efficient conversion of raw materials, human skills & other inputs into finished output.

5.5 Main function of Production Planning & Control department.

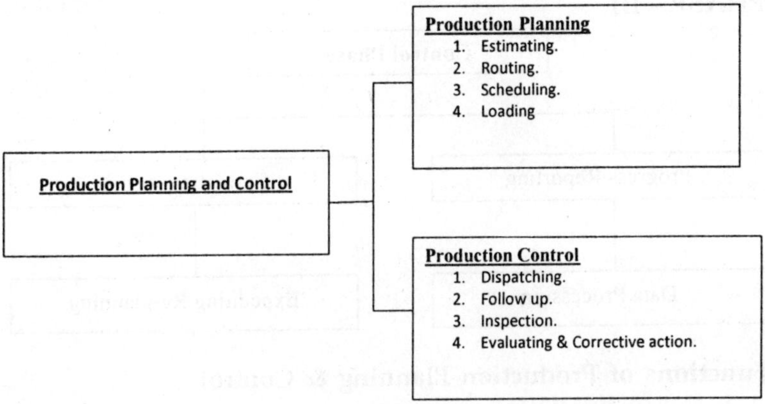

5.6 Phases in Production Planning & Control functions

PHASE – I

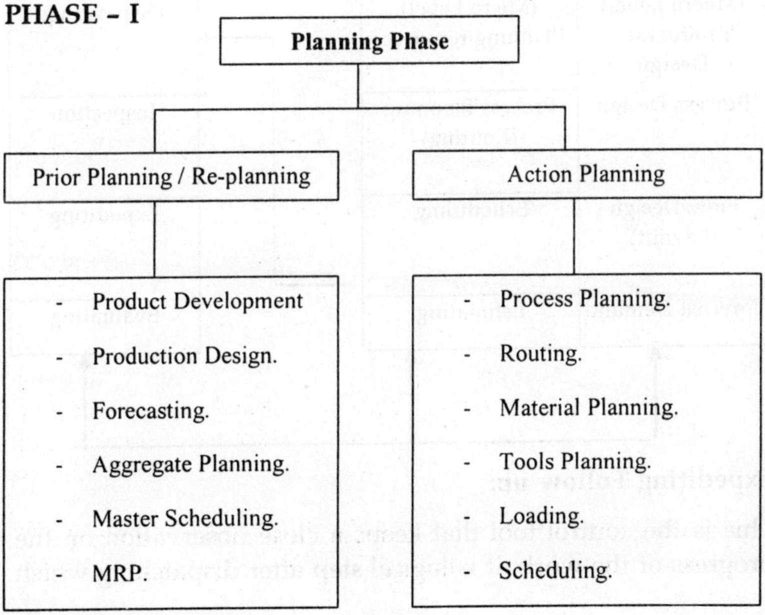

PHASE – II

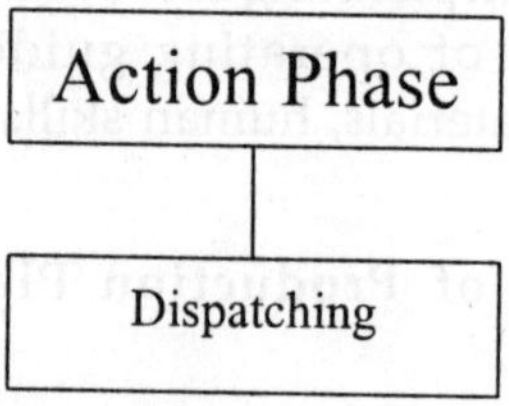

PHASE – III

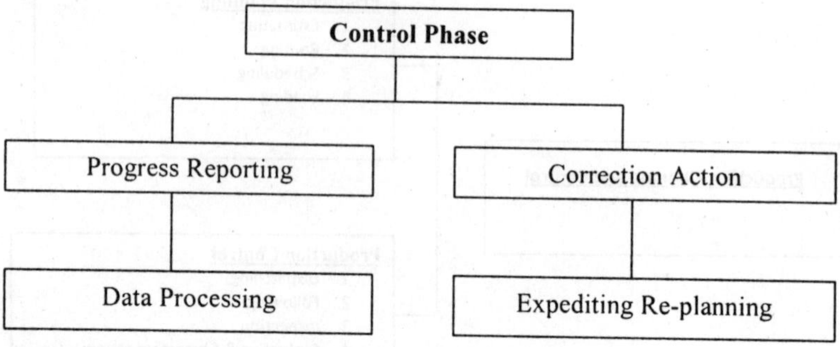

Functions of Production Planning & Control

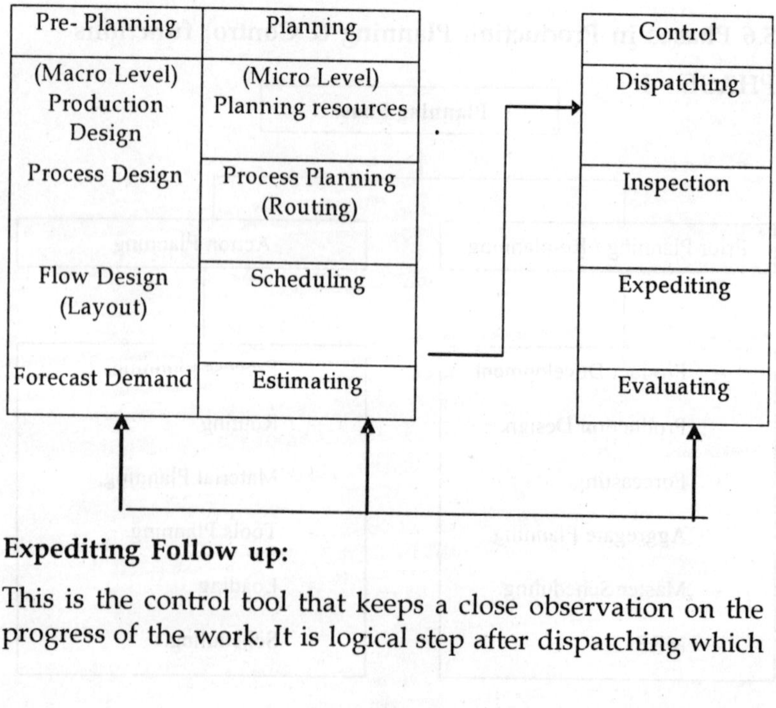

Expediting Follow up:

This is the control tool that keeps a close observation on the progress of the work. It is logical step after dispatching which is called 'follow up'. It coordinates extensively to execute the production plan. Progressing function can be divided in to three parts i.e.,

1. Follow up of materials.
2. Follow up of work in process.
3. Follow up of assembly.

5.7 Factors determining Production Planning Procedures:

The production planning procedures use varies from organization to organization. Production planning activity may begin with a product and a plan for the design of the new product and the entire system to manufacture the product. It also includes the task of planning for the manufacturing of modified version of an existing product, using the existing facilities.

The three major factors determining production planning procedures are:

1. **Volume of Production:** The amount and intensity of Production Planning is defined by the quantity & character of the operations & the nature of the converting the raw material in final goods processes, Production planning is expected to reduce manufacturing costs. The planning of production in case of custom order job shop is limited to planning for purchase of raw materials & components high volume operations, extensive production planning is necessary in planning for the design of both the product & the production processes in order to achieve substantial cost reduction when a large number of products are produced.

2. **Nature of Production Processes:** In job shop, the production planning may be informal & the development of work methods is left to the individual workman who is highly skilled. In high volume production, many production designers, equipment designers, process engineers and methods engineers are involved and they put enormous amount of effort in designing the product & the manufacturing processes.

3. Nature of Operations: Detailed production planning is required for repetitive operations,, for example, in case of continuous production of a single standardized product: The variants in manufacturing approach are:

a. Manufacturing to order which may or may not be repeated at regular intervals.

b. Manufacturing for stock & sell under repetitive batch or mass Production, example – manufacturing of auto mobiles, watches, typewriter etc.

c. Manufacturing for stock & sell, (under continuous process manufacturing) example: Chemical & food products, soap etc.

5.8 Production Control:

Importance of Control function:

The function of production control is to:

1. Provide for the production of parts, assembles & products of required quality quantity at the required time.
2. Co-ordinate, monitor & feed-back to manufacturing management, the result of the production activities, analyzing & interpreting their significance & taking corrective action if necessary.
3. Provide for optimum utilization of all resources.
4. Achieve the broad objectives of low cost production & reliable customer service.

Benefits of Production Control:

1. Improvement in Profits through:

   A. Maintenance of a balanced inventory of materials, parts, work-in-progress & finished goods.

   B. Balanced & stabilized production.

   C. Maximum utilization of equipment, tooling, labour (manpower) & manufacturing & storage space.

   D. Minimum investment in inventory.

E. Reduction in indirect costs.

F. Reduction in setup costs.

G. Reduction in scrap& reworks costs.

H. Reduction in inventory costs.

2. Competitive advantages:

a. Reliable delivery to customers.

b. Shortened delivery schedules to customers.

c. Lower production costs greater pricing flexibility.

d. Orderly planning & marketing of new or improved products.

Elements of Production Control:

1. Control of Planning.
2. Control of materials.
3. Control of tooling.
4. Control of manufacturing capacity.
5. Control of Activities.
6. Control of Quantity.
7. Control of Material handling.
8. Control of Due dates.
9. Control of Information.

5.9 Scope of Production Planning & Control

Production planning & control involved in the following areas:

1. **Materials:** Planning for procurement of raw materials, components and spare parts in the right quantities & specifications at the right time from the right source at the right price. Purchasing, storage, inventory control, variety reduction, value analysis & inspection are the other activities associated with materials.
2. **Methods:** Choosing the best method of processing from several alternatives. It also includes determining the best sequence of operations & planning for tooling, jigs & fixtures etc.

3. **Machines & equipments:** Manufacturing methods are related to production facilities planning, capacity planning, allocation & utilization of plant & equipments, machines etc.
4. **Manpower:** Planning for manpower (labour, supervisory & managerial levels) having appropriate skills and expertise.
5. **Routing:** Determine the flow of work, arterial handling in the plant & sequence of operations or processing steps.
6. **Estimating:** Establishing operations times leading to fixation of performance standards both for workers & machines.
7. **Scheduling:** Scheduling ensures that parts, sub assemblies & finished products are completed as per the required delivery dates. It provides a time table of manufacturing activities.
8. **Dispatching:** Dispatching is the release of order & instructions for the starting of production in accordance with the route sheets & schedule charts.
9. **Expediting / Follow up:** Means chasing, follow-up or progressing which is done after the dispatching functions.
10. **Inspection:** This function is related to maintenance of quality in production & of evaluating the efficiency of the processes, methods & labour so that improvements can be made to achieve the quality standards set by product design.
11. **Evaluating:** The objective of evaluation is to improve performance of machines, processes & labour is evaluated to improve the same.
12. **Lost Control:** Manufacturing cost is controlled by wastage reduction, value analysis, inventory control & efficient utilization of all resource.

5.10 Aggregate Planning & Master Production Scheduling:

Production planning in the range of time is termed as 'Aggregate Planning'. It is thus called because the demand on facilities &

available capacities is specified in aggregate quantities.

In production Process (Problems), the Planning process is normally divided in three categories:

1. Long Range Planning
2. Short range Planning
3. Intermediate Planning or Aggregate Planning.

5.11 The Operation Planning and Scheduling Systems

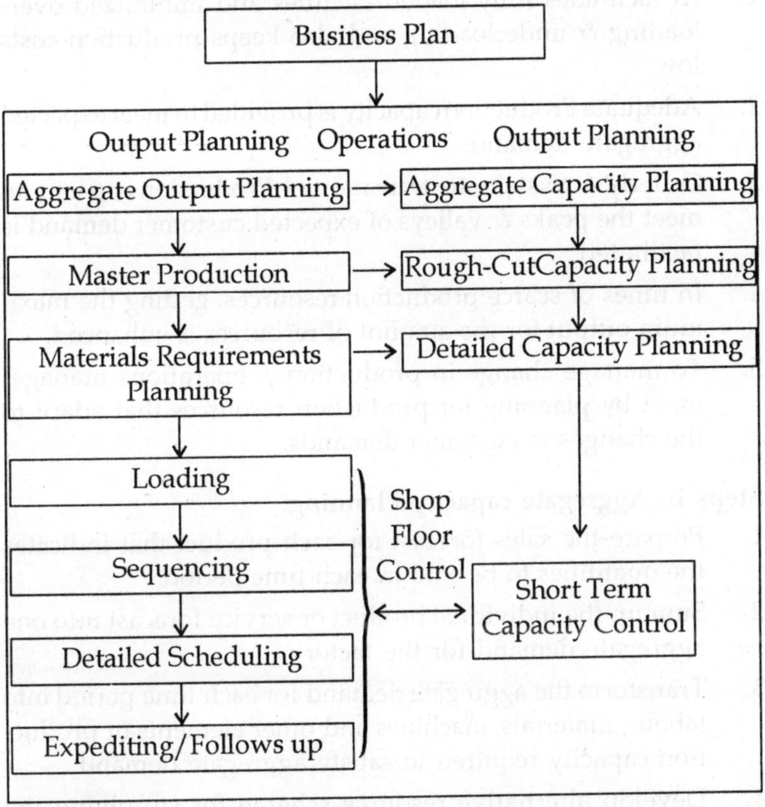

Aggregate Production (Output) Planning: It is the process of determining output levels (units) of product groups over the next 6 to 8 months period on a weekly or monthly basis. The plan indicates the overall level of outputs supporting the business plan.

Aggregate Planning or Aggregate Capacity Planning: It is the process of for formulate a plan for providing a production capacity scheme to support the middle range sales forecast. As forecast demand becomes known in the form of customer orders, aggregate capacity plans may have to be revised upwards & downwards to avoid either overloaded or under loaded facilities.

Need for Aggregate capacity Planning:

1. It facilitates fully loaded facilities and minimized over-loading & underloading and also keeps production costs low.
2. Adequate Production capacity is provided to meet expected aggregate demand.
3. Orderly & Systematic transition of Production capacity to meet the peaks & valleys of expected customer demand is facilitated.
4. In times of scarce production resources, getting the maximum output for the amount of resources is enhanced.
5. To manage change in production / operations management by planning for production resources that adapt to the changes in customer demands.

Steps in Aggregate capacity Planning:

1. Prepare the sales forecast for each product that indicates the quantities to be sold in each time period.
2. Sum up the individual product or service forecast into one aggregate demand for the factory.
3. Transform the aggregate demand for each time period into labour, materials, machines and other elements of production capacity required to satisfy aggregate demand.
4. Develop alternative resource scheme for supplying the necessary production capacity to support the cumulative aggregate demand.
5. Select the capacity plan from among the alternatives considered that satisfies aggregate demand and best meets the objectives of the organization.

Flow Chart of Aggregate Plan:

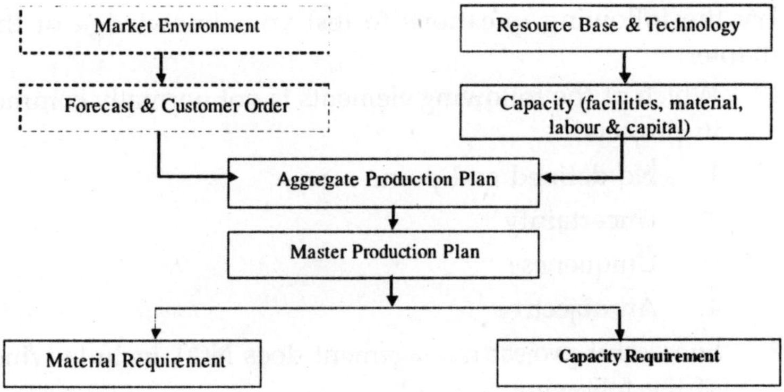

Multiple choice questions

Try the following questions to test your knowledge of this chapter.

1. Which of the following elements is not normally common in projects?
    1. No defined end point
    2. Uncertainty
    3. Uniqueness
    4. An objective
2. Successful project management does NOT include which of the following factors?
    1. Control mechanisms
    2. Interchangeable staff
    3. Competent team members
    4. Responsiveness to clients
3. Which is the first stage in the project management model?
    1. Project definition
    2. Project planning
    3. Understanding the project environment
    4. Project control
4. A clear hierarchy of objectives in the project definition would not normally contain:
    1. Desired end result
    2. Success criteria
    3. Control mechanisms
    4. The purpose
5. A critical path network diagram does not:
    1. Calculate earned-value
    2. Identify the particularly important activities
    3. Help determine the amount of float
    4. Calculate the duration of the whole project

6. Which of the following are features of Belbin's 'resource investigator' role?
   1. Extroverted, enthusiastic and communicative
   2. Sober, unemotional and prudent
   3. Calm, self confident and controlled
   4. Unorthodox, discerning, single-minded
   5. Painstaking, orderly and conscientious
7. Which of the following are features of Belbin's 'coordinator' role?
   1. Calm, self confident and controlled
   2. Mature, confident, delegates
   3. Unorthodox, discerning, single-minded
   4. Sober, unemotional and prudent
   5. Extroverted, enthusiastic and communicative

Discussion questions

1. Would professional services, such as a management consultancy project, benefit from the application of project management principles in the same way as would the manufacturer of a turbine generator set for a power station?
2. Why is the critical path a helpful concept in project planning and control?
3. Identify possible differences between internal and external project performance reports.
4. Evaluate the job of the project manager.
   a. Does project management tend to make people value short-term expediency in order to get the job done?
   b. Why does the project manager tend to resist changes?
   c. Is project management good training for general management?
5. Identify a number of projects with which you have been involved, for example 'project work' as part of the university course, moving house, preparing a large meal, organizing a foreign trip for several people, etc. Assess each of

them in terms of their project elements and the complexity-uncertainty typology.

6. Discuss the problems of managing a large-scale famine relief project.
7. Identify the key project planning phases for a major rock concert.
8. What criteria might you use to monitor a theatrical production?

Short Case (Case Study)

- XYZ Television

XYZ Television is a television production company which specializes in making outside broadcast (OB) 'specials' for a variety of television networks. It was recently commissioned to make a series of 'summer road show' programmes which would be shot at locations around India during the spring and early summer and broadcast by the customer (a satellite broadcasting network) during the summer. The programmes would involve circus acts, displays, events and computer-graphic displays to entertain the crowds and popular entertainment acts and interviews which would be interspersed with contestant games. Managing the preparation for the series was the responsibility of the show's producer, Mr. ABC, who had recently graduated with distinction from her MBA course, knew that he would need to keep a tight grip on the arrangements for the road show series. The shooting would start at the end of May and the final show would be recorded at the end of July. The shows would be broadcast between early July and late August, so any delay either in recording the material or in editing the programmes would cause considerable complications.

The company had known that it would be commissioned to make the programmes since December, but ABC had only been allocated the job in early February! His first act was to list the various jobs which would have to be done before shooting could start. He then discussed each job with the part of the company which would carry it out, to try to understand what decisions would need to be made before they could start on their jobs. The jobs which needed to be done prior to the start of the shooting are listed below together with some details.

The producer's responsibilities (as well as managing the whole project) included:

1. *Scheduling the venues:* would take about two weeks to finalize and could be started straight away.
2. *Defining the design concept:* would need discussions with the chief designer and would take about four weeks of considering alternative designs before finalizing the concept, but could be started straight away.
3. *Specifying computer-graphic displays:* again in consultation with the chief designer, it would take about a week but could not be started until all the detailed planning had been finalized.
4. The design department's responsibility was:
5. *Producing artwork for printed materials:* would take about three weeks but could be started only after completion of the detailed planning.
6. The programme planning department's responsibilities were:
7. *Booking the venues:* a one-week job which could be started as soon as the venues had been decided by ABC.
8. *Detailed planning:* the preparation of detailed plans and schedules, a two-week task which could be started once the design concept had been finalized and the venues booked.
9. *Printing the brochures:* an outside printer could be given this job as soon as the artwork for the printed materials had been prepared by the design department. The printer usually quoted a four-week delivery from receipt of the artwork.
10. *Printing the display posters:* again depended on the preparation of the artwork but could be delivered within two weeks of the artwork being ready.

11. *Ordering the road show vehicles:* several trailer trucks and ancillary vehicles were needed which could be ordered on completion of the detailed planning; delivery of the vehicles would take about six weeks.
12. *Writing the graphic display software:* contracted out to a software house, it would take about four weeks but could only be started after the computer graphics had been specified by the producer and chief designer.
13. *Final testing and rehearsals:* the programme planning department were finally responsible for getting the 'whole act together' immediately prior to shooting. Testing and rehearsals could only start once the brochures had been printed, the vehicles fully fitted out and customized and the promotion staff trained. Final tests and rehearsals should take around a week but, if things went wrong at any stage, could take longer.

The workshop's responsibility was:

Customizing and fitting out the vehicles: after the vehicles are delivered and the artwork agreed and the computer-graphics software finished, the vehicles could be fitted out and customized for the shows; this would normally take around two weeks.

The personnel department was responsible for:

Recruiting the promotion (promo) staff: these were the people (often 'resting' actors) who staffed the exhibits and entertained the crowds; they could be recruited as soon as the detailed planning was completed. Usually it took two weeks to recruit all the promo staff.

Training the promo staff: once all promo staff had been recruited they would need training – a one-week task.

Questions

1. Can ABC get the project together in time to start shooting on schedule?

2. Which are the jobs which she will have to manage particularly closely?
3. What general advice would you give her to help her to manage this project?

Answer

XYZ Television

1. Can Mr. ABC meet the deadline?

In order to answer this question itis necessary to draw a project network diagram. A summary of all the activities in the project is given below. It shows their likely duration and their immediate predecessor.

TV SUMMER ROADSHOW

	Activities	Immediate Predecessor	Estimated Duration in Weeks
a	Schedule venues	-	2
b	Define design concept	-	4
c	Book venues	a	1
d	Detail planning	b,c	2
e	Artwork for printed mail	d	3
f	Print brochures	e	4
g	Print display posters	e	2
h	Order vehicles	d	6
i	Customize vehicles	e,h,k	2
j	Spec. computer graphic displays	d	1
k	Write software	j	4
l	Recruit promo staff	d	2
m	Train promo staff	l	1
n	Final tests and rehearsals	f,i,m	1

The complete network can be drawn from this. It can be seen that the time available is probably just sufficient to plan and organize the road show project, although there is little, if any, room for delay (17 weeks from beginning of February to end of May, 15 weeks for project). This will make the whole project particularly sensitive to delays in any of its constituent activities.

2. Which jobs will have to be managed closely?

The 'critical path' through the network includes the following activities:

a - Define the design concept

b- Detailed planning

c - Ordering (and awaiting delivery) of the vehicles

d - Customizing the vehicles and fitting them out

e - Final tests and rehearsals

Any delay on these will delay the whole project, and savings in time on them might (up to a point) be saved on the whole project. Of particular significant is the final activity which seems, from the narrative, to have a particularly uncertain time estimate. This activity should warrant close attention.

3. What else might ABC do?

The following recommendations are made to ABC with reference to the factors important for successful project management (p.592 of Slack *et al.*):

1. ABC should clearly define the goals of the project to all the organizations involved. He should also stress the critical time scales involved in the project.
2. He should ensure that the project has the support of top management (as the project is for a popular summer programme, this should not present a problem).
3. He needs to establish a project team of competent, experienced members who will be involved for the duration of the whole project. All the organizations involved in the project should be represented in the team to improve communications.
4. Communications between the organizations should be improved to optimize co-operation.

5. The resources allocated to the project should be checked to ensure that the project can be completed within the strict time scales imposed.
6. Effective control mechanisms should be established to provide instant measures of project progress. Thus the problems can be identified as early as possible.
7. Feedback capabilities and trouble-shooting mechanisms should also be installed to identify and solve potential problems as they occur.
8. Methods of reducing the time scales for the critical path should be examined
9. The project budget should be tightly controlled. Problems could be encountered if any part of the project needed to be crashed to ensure on-time completion.

Chapter **6**

Inventory Management

6.1 Inventory

The word inventory was first recorded in 1601. The French term inventories, or "detailed list of goods," dates back to 1415.

6.2 The reasons for keeping stock

There are three basic reasons for keeping an inventory:

1. *Time* - The time lags present in the supply chain, from supplier to user at every stage, requires that you sustain certain amount of inventory to use in this "lead time"
2. *Uncertainty* - Inventories are sustained as buffers to meet uncertainties in demand, supply and movements of goods.
3. *Economies of scale* - Condition of "one unit at a time at a place where user needs it, when he needs it" principle tends to incur lots of costs in terms of logistics. So bulk buying, movement and storing brings in economies of scale, thus inventory

Buffer stock is held in individual workstations against the possibility that the upstream workstation may be a little delayed in long setup or change-over time. This stock is then used while that change-over is happening. This stock can be eliminated by tools like.

6.3 LIFO accounting

In **LIFO accounting**, a historical method of recording the value of inventory, a firm record the last units purchased as the first units sold. LIFO is an acronym for "last in, first out." Sometimes the term **FILO** ("first in, last out") is used synonymously. LIFO accounting is in contrast to the method **FIFO accounting** covered below.

Since prices generally rise over time because of inflation, this method records the sale of the most expensive inventory first and thereby decreases profit and reduces taxes. However, this method rarely reflects the physical flow of indistinguishable items.

LIFO valuation is permitted in the belief that an ongoing business does not realize an economic profit solely from inflation. When prices are increasing, they must replace inventory currently being sold with higher priced goods. LIFO better matches current cost against current revenue. It also defers paying taxes on phantom income arising solely from inflation. LIFO is attractive to business in that it delays a major detrimental effect of inflation, namely higher taxes. However, in a very long run, both methods converge.

6.4 FIFO accounting

FIFO accounting is a common method for recording the value of inventory. It is appropriate where there are many different batches of similar products. The method presumes that the next item to be shipped will be the oldest of that type in the warehouse. In practice, this usually reflects the underlying commercial substance of the transaction, since many companies rotate their inventory (especially of perishable goods). This is still not in contrast to LIFO because FIFO and LIFO are cost flow assumptions not product flow assumptions.

In an economy of rising prices (during inflation), it is common for beginning companies to use FIFO for reporting the value of merchandise to bolster their balance sheet. As the older and cheaper goods are sold, the newer and more expensive goods remain as assets on the company's books. Having the higher valued inventory and the lower cost of goods sold on the company's financial statements may increase the chances of getting a loan. However, as it prospers the company may switch to LIFO to reduce the amount of taxes it pays to the government.

6.5 LIFO liquidation

Notwithstanding its deferred tax advantage, a LIFO inventory systems can lead to LIFO liquidation, a situation where in the absence of new replacement inventory or a search for increased profits, older inventory is increasingly liquidated, or sold. If prices have been rising, for example through inflation, this older inventory will have a lower cost, and its liquidation will lead to the recognition of higher net income and the payment of higher taxes, thus reversing the deferred tax advantage that initially encouraged the adoption of a LIFO system. Some companies who use LIFO have decades-old inventory recorded on their books at a very low cost. For these companies LIFO liquidation would result in an inflated net income and higher tax payments. This situation is usually undesirable; on rare occasions a company in financial stress may abuse this method to temporarily increase income.

6.6 Inventory Control Techniques:

Inventory is maintained in every organization depending on the type of the business. Inventory control techniques are governed by the inventory control department with in the setup of one on the basis inventory models. Viz., fixed order quantity system or fixed order period system. The management view is focused on the proper control over its ordering, procurement, maintenance & Consumption. The control can be for order quality & order frequency. Inventory control is concerned with minimizing the total cost of inventory. In the U.K. the term often used is stock control. The three main factors in inventory control decision making process are:

- The cost of holding the stock (e.g., based on the interest rate).
- The cost of placing an order (e.g., for row material stocks) or the set-up cost of production.
- The cost of shortage, i.e., what is lost if the stock is insufficient to meet all demand.

The third element is the most difficult to measure and is often handled by establishing a "service level" policy, e. g, certain percentage of demand will be met from stock without delay.

The ABC Classification The ABC classification system is to grouping items according to annual sales volume, in an attempt to identify the small number of items that will account for most of the sales volume and that are the most important ones to control for effective inventory management.

Reorder Point: The inventory level R in which an order is placed Where R = D.L, D = demand rate (demand rate period (day, week, etc), and L = lead time.

Safety Stock: Remaining inventory between the times that an order is placed and when new stock is received. If there are not enough inventories then a shortage may occur.

Safety stock is a hedge against running out of inventory. It is an extra inventory to take care on unexpected events. It is often called buffer stock. The absence of inventory is called a shortage.

The different techniques of inventory control are:

1. **ABC** - Always better control analysis.
2. **HML** -High, Medium & Low analysis.
3. **VED** - Vital, Essential & desirable analysis.
4. **SDE** - Scare, difficult & easy to obtain analysis.
5. **FSN** - Fast moving, slow moving & non moving analysis.
6. **EOQ** - Economic order quantity analysis.

6.7 ABC Analysis [Always Better Control]: The materials are divided into a number of categories for adopting a selective approach for material control. It is generally seen that in manufacturing concern, a small percentage of items contribute a large percentage of value of consumption and a large percentage of items of materials contribute a small percentage of value.

Under ABC analysis, the materials are divided into three categories viz, A, B & C. Past experience has shown that almost 10% of the items contributes to 70% of value consumption and

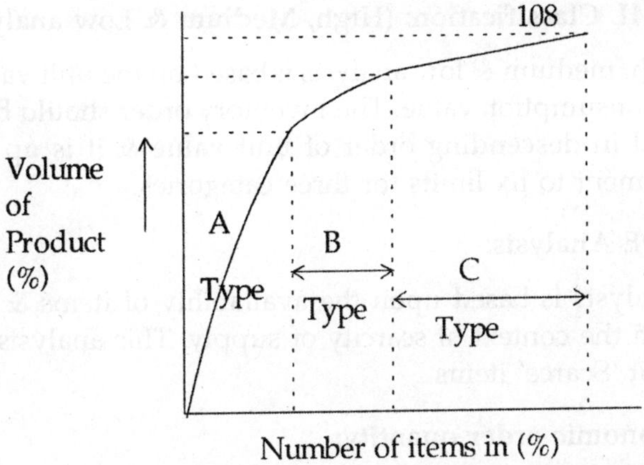

this category is called 'A' category. About 20% of the items contribute about 20% of consumption and this is known as Category 'B' materials Category 'C' covers about 70% of items of materials, which contribute only 10% of value of consumption.

6.8 VED Classification: The VED analysis is done to determine the critically of an item and its effect on production and other services. It is specially used for classification of spare parts. If it is essential, then it is given 'E' classification and if it is not so essential, the part is given 'D' classification. For v items, a large stock of inventory is generally maintained, while for 'D' items, minimum stock is enough.

6.9 Comparison/relationship between ABC Analysis & VED Classification

ABC CLASSIFICATION	VED CLASSIFICATION		
	V	E	D
A	Constant Control; Regular follow up, Low stock and Ordering more frequently	Average stock; No risk of stockouts	No stock.
B	Moderate Stock; No risk of stockout.	Average stock, some risk can be taken	Very low stock; some risk can be taken
C	High stocks; Restricted order; No risk.	Average stock; some risk can be taken.	Low stock; some risk can be taken.

6.10 HML Classification: (High, Medium & Low analysis)

The high, medium & low analysis is based on the unit value not on the consumption value. The inventory order should be/will be listed in descending order of unit value & it is up to the management to fix limits for three categories.

6.11 SDE Analysis:

This analysis is based upon the availability of items & this is useful in the context of scarcity of supply. This analysis refers on 'S' for 'Scarce' items

6.12 Economic order quantity:

Economic order quantity is the level of inventory that minimizes the total inventory holding costs and ordering costs. The framework used to determine this order quantity is also known as **Wilson EOQ Model**. The model was developed by F. W. Harris in 1913. But still R. H. Wilson is given credit for his early in-depth analysis of the model.

Underlying assumptions

1. The ordering cost is constant.
2. The rate of demand is constant
3. The lead time is fixed
4. The purchase price of the item is constant i.e no discount is available

EOQ is the levels of the inventory where ordering cost and carrying cost remains equal.

Variables

- Q = order quantity
- Q^* = optimal order quantity
- D = annual demand quantity of the product
- P = purchase cost per unit
- C = fixed cost per order (*not* per unit, in addition to unit cost)

- *H* = annual holding cost per unit (also known as carrying cost) (warehouse space, refrigeration, insurance, etc. usually not related to the unit cost)

The Total Cost function

The single-item EOQ formula finds the minimum point of the following cost function: EOQ is the level of the inventory where ordering cost and carrying cost remains equal.

Total Cost = purchase cost + ordering cost + holding cost

- **Purchase cost:** This is the variable cost of goods: purchase unit price × annual demand quantity. This is P×D
- **Ordering cost:** This is the cost of placing orders: each order has a fixed cost C, and we need to order D/Q times per year. This is C × D/Q
- **Holding cost:** the average quantity in stock (between fully replenished and empty) is Q/2, so this cost is H × Q/2

$$TC = PD + (CD / Q) + (HQ/2)$$

In order to determine the minimum point of the total cost curve, set its derivative equal to zero:

$$(dTC\,(Q)/d\,Q) = d\,/\,d\,Q\,\{PD + (CD\,/\,Q) + (HQ\,/\,2)\}$$

The result of this derivation is:

$$-CD\,/\,Q^2 + H/2 = 0$$

Solving for Q gives Q* (the optimal order quantity):

$$H/2 = CD\,/\,Q^2$$

$$Q^2 = 2CD\,/\,H$$

Therefore; $Q^* = \sqrt{\frac{2CD}{H}}$

Note that interestingly, Q* is independent of P, it is a function of only C, D, H.

Multiple choice questions

Try the following questions to test your knowledge of this chapter.

1. Buffer inventory is required as:
   1. One or more stages in the operation cannot supply all the items it produces simultaneously
   2. Material cannot be transported instantaneously between the point of supply and the point of demand
   3. Compensation for the uncertainties inherent in supply and demand
   4. Compensation for differences in the timing of supply and demand
2. Cycle inventory is required as:
   1. Compensation for differences in the timing of supply and demand
   2. One or more stages in the operation cannot supply all the items it produces simultaneously
   3. Compensation for the uncertainties inherent in supply and demand
   4. Material cannot be transported instantaneously between the point of supply and the point of demand
3. The EOQ formula has been criticised in a number of areas. Which of the following is not an area of common criticism?
   1. Small errors in estimating will not result in a significant deviation from the EOQ
   2. The assumptions included in the models
   3. The use of the models as prescriptive devices
   4. The real costs of stock in operations
4. What is a two-bin system?
   1. A system in which suppliers deliver two bins at a time
   2. A system in which two full bins of an item are always held in stock

3. A system in which orders are placed when only one complete bin of stock is remaining
4. A system in which everything is split between two storage bins

5. Under the ABC system of inventory priorities a Class A item is:
   1. The 20% of high-value items that account for around 20% the total stock value
   2. The 80% of high-value items that account for around 80% the total stock value
   3. The 80% of high-value items that account for around 20% the total stock value
   4. The 20% of high-value items that account for around 80% the total stock value

6. Order-point or re-order level inventory control is used for:
   1. Inventory quality control
   2. Control of dependent demand inventory items
   3. Monitoring the workings of a MRP system
   4. Control of independent demand inventory items
   5. Production scheduling

7. Which of these statements is correct?

The Economic Order Quantity (EOQ):

1. Will depend on how many related parts are required in the same period
2. Determines the lowest order quantity by balancing the cost of ordering against the cost of holding stock
3. Should be calculated once a year
4. Is a formula that calculates a realistic purchase price for an item
5. Is used to calculate how much safety stock should be carried

8. One of the underlying assumptions of the EOQ model is that :
   1. There is a point where stockholding costs are equal to ordering costs
   2. Demand is unstable and unpredictable
   3. A doubling of demand requires a doubling of the order quantity
   4. Replenishment is non-instantaneous
   5. The purchase price per unit varies with the quantity ordered
9. Which would be the most appropriate method of controlling stock in a retail shop?
   1. Order Point
   2. Materials Requirements Planning
   3. Periodic Review
   4. 4Just-in-Time
   5. Two-Bin System
10. Which would be the most appropriate method of controlling stock in a hotel bar?
    1. Order Point
    2. Poke-Yoka
    3. Materials Requirements Planning
    4. Periodic Review
    5. Two-Bin System
    6. Just-in-Time
11. Periodic review means:
    1. Ordering inventory in consultation with suppliers relative to their available capacity
    2. Ordering inventory at a predetermined re-order level
    3. Ordering inventory to supplier call-offs on an as required basis
    4. Ordering inventory at a fixed and regular time interval

5. Ordering inventory when it falls below the designated safety stock level

Discussion questions

1. Describe and categorize the types of material inventories that might be found in the following organizations:
   1. a theatre
   2. a furniture retailer
   3. a brewery
   4. a city bus company.
2. Talk to an operations manager about the different types of inventory that the organization holds. Find out if there are different ways of planning and controlling some of the different types of inventory.
3. The Shocking Electricity Company uses 3000 metres of wire every month. The cost of placing an order for the wire has been calculated at Rs 40 and the cost of stocking the wire is 5p per metre per year. In what quantities should the company order the wire? If it adopts an EOQ approach to ordering, what would be its annual inventory cost?
4. A university's printing department uses paper at the rate of 86 packets per day. A pack of paper costs Rs 2 and the annual stock-holding cost is calculated at 10 per cent of the cost of the paper. If it costs Rs 25 every time an order is placed and the department works 250 days in the year, what is the EOQ for the paper? If it takes three days between placing an order and receiving it, what is the reorder point at which an order should be placed?
5. The Pride of Scotland Butchers Limited has a haggis machine which can produce at a rate of 1000 haggises per day. Traditionally the company produces a day's worth of haggises which fully satisfies the demand for one week. The company sells its haggises throughout 50 weeks of the year. Each time the haggis machine is set up to produce a batch of haggises it costs Rs 100. The haggises have to be kept in particularly cool and hygienic conditions and therefore it costs the company Rs 0.5 per haggis per day to

store stock. How much money is the company losing by producing 1000 haggises per week in one batch rather than adopting an EBQ policy (make any assumptions you believe reasonable)?

6. A company which has been using the EOQ formula to determine its order quantities has now found that demand has increased by 50 per cent since it last calculated the optimum order quantity. What adjustment will it have to make to its order quantity? What further adjustment will it have to make to its ordering quantity if its stock-holding costs increase by 50 per cent?

7. A university MBA programme keeps sweatshirts in stock for its students with the university's logo emblazoned on the front. On average it sells 200 of these sweatshirts every year. There is a fixed postage and packing charge of Rs 5 every time it places an order. The cost of the sweatshirts is Rs15 and inventory is charged by the university at 30 per cent per year. How many sweatshirts should the university order at a time? The new programme director has responded to complaints from the students that the sweatshirts were out of stock last year by offering to pay Rs 20 into the students' entertainment fund every time there is a stock-out. How would this affect the economic order quantity?

8. An ice-cream seller is required to purchase the ice-creams which are then kept in a cold box at the beginning of a sales day. The seller pays Rs 0.20 for every ice-cream. Ice-creams are sold at Rs 0.50 each but any ice-creams left at the end of the day cannot be returned and go to waste. The ice-cream seller classifies demand as either low, medium or high. Low demand is between 40 and 80 ice-creams, medium demand is between 80 and 120 ice-creams, and high demand is between 120 and 160 ice-creams. The probability of demand being low is 0.2, the probability of demand being medium is 0.5, and the probability of demand being high is 0.3. Approximately how many ice-creams would you advise the ice-cream seller to purchase

every morning? If competition forces down the price the ice-cream seller can charge to Rs 0.40, does this change the decision?

9. A furniture store sells tables which it obtains from a local furniture factory. Each time it places an order on the factory there is a delivery charge and general transaction cost of Rs 60. The stock-holding cost is estimated to be Rs 10 per table per year. Both demand and lead time vary according to the distribution in Table 1. Devise a re-order level policy for the furniture store if it is to have less than a 5 per cent probability of being out of stock in each order cycle.

Table 1. Lead-time usage of tables

Lead time usage	*Probability*
600-650	0.2
650-700	0.2
700-750	0.3
750-800	0.2
800-850	0.05
850-900	0.05

10. Save all your food (and drink) bills over a two-week period (or otherwise make a note of such purchases) and conduct a Pareto analysis of the usage value of the items. How would you use this information to plan an inventory policy for your purchasing and storage of such items?
11. Identify 10 public companies from different industrial sectors and examine their published accounts (you can do this through the internet); calculate the value of their 'stock turn' ratios. What are the implications of the variations in this figure you will observe between the companies?

Short Case

Inventory management at SUN Electrical

Inventory management in some operations is more than just a part of their responsibility; it is their very reason for being in business. SUN Electrical, India's independent supplier and distributor of lamps, is such a business. It stocks over 2900 different types of lamp, which are sourced from 14 countries and distributed to customers throughout the country.

'In effect our customers are using us to manage their stocks of lighting sources for them,' says Mr. Sachin, the Managing Director of Sun Electrical. *'They could, if they wanted to, hold their own stock but might not want to devote the time, space, money or effort to doing so. Using us they get the widest range of products to choose from, and an accurate, fast and dependable service.'*

Central to the company's ability to provide the service its customers expect is its computerized stock management system. The system holds information on all of Sun's customers, the type of lamps they may order, the quality and brand of lamps they prefer, the price to be charged and the location of each item in the warehouse. When a customer phones in to order, the computer system immediately accesses all this information, which is confirmed to the customer. This leaves only the quantity of each lamp required by the customer to be keyed in. The system then generates an instruction to the warehouse to pick up and dispatch the order. This instruction includes the shelf location of each item. The system even calculates the location of each item in the warehouse which will minimize the movement of stock for warehouse staff.

Orders for the replenishment of stocks in the warehouse are triggered by a re-order point system. The re-order point is set for each stocked item depending on the likely demand for the product during the order lead time (forecast from the equivalent period's orders the previous year), the order lead time for the item (which varies from 24 hours to four months) and the variability of the lead time (from previous experience). The size of the replenishment order depends on the lamp being ordered. Sun prefers most orders to be for a whole number of container loads (the shipping costs for part-container loads being more expensive). However, lower order quantities of small or expensive lamps may be used. The order quantity for each lamp is based on its demand, its value and the cost of transportation from the suppliers. However, all this can be overridden in an emergency. If a customer, such as a hospital, urgently needs a particular lamp which is not in stock, the company will even use a fast courier to fly the item in from overseas – all for the sake of maintaining its reputation for high service levels.

'We have to get the balance right,' says Mr. Sachin. *'Excellent service is the foundation of our success. But we could not survive if we did not control stocks tightly. After all we are carrying the cost of every lamp in our warehouse until the customer eventually pays for it. If stock levels were too high we just could not operate profitably. It is for that reason that we go as far as to pay incentives to the relevant staff based on how well they keep our working capital and stocks under control.'*

Questions

1 Define what you think the five performance objectives (quality, speed, dependability, flexibility and cost) mean for an operation such as Sun Electrical.

2 What are the most important of these performance objectives for Sun Electrical?

3 What seems to influence the stock replenishment policy of Sun Electrical?

4 How does this differ from conventional economic order quantity theory?

Answer

Sun Electrical

1. Define what you think the five performance objectives mean for an operation such as Sun Electrical?

Quality

Quality in this case means the quality of service to the customers. This means getting their order right, giving them any relevant information about the product (such as any changes in its design or whether it is available immediately) and being able to suggest alternatives for the customer (this is enabled by the sophisticated computer system the company uses).

Speed

Speed refers to the time between a customer placing an order for lamps and them arriving at their premises.

Dependability

This is the operations ability to stick to its explicit or implicit delivery times. For example, if there is a chance that an item cannot be delivered the next day, the customer needs to be told as soon as possible.

Flexibility

This could mean various things such as the operations ability to change its level of output when demand fluctuates, its ability to find substitute products if the customer's first choice is not available, or the ability to override its normal procedures in an emergency (such as when a hospital wants a special lamp).

Cost

As the owner of the company says, an important cost is the working capital costs of holding the stock. Other costs include the cost of the warehouse and the computer system which takes inventory decisions.

2. What are the most important of these performance objectives for Sun Electrical?

Cost is clearly important to it, which is why it even pays incentives on how well costs and working capital are kept under control. At the same time 'excellent service' is also mentioned. Partly this is quality but it is also availability. Availability is a combination of speed and dependability.

3. What seems to influence the stock replenishment policy of Sun Electrical?

The company uses the re-order point system. In other words, when stocks of an item get below a certain point they are re-ordered. Re-order points are set on the basis of predicted demand, the order lead time, the variability of lead time, the physical size of the lamp, and the transportation cost.

4. How does this differ from conventional economic order quantity theory?

The main departure from conventional EOQ theory is the influence of the 'container load'. Shipping items where the total load is less than a full container is relatively expensive. Thus, if the theoretical EOQ is slightly less than a full container load, the order quantity would be possibly increased to fill the whole container.

Chapter 7

Quality

7.1 Introduction

What does the word "Quality" means to you? Quality is what customer wants. Quality is the perception of the customer about the product/service's degree, which meets the customer's expectations. Therefore, quality is defined by customer needs and expectations. Likely *beauty, quality lies in the eyes of the beholder.*

American Society of Quality Control defines *(1) "Quality" is the totality of features and characteristics of a product or service that bear on its ability to satisfy a given need. (2) A product or service free of deficiencies.*

Another definition of quality is given by Badiru and Ayeni (1993):

"Quality refers to an equilibrium level of functionality possessed by a product or service based on the producer's capability and customer's need"

Dr. Joseph M. Juran defines in his book Juran's Quality Control hand book about quality he said *quality as fitness for use.* In his text, *Quality Is Free,* Philip Crosby discusses *quality as conformance to requirements and non quality as non conformance.*

Armand Feigenbaum, written a book " Total Quality Control", states that *quality is a customer determination which is based on the customer's actual experience with the product or service, measured against his or her requirements – stated or unstated, conscious or merely sensed, technically operational or entirely subjective and always representing a moving target in a competitive market.*

7.2 Dimensions of Quality:

Quality represents many aspects of what customer want. Some dimensions of quality are:

1. The primary operating characteristics is **performance**, which determines- how well the product or service performs the intended function. Example: Durability of batteries, fuel economy of bikes, breaks horse power of an engine etc.

2. **Features** are the second dimension of quality. Example: looks and design of a car, interior of the refrigerator etc.

3. Durability is the time – duration or amount of use before being replaced or repaired.

4. **Reliability** means likelihood of breakdown, repair or expected time of fault- free operation.

5. Convenience and cost of repair and maintenance and is related to ease in resolving the customer complains, in short we can say it a **Serviceability**.

6. **Appearance** means look, taste, smell, sound or any other effect which is felt by human senses.

7. **Uniformity** called as limited variations among different products of same type.

8. **Consistency**, conformance with standards, being on time etc.

9. **Time** means lead time, waiting time, etc.

10. **Safety** means harmless from health and environment during performance.

11. **Customer Service**, after sales service, treatment with customer during or before sales.

12. **Compatibility** of the product/service with existing or standards interfaces.

Customer determines Quality in two ways: Requirement and Assessment

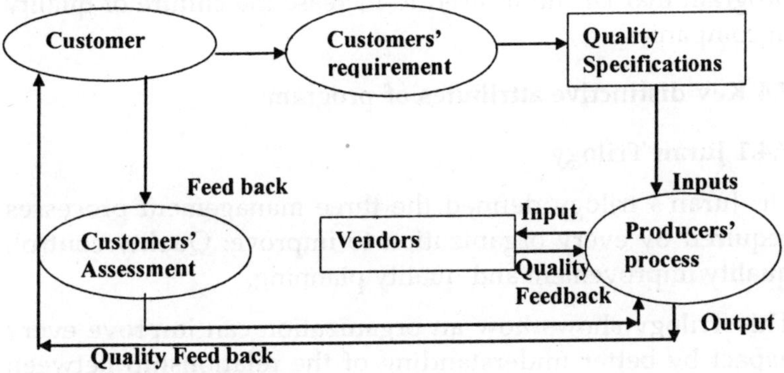

7.3 Dr. Juran quality program

Background of program

Dr. Joseph M. Juran was born in December 24th of 1904 at Braila, Rumania, he graduated as an Electrical Engineer in 1924 and now a day he is considered the leader of the quality management of the last 70 years. The influence of the scripts he has written is considered the core of quality management, i.e. Juran's Quality Handbook 5th edition.

The relevant things that Dr. Juran did was conceptualized the Pareto Principal to apply it in quality management. He also spent some years with the reengineering concepts. During this time he observed that an organization could work better if they standardized the process and give more importance to the quality.

After the Second World War, he started to get rename in Japan. Japanese executives were preoccupied for giving to their companies an aggregated value and maintain them between the best companies worldwide. Dr. Juran had a set of principals and methodologies that helped to the companies stay over their competitors and implement them in Japan with great success. Dr. Juran got recognized in countries like Japan and USA because the executives got excellent results with his programs.

Dr. Juran worked together with tools like Pareto Principle and Total Quality Management and others that are part of the program that Dr. Juran used to increase the culture of quality in companies.

7.4 Key distinctive attributes of program

7.4.1 Juran Trilogy

Dr. Juran's trilogy defined the three management processes required by every organization to improve: Quality control, quality improvement and quality planning.

This Trilogy shows how an organization can improve every aspect by better understanding of the relationship between processes that plan, control and improve quality as well as business results. It was created in the 1950's and defines managing for quality as three basic quality-oriented, interrelated processes:

7.4.1.1 Quality Planning – To determine customer needs and develop processes and products required to meet and exceed those of the customer needs. The processes are called Design for Six Sigma or Concurrent Engineering. This can be particularly challenging for a planning team, because customers are not always consistent with what they say they want. The challenge for quality planning is to identify the most important needs from all the needs expressed by the customer.

- Identify who are the customers.
- Determine the needs of those customers.
- Translate those needs into our language.
- Develop a product that can respond to those needs.

Optimize the product features so as to meet our needs and customer needs.

7.4.1.2 Quality Control – The purposes of quality control is to ensure the process is running in optimal effectiveness, or to ensure that any level of chronic waste inherent in the process does not get worst. Chronic waste, which is a cost of poor quality that can exist in any process, may exist due to various factors including deficiencies in the original planning. It could cost a lot of money to the company, from rework time to scrap product to overdue receivables. If the waste does get worst (sporadic spike), a corrective action team is brought in to determine the cause or causes of this abnormal variation. Once the cause or causes had been determined and corrected, the process again falls into the zone defined by the "quality control" limits.

This proves that the process can produce the product under operating conditions with minimal inspection.

Transfer the process to Operations.

7.4.1.3 *Quality Improvement* – Eliminate waste, defects and rework that improves processes and reduces the cost of poor quality. The processes have to be constantly challenged and continuously improved. Such an improvement does not happen of its own accord. It results from purposeful Quality Improvement or "Breakthrough."

Develop a process which is able to produce the product.

Optimize the process.

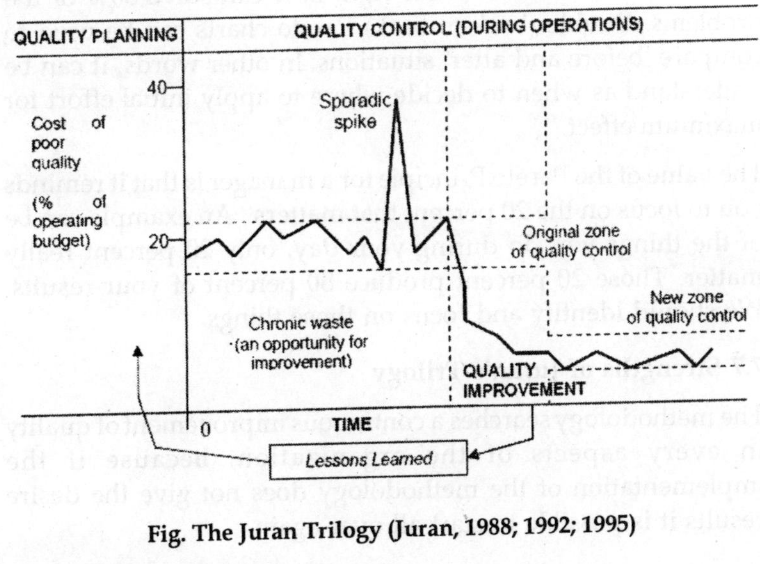

Fig. The Juran Trilogy (Juran, 1988; 1992; 1995)

7.5 Juran's ten steps to Quality improvement

1. Build awareness of the need and opportunity for improvement
2. Set goals for improvement
3. Organize to reach the goals
4. Provide training
5. Carry out projects to solve problems
6. Report progress
7. Give recognition
8. Communicate results
9. Keep score
10. Maintain momentum by making annual improvement part of the regular systems and processes of the company

7.6 Pareto's principle

The Pareto principle suggests that most effects come from relatively few causes. In quantitative terms: 80% of the problems come from 20% of the causes (machines, raw materials, operators etc.); 80% of the wealth is owned by 20% of the people etc. Therefore effort aimed at the right 20% can solve 80% of the problems. Double (back to back) Pareto charts can be used to compare 'before and after' situations. In other words, it can be understand as when to decide where to apply initial effort for maximum effect.

The value of the Pareto Principle for a manager is that it reminds you to focus on the 20 percent that matters. An example can be of the things you do during your day, only 20 percent really matter. Those 20 percent produce 80 percent of your results. We should identify and focus on those things.

7.7 Strengths of Juran's Trilogy

The methodology searches a continuous improvement of quality in every aspects of the organization, because if the implementation of the methodology does not give the desire results it is possible to start all over again.

The methodology allows using different quality tools to cover the steps of Juran's Trilogy. It allows a better understanding of the relationships of every stage of the company.

The methodology is well structured and allows the companies that implement it, an easy understanding and application.

7.8 Weaknesses of Juran's Trilogy

To have quality control it is necessary to have a trained person with knowledge in statistical processes or train a special person to be in charge of quality.

The program is focus in the company process and not in labor force.

- Analyzing the requirements of the program we found that the companies who apply the program have a complex level of organization.
- This kind of methodologies show results in a long term; this represents a risk for the company because the implementation of the quality program can be a waste of time, money and resources.
- Examples of use and where it is used.

The Juran quality program is used in health care improvement. The Institute of Juran has been helping health care providers like hospitals and clinics improve the quality of their care as well as reducing costs. The institute provides consulting and training, so organizations can understand the importance of improving their main processes and help them to create a plan for it.

One example of Juran quality program was used in patient care program. The Juran center gather several health care executives from several regions of Minnesota in order to improve several aspects like health care cost, patients safety and worker shortages. The Juran center launched a research project called Leading to Perfect Patient Care or LPPC, to test and implement a plan to eliminate medical errors this was made for a 90 day period of time, in some important clinics and hospitals. The results expected with this program are an improvement in the safety and other organizational outcomes.

The Dr. Juran quality program is also used in benchmarking, change management, design for six sigma, lean techniques, performance improvement, quality management and six sigma deployments.

Training requirements and maintenance needs of the program before and after implementation

The major problem in training for quality is that there needs to be an organized and integrated approach to management. In order to succeed the following steps can be followed:

7.9 The following steps were obtained from the Juran's Quality Handbook 5th edition.

A delineation of responsibilities for who contributes and in what ways

7.9.1 Executive leadership

The executive team takes the responsibility for creating a quality culture in the organization. A quality culture is a product of behaviors, skills, tools, and methods as they are applied to the work. These changes don't come about without showing people how to implement and sustain this culture.

7.9.2 Human resources

The human resources function bears the responsibility for implementing the quality training strategy. The implementation activities include the selection of subject matter, training design and delivery, and establishing an evaluation process.

7.9.3 The quality professionals

The quality professionals bear the responsibility to collaborate with the Human Resources professionals to share their technical expertise on quality, much the same as key sales professional would share their expertise in developing the curriculum for sales training.

7.9.4 A strong and reliable focus on the customer—internal and external

It's necessary to know who the customers are, what their needs are, and what the features should be of a training strategy.

An integrated training system for quality requires an organization to design the system using a process that incorporates all of the basics of quality planning.

7.9.5 A plan established with clear strategies and tactics for quality training

Developing the strategic training plan for quality is critical to the success of any TQM implementation. A strategic training plan addresses these key areas: quality awareness, executive education, management training, technical training, resources, budgeting, and staffing. Strategic training plan uses different types of training like: Modular training: just-in-time training, mentoring, lectures by peers, self-study and conferences.

7.9.6 Resources

Every quality training program needs resources. There must be a purposeful effort to identify the staffing and materials funding necessary to achieve quality training goals.

A budget to fund the plan

They need to be committed specifically to the strategy and tactics that support training for quality.

7.9.7 Staffing

It's the personnel requirements necessary to support training for quality. There are many basic types of staffing options that organizations utilize. There is, however, one constant trend: quality departments and the training function for quality are leaner and multifunctional. Various staffing structures are described below.

7.9.8 Centralized

There is a dedicated group of individuals that research, develop, instruct, and evaluate the quality-training curriculum. This structure tends to segregate the quality-training strategy from the general education strategies, creating a learning barrier. Participants view the quality training as something distinctly different from other professional development activities.

7.9.9 Hub and spoke

It consists of a training coordinator or manager at the headquarters unit with a "dotted line" relationship to training professionals in other divisions or business units. These individuals are usually part of the quality department infrastructure that is deployed throughout the organization.

7.9.10 Decentralized

In this model, each department, division, or business unit has its own approach to training for quality. However each unit is charged with developing its own tactics and deploying them within their areas of responsibilities. This is not an effective approach to quality training and takes a much higher level of coordination.

7.9.11 Shared

This is similar to the hub-and-spoke model, with slight enhancements. The trainers draft volunteers from the organization to support the training plan. These volunteers are selected from those who have received quality training in the past and may be supporting the quality system implementation as facilitator, team leader, or team member.

7.9.12 External quality consultants

External quality consultants provide an immediate, qualified resource that can support the organization's planning, development, delivery, and evaluation of training for quality.

7.9.13 Evaluation

Evaluation is critical to effective training for quality. Evaluation is not just an afterthought but a necessary and systematic part of an effective training process for quality.

To maintain the quality program based on the Juran's Trilogy Methodology is necessary follow the ten steps of Juran. Quality is a continuous improvement issue, so following the ten steps is possible maintain the methodology before and after the implementation.

7.10 Deming's 14 principles:

Dr. W. Edwards Deming (1900-1993) made it his mission to spread the true functioning of quality control and quality management. Dr. Deming motivates top level management to take interest in the process of creating an environment that supports the concept of total quality and continuous improvement. Dr. Deming was Graduate from Yale University in 1928. He first began spreading his message shortly after World War II. His work with the census Bureau & other government agencies led to his eventual contacts with Japan as the nation was beginning to rebuild. When this message was refused by United States Dr. Deming took it to Japan. There Dr. Deming helped turn Japan into an industrial force to be reckoned with. After some time he became one of the most influential experts on quality assurance.

Deming's all 14 points focus heavily on management involvement, continuous improvement, statistical analysis, goal setting and communication. Management used those 14 points as a guideline for improvement of the product or services. Dr. Deming try to change people's attitude about quality and removing any barriers preventing employees from their job well, management maintain an environment supportive of continuous improvement. Deming's 14 points motivates company leaders to dedicate themselves and their companies to the long term improvement of the quality of their goods and/or services.

Dr. Deming's first point- create a constancy of purpose - motivates top management to accept the obligation to continuously improve the product or services through novelty, research, learning, and continual development in all facts of the company. This commitment essentially leads to Deming's second point: accept a new philosophy that rejects "acceptable" quality level and poor service as a way of life. The 12 other points ask management to reorganize past practices such as awarding business on the basis of price tag alone, using mass scrutiny, setting statistical goals and quotas, enforcing work time standard, allowing incomplete guidance or education, and using outdated methods of management.

7.10.1 Deming's 14 points:

1. Create a constancy of purpose towards improvement of products and service, with the aim to become competitive and to stay in business and to provide jobs.
2. Adopt the new philosophy.
3. Cease dependence on inspection to achieve quality.
4. End the practice of awarding business on the basis of price tag alone. Instead minimize total cost.
5. Constantly and forever improve the system of production and service.
6. Institute training on the job.
7. Institute leadership.
8. Drive out fear.
9. Break down barriers between departments
10. Eliminate slogans, exhortations, and targets for the work force.
11. Eliminate work standards and numerical quotas. Substitute leadership.
12. Remove barriers that rob people of their right to pride of workmanship.
13. Institute a vigorous program of education and self-improvement.
14. Put everybody in the company to work to accomplish the transformation.

7.11 Quality Improvement:

Improvement in the continual process in this earth so

improvement in quality is also a continual process. It starts with a mission statement stating quality objective. Then customer needs follows then after. In the next step quality improvement identifies organizational capabilities and development of overall corporate strategy follows. In the next step quality improvement program emphasizes on functional activities like- Engineering approach, manufacturing approach, marketing approach, business approach. After the establishment of above strategy the quality improvement team establishes a relation with other parameters like communication, cooperation, coordination, self evaluation, customer evaluation vendor evaluation etc.

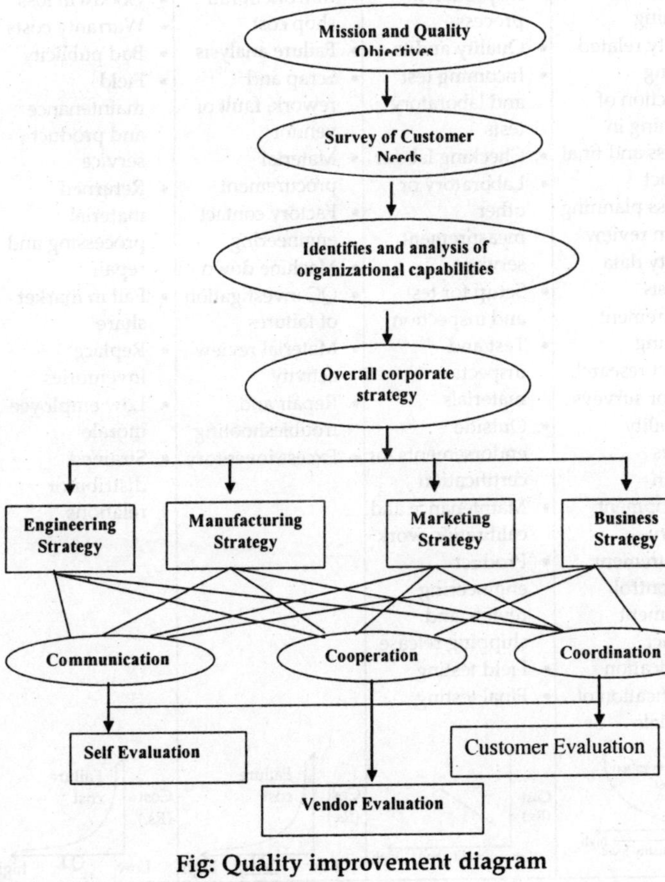

Fig: Quality improvement diagram

7.12 Quality Cost:

It is the cost in ensuring and assuring qualities as well as loss incurred when quality is not achieved. Different component of cost of quality assurance may be classified by Gavett 1968, Adam and Evertt-1998 in to four categories (table given below) of prevention cost, appraisal cost, internal failure cost and external failure cost.

Prevention Cost	Appraisal Cost	Internal Failure Cost	External Failure Cost
• Quality Planning • QC administration and system planning • Quality related training • Inspection of Incoming in process and final product • Process planning • Design review • Quality data analysis • Procurement planning • Market research • Vendor surveys • Reliability studies • System development • Quality measurement and control equipment • Product qualification • Qualification of materials	• Incoming inspection • Testing • Inspection in process • Quality audits • Incoming test and laboratory tests • Checking labour • Laboratory or other measurement services • Setup for test and inspection • Test and inspection materials • Outside endorsements for certification • Maintenance and calibration work • Product engineering review and shipping release • Field testing • Final testing	• Rejections • Scrap at full shop cost • Rework at full shop cost • Failure analysis • Scrap and rework, fault of vendor • Material procurement • Factory contact engineering • Machine down • QC investigation of failures • Material review activity • Repair and troubleshooting • Excess inventory	• Recall • Complaints handling • Goodwill loss • Warranty costs • Bad publicity • Field maintenance and product service • Returned material processing and repair • Fall in market share • Replace inventories • Low employee morale • Strained distributor relations
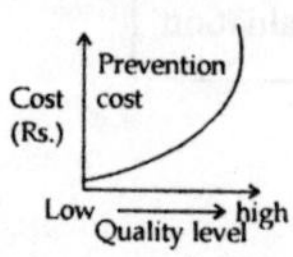 	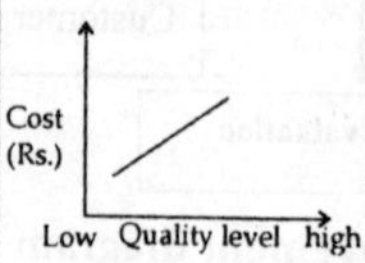 	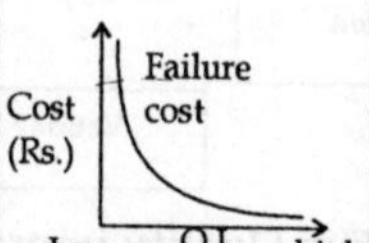 	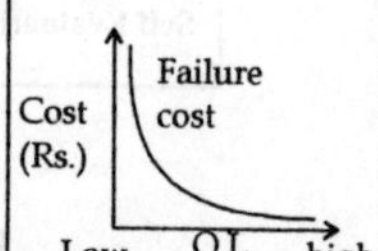

Source: Cost of quality assurance (Compiled from Gavett 1968, Adam and Evertt 1998)

7.13 7 (Seven) Quality Control Tools:

Seven quality tools are used in the quality improvement process. These seven tools are very useful in the identification of problem and establishment of measures for the improvement. These seven quality control tools are:

1. Scatter Diagram
2. Check Sheet
3. Graph and Charts
4. Histograms
5. Pareto Diagram
6. Cause Effect Diagram
7. Control Charts

7.13.1 Scatter Diagram:

It is prepared by plotting paired set of data such as temperature and elongation, porosity and insulation, etc against each other on an X and Y axes.

It is used to collect paired set of data on cause and effect and also use scatter diagram to check the correlation between the set of data. It must be used for a sufficiently large data set, say 50 or more.

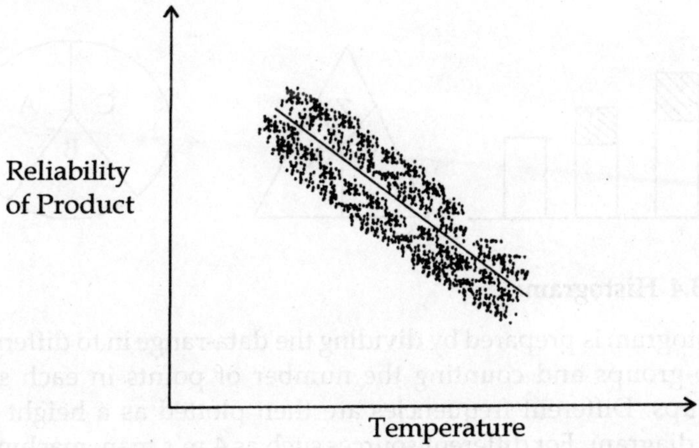

7.13.2 Check Sheets:

A check sheet is a data recording device. It is not to be confused with checklist, which lists all of the important steps, actions that need to take place, or things that need to be remembered. It is used tallying the happening of the defects or causes being addressed and graphing or charting straightly. Check sheets are to be designed only after clarity about the objective is known.

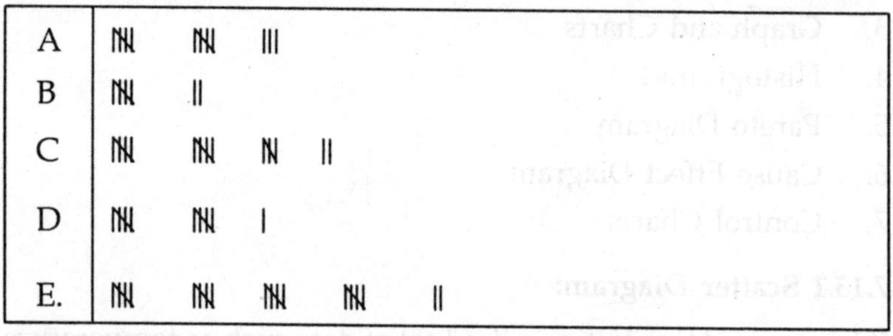

7.13.3 Graphs and Charts:

These are the diagrams for platting data and showing statistical breakdowns with relationship between different quantities. These are used for organized set of observations. Line-graph used to know trend, bar and pie charts for comparing quantities and showing relative proportions.

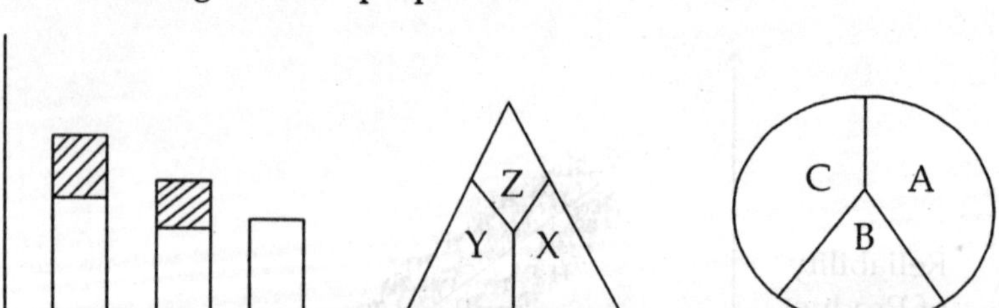

7.13.4 Histogram:

Histogram is prepared by dividing the data-range in to different sub-groups and counting the number of points in each sub groups. Different frequencies are then plotted as a height on the diagram. For different sources such as 4 m's man, machines, material & method separate but stratified histogram may be prepared. Histogram may be used to understand the relationship between shapes of distribution and the specifications. Histogram usually requires reasonable large data set for plotting.

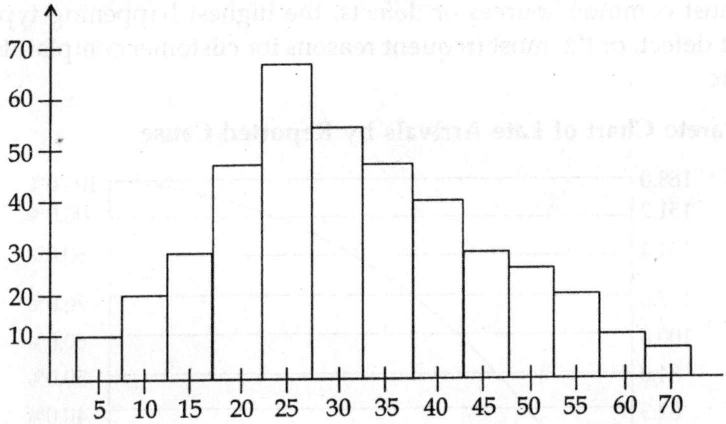

7.13.5 Petro chart

Pareto chart

Simple example of a Pareto chart using imaginary data showing the relative occurrence of reasons for in ward late at work.

A Pareto chart is a special kind of bar chart where the values being plotted are arranged in descending order. The graph is accompanied by a line graph which shows the collective totals of each grouping, left to right. The chart is named after Vilfredo Pareto, and its use in quality pledge was popularized by Joseph M. Juran and Kaoru Ishikawa.

The Pareto chart is one of the seven basic tools of quality control, which include the histogram, Pareto chart, check sheet, control chart, cause-and-effect diagram, flowchart, and scatter diagram. See glossary of quality management. These charts can be generated in Microsoft Office or Open Office as well as many free software tools establish online.

Characteristically on the left vertical axis is frequency of incidence, but it can alternatively represent cost or other important unit of measure? The right upright axis is the cumulative percentage of the total number of occurrences, total cost, or total of the particular unit of measure. The purpose is to highlight the most important in the middle of a set of factors. In quality control, the Pareto chart frequently represents the most common sources of defects, the highest happening type of defect, or the most frequent reasons for customer complaints, etc.

Pareto Chart of Late Arrivals by Reported Cause

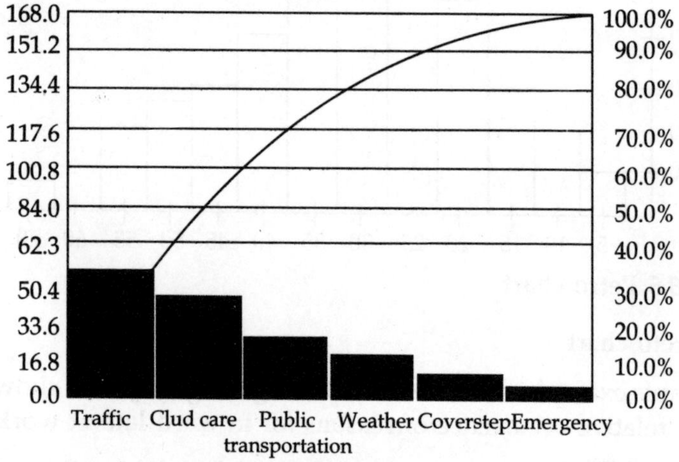

7.13.6 Cause and Diagram (Is ikawa diagram)

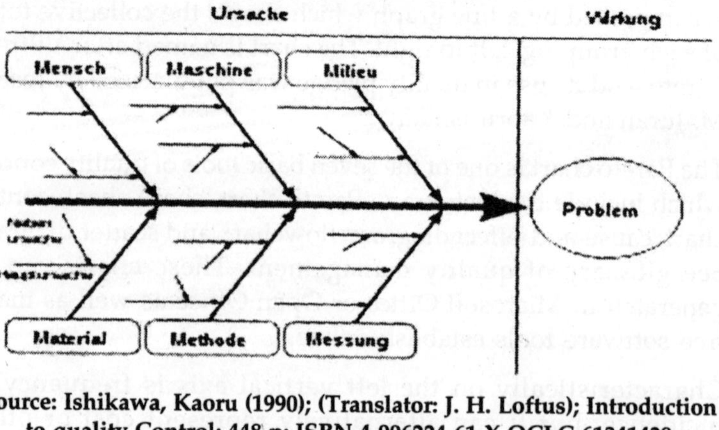

Source: Ishikawa, Kaoru (1990); (Translator: J. H. Loftus); Introduction to quality Control; 448 p; ISBN 4-906224-61-X OCLC 61341428

Ishikawa diagram, in fishbone shape, showing factor of men, machines, milieu (workplace), materiel, methods measurement, all affecting the overall problem. Smaller arrows connect the sub-causes

The Ishikawa diagram (or fishbone diagram or also cause-and-effect diagram) are diagrams, that shows the causes of a certain event. A common use of the Ishikawa diagram is in product design, to identify potential factors causing an overall effect.

Ishikawa diagrams were proposed by Kaoru Ishikawa in the 1960s, which pioneered quality management processes in the Kawasaki shipyards, and in the procedure became one of the founding fathers of modern management.

It was first used in the 1960s, and is considered one of the seven basic tolls of quality management, long with the histogram, Pareto chart, check sheet, control chart, flowchart and scatter diagram. See Quality Management Glossary. It is known as a fishbone diagram because of its shape, similar to the side view of a fish skeleton.

Mazda Motors famously used an Ishikawa diagram in the development of the Miata sports car, where the required result was "Jinba Ittai" or "Horse and Rider as One". The main causes included such aspects as "touch" and "braking" with the lesser causes including highly granular factors such as "50/50 weight distribution" and "able to rest elbow on top of driver's door". Every factor identified in the diagram was included in the final design.

Causes

Causes in the diagram are often based on a certain set of causes, such as the 6 M's 8 P's or 4 S's, described below. Cause-and-effect diagrams can reveal key relationships among various variables, and the possible causes provide additional insight into process behaviour.

Causes in a typical diagram are normally grouped into categories, the main ones of which are:

The 6 M's

Machine, Method, Materials, Maintenance, Man and Mother Nature (Environment) (recommended for the manufacturing industry).

1. The 8P's

Price, promotion, People Processes, Place/ Plant, Policies, Procedures, and Product (or Service) (recommended for the administration and service industries).

2. The 4 S's

Surroundings, suppliers, Systems, Skills (recommended for the service industry).

It can also be used in connection with the Neuro-linguitic programming model of the neurological levels created by Robert Dilts: with Identity, Beliefs and Values, Capability, Behaviour, Environment.

Causes should be derived from brainstorming sessions. Then causes should be sorted through affinity-grouping to collect similar ideas together. These groups should then be labeled as categories of the fishbone. They will typically be one of the traditional categories mentioned above but may be something unique to your application of this tool. Causes should be specific, measurable, and controllable appearance.

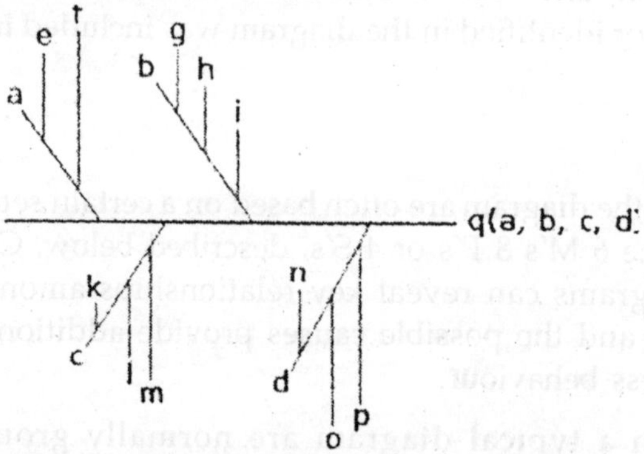

Source: Ishikawa, Kaoru (1990); (Translator: J. H. Loftus); Introduction to Quality Control; 448 p; ISBN 4- 906224-61-X OCLC 61341428

A basic Ishikawa diagram showing general and more advanced causes for an event. Most Ishikawa diagrams have a box at the right hand side, where the effect to be examined is written. The main body of the diagram is a horizontal line from which stems the general causes, represented as "bones". These are drawn towards the left-hand side of the paper and are each labeled with the causes to be investigated, often brainstormed beforehand and based on the major causes listed above.

Off each of the large bones there may be smaller bones highlighting more specific aspects of a certain cause, and sometimes there may be a third level of bones or more. These can be found using the '5 Whys' technique. When the most probable causes have been identified, they are written in the box along with the original effect. The more populated bones generally outline ore influential factors, with the opposite applying to bones with fewer "branches". Further analysis of the diagram can be achieved with a Pareto chart.

7.13.7 Control Charts

The control chart was introduced by Walter A. Shewhart while working with Bell Labs in te 1920s. The company's engineers had been seeking to get better the consistency of their telephony broadcast systems. Because amplifiers and other equipment had to be covered underground, there was a business need to reduce the frequency of failures and maintenance. By 1920 they had already realized the importance of reducing variation in a mechanized process. Moreover, they had realized that frequent process-adjustment in reaction to non-conformance actually increased variation ad tainted quality. Shewhart framed the problem in terms of Common -and special-causes of variation and, on May 16, 1924, wrote an internal memo introducing the control chart as a tool for distinguishing between the two. Dr. Shewhart's boss, George Edwards, recalled: "Dr. Shewhart prepared a little memorandum simply concerning a page in length.

About a third of that page was given over to a simple diagram which we would all recognize today as a schematic control chart. That diagram, and the short text which preceded and followed it, set forth all of the essential principles and considerations which are involved in what we know today as procedure quality control. "Shewhart stressed that bringing a construction procedure into a state of statistical control, where there is only common-cause difference, and keeping it in control, is necessary to predict future output and to manage a process economically.

A control chart consists of the following:

- Points representing measurements of a quality characteristic in samples taken from the process at different times [the data]
- A centre line, drawn at the process characteristic mean which is calculated from data
- Upper and lower control limits (sometimes called "natural process limits") that indicate the threshold at which the process output is considered statistically 'unlikely'
- The chart may contain other optional features, including:
- upper and lower warning limits, drawn as separate lines, typically two standard deviations above and below the centre line
- Division into zones, with the addition of rules governing frequencies of observations in each zone
- Annotation with events of interest, as determined by the Quality Engineer in charge of the process's quality
- However in the early stages of use the inclusion of these items may confuse inexperienced chart interpreters.

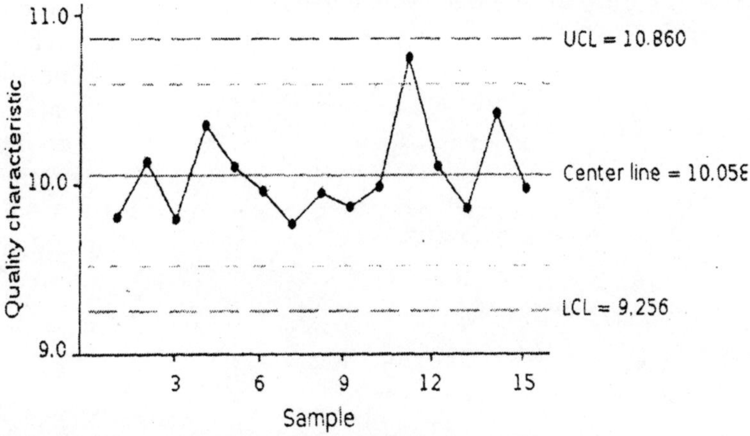

Source: Shewhart, W A (1931) Economic Control of Quality of Manufactured Product ISBN 0- 87389-076-0.

Chapter 8

Six Sigma (6σ)

8.1 Historical overview

Six Sigma (6σ) was developed as a set of practices formulated to develop modified manufacturing processes and minimize or eliminate defects, but its application was subsequently applied to other types of business processes as well. In Six Sigma philosophy, a defect is defined as anything that could lead to customer dissatisfaction.

The particulars of the philosophy were first formulated by *Bill Smith* at Motorola in 1986. Six Sigma was influenced by six preceding decades of quality improvement philosophies such as quality control, Total Quality Management, and Zero Defects, based on the work of pioneers such as Shewhart, Deming, Juran, Ishikawa, Taguchi and others.

Like its predecessors, Six Sigma asserts that –

1. Continuous process to achieve stable and predictable procedure results (i.e. minimize process variation) are of vital importance to business success.
2. Manufacturing and production business procedures have characteristics that can be evaluate, measured, analyzed, improved and controlled.
3. Achieving stabilized quality improvement requires dedication from the entire organization, particularly from top-level management.

8.2 Features that set Six Sigma apart from previous quality improvement initiatives include –

- A clear focus on achieving computable and quantifiable financial returns from any Six Sigma assignment
- An increased stress on strong and enthusiastic management leadership and support
- A special infrastructure of "Champions," "Master Black Belts," "Black Belts," etc. to lead and implement the Six Sigma approach.
- A clear commitment to making decisions on the basis of verifiable data, rather than assumptions and estimation.
- The term "Six Sigma" is derived from a field of statistics known as process capability studies. Formerly, it referred to the ability of production processes to produce a very high amount of output within specification. Processes that operate with "six sigma quality" over the short period are assumed to produce long-time defect levels below 3.4 defects per million opportunities (DPMO). Six Sigma's contained goal is to improve all procedures to that level of quality or better.
- Six Sigma is a registered service mark and trademark of Motorola, Inc. Motorola has reported over US$17 billion in savings from Six Sigma as of 2006.
- Other early accepters of Six Sigma who achieved well-publicized success include Honeywell (previously known as AlliedSignal) and General Electric, where the method was introduced by Jack Welch. By the late 1990s, about two-thirds of the Fortune 500 companies had established Six Sigma initiatives with the aim of reducing costs and improving quality and profits.
- In recent years, Six Sigma has sometimes been combined with lean manufacturing to yield a philosophy named Lean Six Sigma.

8.3 Origin and meaning of the term "six sigma processes"

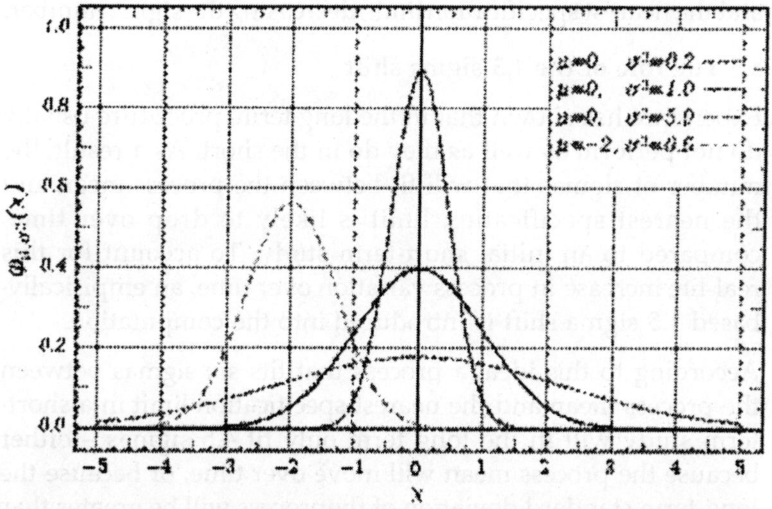

Graph of the normal distribution curve, which underlies the mathematical assumptions of the Six Sigma model. The Greek letter "ó" marks the distance on the horizontal axis between the mean, "μ", and the curve's inflection point. The greater this distance is the greater the spread of values encountered. For the curve shown in red above, μ = 0 and ó = 1. The other curve shows different values of μ and ó.

8.4 The given outlines the statistical background of the term Six Sigma:

Sigma (the lower-case Greek letter ó) is used to represent the standard deviation (a measure of variation) of a statistical population. The term "six sigma process" comes from the notion that if one has six standard deviations between the mean of a process and the nearest specification limit, there will be almost no items that fail to meet the requirement. This is based on the computation method employed in a process capability study.

In a capability study, the number of standard deviations between the process mean and the nearest specification limit is given in sigma units. As activity standard deviation goes up, or the mean of the activity moves away from the center of the tolerance, fewer standard deviations will fit between the mean and the nearest specification limit, decreasing the sigma number.

8.5 The role of the 1.5 sigma shift

Experience has shown that in the long term, procedure usually do not perform as well as they do in the short. As a result, the number of sigmas that will fit between the process mean and the nearest specification limit is likely to drop over time, compared to an initial short-term study. To account for this real-life increase in process variation over time, an empirically-based 1.5 sigma shift is introduced into the computation.

According to this idea, a process that fits six sigmas between the process mean and the nearest specification limit in a short-term study will in the long term only fit 4.5 sigmas - either because the process mean will move over time, or because the long-term standard deviation of theprocess will be greater than that observed in the short term, or both. Hence the largely accepted description of a six sigma procedure is one that produces 3.4 *defective parts per million opportunities* (DPMO). This is based on the fact that a procedures that is usually distributed will have 3.4 parts per million beyond a point that is 4.5 standard deviations above or below the mean (one-sided capability study). So the 3.4 DPMO of a "Six Sigma" process in fact corresponds to 4.5 sigmas, namely 6 sigmas minus the 1.5 sigma shift introduced to account for long-term variation. This is designed to prevent underestimation of the defect levels likely to be encountered in real-life operation.

8.6 Sigma levels

Taking the 1.5 sigma shift into account, short-term sigma levels communicate to the following long-term DPMO values (one-sided):

- **One Sigma** = 690,000 DPMO = 31% efficiency
- **Two Sigma** = 308,000 DPMO = 69.2% efficiency
- **Three Sigma**= 66,800 DPMO = 93.32% efficiency
- **Four Sigma** = 6,210 DPMO = 99.379% efficiency
- **Five Sigma** = 230 DPMO = 99.977% efficiency

- **Six Sigma** = 3.4 DPMO = 99.9997% efficiency

8.7 Philosophy

Six Sigma has two key philosophies:

DMAIC and DMADV both philosophies are influence by Deming's Plan-Do-Check-Act Cycle. DMAIC is used to improve an existing business process; DMADV is used to create new product or process designs.

8.7.1 DMAIC

The basic methodology consists of the following five steps:

1. *Define* process improvement goals that are consistent with customer demands and the enterprise strategy.
2. *Measure* key aspects of the current process and collect relevant data.
3. *Analyze* the data to verify cause-and-effect relationships. Determine what the relationships are, and attempt to ensure that all factors have been considered.
4. *Improve* or optimize the process based upon data analysis using techniques like Design of experiments.
5. *Control* to ensure that any deviations from target are corrected before they result in defects. Set up pilot runs to establish process capability, move on to production, set up control mechanisms and continuously monitor the process.

8.7.2 DMADV

The basic methodology consists of the following five steps:

1. *Define* design goals that are consistent with customer demands and the enterprise strategy.
2. *Measure* and identify characteristics that are Critical to Quality, product capabilities, production process capability, and risks.
3. *Analyze* to develop and design alternatives, create a high-level design and evaluate design capability to select the

best design.

4. *Design* details, optimize the design, and plan for design substantiation. This phase may require simulations.
5. *Verify* the design, set up pilot runs, implement the production process and hand it over to the process owners.

DMADV is also known as DFSS, a short form of "*Design for Six Sigma*".

8.8 Implementation roles

One of the key innovations of Six Sigma is the professionalizing of quality management functions. Prior to Six Sigma, quality management in practice was largely relegated to the production floor and to statisticians in a separate quality department. Six Sigma borrows martial arts ranking expressions to define a hierarchy that cuts across all business functions and a promotion path straight into the executive suite.

Six Sigma identifies several key roles for its successful implementation.

8.8.1 Executive Leadership includes the CEO and other top management. They are responsible for setting up a vision and mission for Six Sigma execution. They also empower the other role holders with the freedom and resources to discover new ideas for breakthrough improvements.

Champions are responsible for Six Sigma implementation across the organization in an integrated manner. The Executive Leadership draws them from upper management. Champions also act as mentors to Black Belts.

8.8.2 Master Black Belts, identified by champions, act as in-house coaches on Six Sigma. They devote 100% time to Six Sigma. They assist champions and guide Black Belts and Green Belts. Apart from numerical tasks, their time is spent on ensuring dependable application of Six Sigma across various functions and departments.

Black Belts operate under Master Black Belts to apply Six Sigma philosophy to specific projects. They devote 100% time to Six

Sigma. They primarily focus on Six Sigma project implementation, whereas Champions and Master Black Belts focus on identifying projects/functions for Six Sigma.

8.8.3 ***Green Belts*** are the employees who take up Six Sigma execution along with their other job tasks. They operate under the guidance of Black Belts.

Chapter 9

Quality Circle

9.1 Quality Circle:

Community are the greatest resources of an organisation, because, through people all other resources are transformed into utilities. However, management of 'People Resources' has always been a vexed difficulty ever since the beginning of organised human behavior. A number of managerial responses have been developed to counter this problem.

Contribute methods in the workplace are one way to get better both the work atmosphere for workers, output and quality for the business.

Quality Circle is one of the worker contribution methods. It implies the development of skills, capabilities, confidence and creativity of the people through snowballing process of education, training, work experience and contribution. It also implies the formation of facilitative conditions and atmosphere of work, which creates and sustains their motivation and commitment towards work quality.

Quality Circles have emerged as a mechanism to develop and utilize the great potential of public for development in product worth and efficiency.

9.2 Origin of Quality Circles

After the Second World War Japanese economy was in the depression. Seeing this unfortunate effect of war, Americans decided to help Japan in improving the quality standards of their products. General Douglas Mac Arthur who, at that time, was the commander of the occupational forces in Japan took up the job of imparting quality alertness among Japanese to help them get better their products and the consistency of manufacturing systems including men, machine and materials. Thus, by 1975, they were topping the world in value and output. This surprising and exclusive achievement in modern history became an eye - opener to the world. Industrialists and politicians from all over the world started visiting Japan to know how they have achieved such miraculous results in such a short duration. The answer to this was conscientious and unrelenting efforts of the Japanese leaders and workers and the enlargement and development of the philosophy of small working groups. This resulted in the Quality Circle concept being accepted all over the world as a very successful procedure to improve the total quality of work life.

9.3 Definition

Quality Circle is a small group of 6 to 12 workers doing alike work who willingly meet together on a regular basis to recognize improvements in their respective work areas using established techniques for analyzing and solving job related troubles coming in the way of achieving and supporting quality leading to reciprocated upliftment of employees as well as the organisation. It is "a technique of capturing the inspired and pioneering power that lies within the work force".

9.4 Philosophy

Quality Circles are a public - structure philosophy, provide self-motivation and pleasure in improving environment without any obligation or financial benefits. It represents a idea of managing public specially those at the grass root height as well as a clearly defined instrument and attitude for translating this philosophy into practice and a required construction to make it a way of life. It is bound to succeed where people are respected and are involved in decisions, concerning their work life, and in environments where peoples' capabilities are looked upon as assets to solve work-area problems.

The Quality Circle philosophy calls for a progressive attitude on the part of the management and their willingness to make adjustments, if necessary, in their style and culture. If workers are ready to add their ideas, the management must be eager to make a friendly atmosphere to encourage them to do so.

9.5 Concept

The concept of Quality Circle is mostly based upon acknowledgment of the assessment of the worker as a human being, as someone who willingly activises on his job, his wisdom, intelligence, knowledge, approach and outlook. It is based upon the human resource management measured as one of the key factors in the development of product value & efficiency. Quality Circle concept has three major attributes:

1. Quality Circle is a form of contribution management.
2. Quality Circle is a human resource expansion method.
3. Quality Circle is a trouble solving approach.

9.6 Objective

The objectives of Quality Circles are multi-faced.

A) Change in Attitude.

From "I don't care" to "I do care"

Nonstop development process in quality of work life through humanization of work is called Change in attitude.

b) Self Development

Bring out 'Hidden Potential' of people
public get to be trained supplementary skills.

C) Growth of Team strength

Individual Vs Team – "I could not do but we did it"

abolish inter departmental conflicts.

D) Enhanced Organisational Culture

optimistic working atmosphere.
Total participation of people at all levels.

Advanced motivational level
Join Management process.

9.7 Organisational Arrengement

A Quality Circle has an proper organisational arrangement for its effective and efficient performance. It varies from industry to industry, organisation to organisation. But it is useful to have a basic structure as a model. The arrangement of a Quality Circle consists of the following elements.

- **A steering committee:** This is at the top of the structure. It is headed by a senior manager and includes representatives from the top management personnel and human resources development public. It establishes strategy, plans and directs the program and meets usually once in a month.
- **Co-ordinator:** He may be a Personnel or managerial officer who co-ordinates and supervises the work of the facilitators and administers the programme.
- **Facilitator:** He may be a senior administrative officer. His co-ordinates the works of several quality circles through the Circle leaders.
- **Circle leader:** Leaders may be from lowest level workers or Supervisors. A Circle leader organises and conducts Circle activities.
- **Circle members:** They may be staff workers. Without circle members the porgramme cannot exist. They are the lifeblood of quality circles. They should attend all meetings as far as possible, offer suggestions and ideas, participate actively in group process, and take training seriously with a receptive attitude. The roles of Steering Committee, Co-0rdinator, Facilitator, Circle leader and Circle members are well defined.

9.8 Introduction of the Quality Circles

The major requirement for initiating Quality Circles in any organisation is the total understanding of, as well as complete conviction and faith in the participative philosophy, on the part of the top and senior management. In the lack of an assurance from the Chief Executive to support the Quality Circle movement totally, it would be inadvisable to seriously attempt the starting of Quality Circles. The introduction of Quality Circles involves the following steps:

Expose middle level executives to the concept.

Explain the concept to the employees and invite them to volunteer as members of Quality Circles.

Nominate senior officers as facilitators.

Form a steering committee

Organize training of coordinators, facilitators in fundamentals of Quality Circle approach, execution, techniques and process. Afterward facilitator may provide training to Circle leaders and Circle members.

A assembly should be fixed if possible one hour a week for the Quality Circle to meet. Officially install the Quality Circle. Arrange the essential amenities for the Quality Circle assembly and its process.

9.9 Training

Appropriate training for different sections of employees desires to be imparted. Without a appropriate perceptive of the real concept of Quality Circles, both the workers and management strength look at this attitude with doubt. Each group should know earlier the commitments and implications occupied as well as the advantage that can be obtained from Quality Circles.

Such training comprises of:

1. Brief direction programme for top management.
2. Programme for middle level executives.
3. Training of facilitators.
4. Training for Circle leaders and members.

9.10 Process Of Operation

The operation of quality circles involves a set of sequential steps as under:

1. **Problem identification:** Identify a figure of problems.
2. **Problem selections:** Decide the priority and select the problem to be taken up foremost.

3. **Problem Analysis:** Problem is clarified and analysed by basic problem solving methods.
4. **Generate alternative solutions:** recognize and assess causes and generate number of possible alternative solutions
5. **Select the most appropriate solution:** Converse and assess the alternative solutions by comparison in terms of asset and return from the investment. This enables to select the most appropriate solution.
6. **Prepare plan of action:** Prepare plan of action for converting the solution into reality which includes the considerations "who, what, when, where, why and how" of solving problems.
7. Present solution to management circle members present solution to management fore approval.
8. **Implementation of solution:** The management evaluates the recommended solution. Then it is tested and if successful, implemented on a full scale.

9.11 Basic Problem Solving Techniques

The following techniques are most commonly used to examine and resolve work related problems.

1 Brain storming

2 Pareto Diagrams

3 Cause & Effect Analysis

4 Data Collection

5 Data Analysis

The tools used for data analysis are:

1 Tables

2 Bar Charts

3 Histograms

4 Circle graphs

5 Line graphs

6 Scatter grams

7 Control Charts

The Quality Circles also are predictable to expand internal leadership, reinforce worker morale and motivation, and push a strong sense of teamwork in an organisation.

A mixture of benefits have been attributed to Quality Circles, including higher quality, improved productivity, greater upward flow of information, broader enhanced worker attitudes, job enrichment, and greater teamwork.

Problem quality circles frequently suffer from impractical potential for fast results, lock of management commitment and support, resistance by middle management, dislike by non participants, insufficient training, lack of clear objectives and breakdown to get solutions implemented.

9.12 Benefits and Limitations of Quality Circles

It took more than two decades for the quality control idea to get recognition in India, after its beginning in Japan. This may be due to the differences in the industrial background in the two countries. Japan needed it for its continued existence in a competitive market. India had a reasonably protected, sellers market, with resulting exhaustion towards efforts to improve quality and output. However, with the policy of liberalization of economy and privatization of infrastructure development, contexts changed. The idea now needs to be looked upon as a obligation.

9.13 Applicability in Government Organisations

The Public Works Department of Government of Maharashtra is accountable for the manufacture and repairs of about 2.00 lakhs km. of road net work in the state and a large number of Government-owned buildings extend all over the state. The road net work caters for national level traffic to the rural area traffic. The climatic and environmental features also differ from place to place in the state. The final customer of the Department is the ordinary man and it is not generally easy to satisfy the final needs of this customer to the fullest extent merely by taking decision at the top management level. The sub-ordinate officers and staff working in the field and who are well-acquainted with the day-to -day problems in their work areas are the best judges to decide upon the line of action. The top management in Maharashtra P.W.D. realized this need of the time and introduced the concept of Quality Circle as employee participation method in the organisation. The concept of Quality Circle was launched in the Public Works Department of Govt. of Maharashtra on 18-11-1997. In a length of about a year 17 Quality Circles have been formed in Mumbai Region wherein 22 problems have been solved so far. 48 Quality Circles have been formed in Pune Region wherein, 8 problems have been solved. Nashik Region of the P.W.D. has formed 9 Quality Circles and solutions to 3 problems have been established out. Aurangabad Region has formed 21 Quality Circles and solved 7 problems. Nagpur Regions have formed 47 Quality Circles and have found out solution to 57 problems, so far.

The results of a short time of one year are found to be very hopeful so far and many of these Circles have already come up with solutions to the various work related problems as evidenced from the last two state level conventions held at Mumbai and Aurangabad in that order. The presentations by the various Quality Circles at these conventions bear testimony to the fact that the concept of Quality Circle has been received with much eagerness at the grass root level. These presentations also provide real facts fulfilling the expected benefits of the Quality Circle. Taking inspirations from these conventions, more staffs of the Department have come forward to form Quality Circles, emphasizing the fact that Quality Circles have come to stay in the Department.

Some of the problems solved by the Quality Circles in P.W.D. of Maharashtra are as follows-

1 Eliminating delay in issuing observation memos after inspection of site.

2 Preventing accidents on highways.

3 Reducing electricity bill in office.

4 Avoiding duplication of work.

5 Removal of encroachment from Govt. land.
6 Speeding up pot-hole filling on roads during monsoon.
7 Up keeping of service records of employees.
8 Maintaining Govt. offices clean.
9 Stream-lining reservation system of Govt. rest houses.
10 Improvement in maintenance of Govt. Hospital at Solapur.

9.14 Some of the problems and the solutions thereof are explained briefly below:

(I) Delay in issue of observation memos:

The Public Works Department of Maharashtra is divided into six regions each headed by a Chief Engineer. Each regional Chief Engineer is assisted by a Superintending Engineer, Vigilance & Quality Circle who with the help of two Executive Engineer and about 6 Deputy Engineers carries out inspection of the ongoing projects. The samples of the construction material being used on project are collected and independently tested in the Regional Testing Laboratories to ascertain the level of acceptance. The findings of the inspections are communicated to the field engineers in the form of 'observation memo'. It is contemplated that the Execution Engineer in charge of the project ensures immediate compliance of the remarks raised in the observation memo and carries out corrective measures in the ongoing project as well as preventive measures for the future works.

However, very often the observation memos are issued after much delay defeating the very purpose of the observation memo. This problem was identified by the 'OMKAR' Quality Circle formed in the office of Superintending Engineer, Vigilance & Quality Control Circle, Navi Mumbai. The members used various tools and methodology, identified the various root causes that led to this problem and finally solved the problem with requisite foolproofing.

By solving this problem, it became possible to improve the quality of work in the field which ultimately brightened the image of the Department. The formation of Quality Circle also benefited employees by providing.

a) A systematic style of education that helped them grows.

b) Freedom to modify their work habits.

c) Opportunity to use their brain for development of the Department; and

d) Opportunity to work as a team.

e) The employees were also motivated to improve work culture, self improvement recognition and creativity in work.

(II) Preventing accidents on highways:

It was observed that the accident rate on Sion-Panvel Highway passing through New Mumbai had disappeared up harshly. The Circle members collect the data from the particular police stations and identified the important causes of accidents by using Pareto Analysis. They segregated the causes under Man, Machine, Material and Method. The Circle members found out solutions to the problem such as finishing of central verge at all locations except junction, frequent lane marking, installation of concern boards, providing lay-byes for buses etc.

The data collection of accidents for a period three months after completion of solutions near Shirvane and Turbhe exposed that the reason of accident had been eliminated and no more accidents occurred at those locations had been eliminated and no more accidents accorded at those locations again. This way the Circle members ensured the effectiveness of the solution implemented. They made presentation to their steering committee for obtaining sanction to other solutions involving more funds.

Multiple choice questions

Try the following questions to test your knowledge of this chapter.

1. The concept of total quality control, i.e. that quality must be attended to at all stage of the industrial cycle and throughout the organization, is the creation of which of the following pioneers?
   1. W Edwards Deming
   2. Genichi Taguchi
   3. Joseph M Juran
   4. Armand Feigenbaum
2. The so-called 'Quality Gurus' of total quality management (TQM) do NOT include one of the following:
   1. Joseph M Juran
   2. W Edwards Deming
   3. Bill Cosby
   4. Kaoru Ishikawa
3. The specific concerns of total quality management (TQM) include a number of aspects. Which is not normally associated with TQM?
   1. Covering all parts of the organization
   2. Meeting the needs and expectations of customers
   3. Primarily a "worker" rather than a management activity
   4. Inclusion of every person in the organization
4. The preferred method for achieving total quality in process output is:
   1. Build and install an error-proof process and maintain it
   2. Perform inspection at the next process
   3. Rely on a team of highly trained and dedicated inspectors
   4. Rely on operator self-inspection and self-correction

5. Total quality management (TQM) programmes are more likely to remain effective if a number of prescriptions are followed. Which of the following prescriptions should not be followed?
   1. Slogans and exhortations about TQM's effectiveness are avoided
   2. TQM should become a substitute for normal managerial leadership
   3. TQM does not become a separate 'bolt-on' set of activities
   4. Quality improvement relates to operation's performance objectives
6. Which of the following would <u>not</u> normally be considered as a 'costs of quality'?
   1. Internal failure costs
   2. Research and development costs
   3. Warranty costs
   4. Inspection costs
   5. Marketing costs
   6. Prevention costs
7. Which one of the following would normally be considered as one of the 'costs of quality'?
   1. Marketing costs
   2. Distribution costs
   3. Research and development costs
   4. Stockholding costs
   5. Internal failure costs
8. Which one of the following would normally be considered as one of the 'costs of quality'?
   1. Overhead costs
   2. Transport costs
   3. Appraisal costs
   4. Marketing costs
   5. Transaction costs

9. Which one of the following would normally be considered as one of the 'costs of quality'?
    1. Purchase order discounts
    2. Appraisal costs
    3. Performance related pay
    4. The Economic Order Quantity
    5. Relocation costs
10. Which of the following would most commentators not regard as a 'quality guru'?
    1. FW Taylor
    2. Joseph Juran
    3. Genichi Taguchi
    4. Charles Handy
    5. Philip Crosby
    6. Arnaud Feigenbaum
    7. W.E. Deming
11. Which of the following would most commentators regard as one of the 'quality gurus'?
    1. Henri Gantt
    2. Terry Hill
    3. Charles Handy
    4. Joe Pine
    5. Joseph Juran

Total quality management

Discussion questions

1. Find out more about one of the 'quality gurus'. Describe his background, his approach to quality and his key contributions to the subject.
2. Talk to an operations manager about TQM. Try to assess what TQM means for that organization and the benefits and problems that have resulted.

3. Identify some of the micro operations that might be found in a high-class restaurant operation. Describe some of the things that might go wrong in each of them and assess the impact of them on the final, external customer.
4. A university is considering creating service-level agreements for its lecturing staff. Explain what is meant by a service-level agreement and suggest some performance measures that might be used.
5. What resistance might there be in an organization to Matsushito's assertion that 'the core of management is precisely the art of mobilizing and pulling together the intellectual resources of all employees in the service of the firm'?
6. Discuss the differences between the 'traditional' and the TQM views on the cost of quality.
7. Get hold of a copy of ISO 9000 or an equivalent and assess its potential impact on quality.
8. Ask an operations manager to describe how quality has been improved in the organization over the last few years. Compare and contrast your findings with the section in this chapter on TQM implementation.
9. Discuss the advantages and disadvantages for an organization considering applying to be assessed for a major quality award.
10. Why do you think that quality award procedures are now used predominantly as self-assessment vehicles?
11. The worldwide fast-food restaurant chain McDonalds has never actually used TQM as such. Yet their quality is renowned for being excellent throughout the world. How do you explain this?

Short Case (Case Study)

- XYZ Travel

XYZ Travel, which provides family camping holidays, has a reputation for the high-quality of its equipment and services, and has become market leader in this rapidly growing holiday sector. In recent years, sales offices have been opened in the India and Germany, and XYZ's geographic coverage has been extended from its original Indian sites to include sites throughout Europe. As the business has become larger and more complex, the demands placed on the office systems have also become greater, reinforcing the need for functional specialization of staff, yet requiring more interdepartmental understanding and cooperation. When it became clear that XYZ's service package could be copied by competitors eager to attract premium customers, the company decided to reinforce quality at every stage in their process. This was, they believed, the main criterion that already differentiated XYZ, and this was also potentially the most difficult for lower priced competitors to follow. A consultant was brought in to facilitate a major quality improvement programme. This was conceived as a 'top-down' approach, whereby important projects were identified and tackled by trained teams, but soon it became apparent that these early projects were not achieving the anticipated sustainable improvements. It also became clear that the failure was largely the result of only involving senior managers, who could not devote the time, required to projects, and did not fully understand the process concerned. Those employees who did have a very detailed understanding of the process had been excluded from problem definition, evaluation and implementation of changes. So, the company launched their quality management system (QMS) initiative. Each department established a quality steering committee which comprised at least one director, a trained facilitator and volunteers from every grade of employee. The emphasis at this stage was on the identification and improvement of internal processes with further emphasis on satisfying the internal customer. Early success demonstrated the validity of this approach and generated a high level of enthusiasm throughout the company.

Questions

1 Why are the differences between the first 'top-down' attempt, and the second attempt at establishing a quality initiative?

2 What do you think are the main advantages and problems with the more participative approach?

Answer

XYZ Travel

1. What are the differences between the first 'top-down' attempt, and the second attempt at establishing a quality initiative?

There are two important points about this case. Firstly that XYZ recognised one of the important aspects of a TQM approach that all parts of an organisation have a role to play in ensuring high quality. Second, like many organisations they try differing initiatives to improve quality, some work and some don't. This in itself can undermine TQM initiatives. TQM has itself to be done right first time too!

The key differences between the first attempt and second attempt are as follows:

	First attempt	*Second attempt*
Leadership	Used a consultant	Company-led
Overseen by	Senior managers	Departments
Team composition	Senior managers	All grades of employees
Team selection	Selected	Voluntary
Training	Used trained teams	Used trained facilitators
Understanding of processes	Little	Great
Focus	'Important' projects	Internal processes
Approach	'top-down'	'bottom-up'
Sustainability	Momentum not sustained	High level enthusiasm
Success	unsuccessful	successful

2. What do you think are the main advantages and problems with the more participative approach?

Advantages:

- involved all employees
- included the people who knew most about the processes
- it is in the interest of those employees to have the internal process problems resolved
- non-threatening and inclusive
- sustainable and successful

Problems:

1. The problems may not be solvable by 'Low Level' teams.
2. Employees will be demoralized if changes do not take place spending time on the projects will reduce the time spent on the actual jobs.

Chapter **10**

Total Productive Maintenance

10.1 What is Total Productive Maintenance (TPM)?

Total Productive Maintenance (TPM) is a maintenance plan which involves a recently defined theory for maintaining plants and equipment. The aim of the TPM program is to noticeably increase production while, at the same time, increasing employee morale and job satisfaction.

TPM brings maintenance into focus as an essential and critically important part of the business. It is no longer regarded as a non-profit activity. Down time for maintenance is scheduled as a part of the developed day and, in some cases, as an integral part of the manufacturing process. The aim is to hold crisis and spontaneous maintenance to a minimum.

10.2 Pillars of TPM

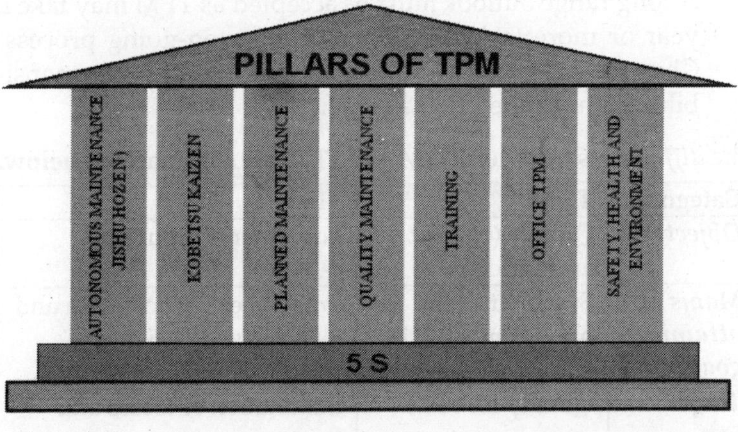

Source: An introduction to total productive maintenance by Venketesh J.

Why TPM?

TPM was introduced to accomplish the following objectives. The important ones are listed below.

1. Avoid wear and tear in a rapidly varying economic environment.
2. Producing commodities without dropping product quality.
3. Reduce price.
4. Produce a short batch quantity at the initial possible time.
5. Goods send to the customers must be non imperfect.

10.3 Similarities and differences between TQM and TPM:

The TPM program closely resembles the accepted Total Quality Management (TQM) program. Many of the tools such as employee empowerment, benchmarking, documentation, etc. used in TQM are used to implement and optimize TPM. Following are the similarities between the two.

1. Total commitment to the plan by upper level management is essential in both programmes.
2. Employees must be empowered to initiate counteractive action, and
3. A long range outlook must be accepted as TPM may take a year or more to implement and is an on-going process. Changes in employee mind-set toward their job responsibilities must take place as well.

The *differences* between TQM and TPM are summarized below.

Category	TQM	TPM
Object	Quality (Output and effects)	Equipment (Input and cause)
Mains of attaining goal	Systematize the management. It is software oriented	Employees participation and it is hardware oriented
Target	Quality for PPM	Elimination of losses and wastes.

Source: An introduction to total productive maintenance by Venketesh J.

10.4 Types of maintenance:

1. Breakdown maintenance:

It means that people waits until equipment fails and repair it. Such a thing could be used when the equipment failure does not extensively affect the operation or production or generate any important loss other than repair cost.

2. Preventive maintenance (1951):

It is an every day maintenance (cleaning, checking, oiling and re-tightening), design to retain the healthy situation of equipment and prevent failure through the prevention of deterioration, periodic inspection or equipment condition analysis, to measure worsening. It is further divided into episodic maintenance and prognostic maintenance. Just like human life is comprehensive by precautionary medicine, the equipment service life can be prolonged by doing preventive maintenance.

2a. Periodic maintenance (Time based maintenance - TBM):

Time based maintenance consists of periodically inspecting, servicing and cleaning equipment and replacing parts to prevent sudden failure and process problems.

2b. Predictive maintenance:

This is a method in which the service life of important part is predicted based on inspection or diagnosis, in order to use the parts to the limit of their service life. Compared to periodic maintenance, predictive maintenance is condition based maintenance.

It manages trend values, by measuring and analyzing data about deterioration and employs a surveillance system, designed to monitor conditions through an on-line system.

3. Corrective maintenance (1957):

It improves equipment and its components so that preventive maintenance can be carried out consistently. Equipment with design weakness must be redesigned to improve reliability or improving maintainability

4. Maintenance prevention (1960):

It indicates the design of new equipment. Weakness of current machines are adequately studied (on site information leading to failure prevention, easier maintenance and prevents of defects, safety and ease of manufacturing) and are included before commissioning a new equipment.

10.5 TPM - History:

TPM is an innovative Japanese concept. The origin of TPM can be traced back to 1951 when preventive maintenance was introduced in Japan. However the concept of preventive maintenance was taken from USA. Nippon denso was the first company to introduce plant wide preventive preservation in 1960. Preventive maintenance is the concept wherein, operators produced goods using machines and the maintenance group was dedicated with work of maintaining those machines, however with the computerization of Nippon denso, maintenance became a problem as more maintenance personnel were required. So the management decided that the routine maintenance of equipment would be carried out by the operators. (This is Autonomous maintenance, one of the features of TPM). Maintenance group took up only essential maintenance works.

Thus Nippon denso which previously followed preventive maintenance also added independent maintenance done by production operators. The repairs crew went in the equipment modification for improving reliability. The modifications were made or incorporated in new equipment. This guide to maintenance avoidance. Thus *preventive maintenance* along with *Maintenance prevention* and *Maintainability Improvement* gave birth to *Productive maintenance*. The aim of productive maintenance was to maximize plant and equipment effectiveness to achieve optimum life cycle cost of production equipment.

By then Nippon Denso had made quality circles, involving the employees' participation. Thus all employees took part in implementing Productive maintenance. Based on these developments Nippon denso was awarded the distinguished plant prize for developing and implementing TPM, by the *Japanese Institute of Plant Engineers* (JIPE). Thus Nippon denso of the Toyota group became the first company to obtain the TPM certification.

10.6 TPM Targets:

P

Obtain Minimum 80% OPE.

Obtain Minimum 90% OEE (Overall Equipment Effectiveness)

Run the machines even during lunch. (Lunch is for operators and not for machines!)

Q

Operate in a manner, so that there are no customer complaints.

C

Reduce the manufacturing cost by 30%.

D

Achieve 100% success in delivering the goods as required by the customer.

S

Maintain a accident free environment.

M

Increase the suggestions by 3 times. Develop Multi-skilled and flexible workers.

Source: An introduction to total productive maintenance by Venketesh J.

OEE (Overall Equipment Efficiency):

$$OEE = A \times PE \times Q$$

A - Availability of the machine. Availability is proportion of time machine is actually available out of time it should be available.

Motives of TPM	Adoption of life cycle approach for improving the overall performance of production equipment. Improving productivity by highly motivated workers which is achieved by job enlargement. The use of voluntary small group activities for identifying the cause of failure, possible plant and equipment modifications.
Uniqueness of TPM	The major difference between TPM and other concepts is that the operators are also made to involve in the maintenance process. The concept of "*I (Production operators) Operate, You (Maintenance department) fix*" is not followed.
TPM Objectives	Achieve Zero Defects, Zero Breakdown and Zero accidents in all functional areas of the organization. Involve people in all levels of organization. Form different teams to reduce defects and Self Maintenance.
Direct benefits of TPM	Increase productivity and OPE (Overall Plant Efficiency) by 1.5 or 2 times. Rectify customer complaints. Decrease the manufacturing cost by 30%. Satisfy the customers' needs by 100 % (Delivering the right quantity at the right time, in the required quality.) Reduce accidents. Follow pollution control measures.
Indirect benefits of TPM	Higher confidence level among the employees. Keep the work place clean, neat and attractive. Favorable change in the attitude of the operators. Achieve goals by working as team. Horizontal deployment of a new concept in all areas of the organization. Share knowledge and experience. The workers get a feeling of owning the machine.

$$A = (MTBF - MTTR) / MTBF.$$

$$\text{MTBF - Mean Time between Failures} = \frac{\text{(Total Running Time)}}{\text{Number of Failures}}$$

MTTR - Mean Time to Repair.

Performance Efficiency (PE). It is given by **RE X SE**.

Rate efficiency (RE): Actual average cycle time is slower than design cycle time because of jams, etc. Output is reduced because of jams

Speed efficiency (SE): Actual cycle time is slower than design cycle time machine output is reduced because it is running at reduced speed.

Q - Refers to quality rate. Which is percentage of good parts out of total produced sometimes called "yield".

Steps in introduction of TPM in an organization:

Step A - PREPARATORY STAGE:

STEP 1 - *Announcement by Management to all about TPM introduction in the organization:*

Proper understanding, commitment and active involvement of the top management in needed for this step. Senior management should have awareness programmes, after which announcement is made to all. Publish it in the house magazine and put it in the notice board. Send a letter to all concerned individuals if required.

STEP 2 - *Initial education and misinformation for TPM:*

Training is to be done based on the need. Some need intensive training and some just an awareness. Take people who matters to places where TPM previously productively implemented.

STEP 3 - Setting up TPM and departmental committees:

TPM includes improvement, independent maintenance, quality maintenance etc., as part of it. When committees are set up it should take care of all those needs.

STEP 4 - Establishing the TPM working system and target:

Now each area is benchmarked and fix up a target for achievement.

STEP 5 - A master plan for institutionalizing:

Next step is implementation leading to institutionalizing wherein TPM becomes an managerial culture. Achieving PM award is the proof of reaching a satisfactory level.

STEP B - INTRODUCTION STAGE

This is a ceremony and we should invite all. Suppliers as they should know that we want quality supply from them. Related companies and associated companies who can be our customers, sisters concerns etc. Some may study from us and some can help us and customers will get the communication from us that we care for quality output.

STAGE C - IMPLEMENTATION

In this stage eight activities are carried which are called eight pillars in the development of TPM activity. Of these four activities are for establishing the system for production efficiency, one for initial control system of new products and equipment, one for improving the efficiency of administration and are for control of safety, sanitation as working environment.

STAGE D - INSTITUTIONALISING STAGE

By all there activities one would has reached maturity stage. Now is the time for applying for PM award. Also think of challenging level to which you can take this movement.

Organization Structure for TPM Implementation:

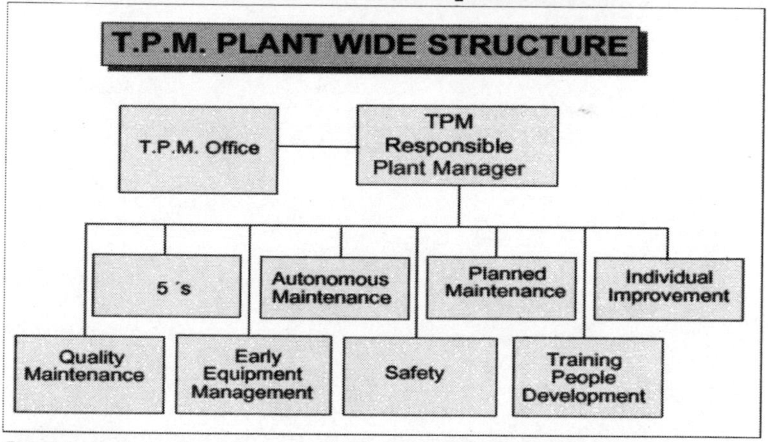

Source: An introduction to total productive maintenance by Venketesh J.

Chapter 11

Business Cycle

11.1 Introduction

The term **business cycle** or **economic cycle** refers to the fluctuations of economic activity (**business fluctuations**) around a long-term growth trend. The cycle involves shifts over time between periods of relatively rapid growth of output (recovery and prosperity), and periods of relative stagnation or decline (contraction or recession). These fluctuations are often measured using the real gross domestic product. Despite being termed cycles, these fluctuations in economic growth and decline do not follow a purely mechanical or predictable periodic pattern.

11.2 Type of business cycle

A number of types of business cycles, in the traditional sense of a fluctuation within a regular period have been proposed. The main types of business cycles enumerated by Joseph Schumpeter, and others in this field, have been named after their discoverers or proposers:

1. the Kitchin inventory cycle (3–5 years) — after Joseph Kitchin,
2. the Juglar fixed investment cycle (7–11 years) — after Clement Juglar,
3. the Kuznets infrastructural investment cycle (15–25 years) — after Simon Kuznets, Nobel Laureate,
4. the Kondratieff wave or cycle (45–60 years) — after Nikolai Kondratieff.
5. the Forrester cycles (200 years) - after Jay Wright Forrester.
6. the Toffler civilisation cycles (1000-2000 years) - after Alvin Toffler.

Even longer cycles are occasionally proposed, often as multiples of the Kondratieff cycle. Interest in traditional business cycles was strongest before World War II. However, interest has waned since the development of modern macroeconomics, which generally gives little support to the idea of regular periodic cycles.

11.3 Juglar cycle

In 1860, French economist Clement Juglar identified the presence of 8 to 11 year cycles. In *Business Cycles,* Schumpeter suggested this cycle be named after Juglar. These cycles are made up of four stages, each linked to the variation in prices, production and interest rates:

1. expansion = increase in production and prices , and low interests rates.
2. crisis = stock exchanges crash and bankruptcies of several companies occur.
3. recession = decrease in price and in output, high interests rates.
4. recovery = stocks recover thanks to the fall in prices and incomes.

In the Juglar cycle, which is sometimes called "the" business cycle, recovery and prosperity are associated with increases in productivity, consumer confidence, aggregate demand, and prices. In the cycles before World War II or that of the late 1990s in the United States, the growth periods usually ended with the failure of speculative investments built on a bubble of confidence that bursts or deflates. In these cycles, the periods of contraction and stagnation reflect a purging of unsuccessful enterprises as resources are transferred by market forces from less productive uses to more productive uses. Cycles between 1945 and the 1990s in the United States were generally more restrained and followed political factors, such as fiscal policy and monetary policy. Automatic stabilisation due to the government's budget helped defeat the cycle even without conscious action by policy-makers.

A usual term for a crisis of this time scale is a "decennial crisis" (meaning one that occurs after about ten years). This phrase was used during the Great Depression due its similarity with the Panic of 1825 in London ten years after the end of the Napoleonic Wars. After the Second World War, however, the nearest equivalent in time and intensity was the recession of 1958.

11.4 Cycles or fluctuations?

In topical years economic theory has moved towards the study of **economic fluctuation** rather than a 'business cycle- though some economists use the phrase 'business cycle' as a convenient shorthand. Milton Friedman stated on a number of occasions that calling the business cycle a "cycle" is a misnomer, because of its non-cyclical nature. He believed that for the most part, excluding very large supply shocks, business declines are more of a monetary phenomenon.

Balanced outlook theory states that no deterministic cycle can persist because it would consistently create arbitrage opportunities. Much economic theory also holds that the economy is usually at or close to equilibrium. These views led to the formulation of the idea that observed economic fluctuations can be modelled as shocks to a system.

A moving standard of a stochastic motionless variable also bears resemblance to a graph of an economic time-series, such as inflation, unemployment, or investment. Such graphs arguably resemble actual events more closely than deteministic cycle formulae.

11.5 Random walks and chaotic patterns

In 1900 Louis Bachelier planned that the fluctuations in share prices follow random walks, being totally random with no cyclic properties. It has been claimed that Bachelier's model failed to account for big fluctuations such as the Great Despair In the 1960s, Benoît Mandelbrot proposed that fluctuation in cotton prices follow a Lévy flight allocation, which have a fat tail allowing greater likelihood for large fluctuations. In 1995, physicists R. Mantegna and G. Stanley analyzed over a million records of stock market indices from the previous five years, and they found that the actual distribution lay between the Gaussian random walks and Lévy flights. They also found that comparable distributions were found regardless of the time scale exhibiting self-similarity. An accurate representation is yet to be found.

11.6 Explanation of business cycles

The explanation of fluctuations in the cumulative level of economic activity is one of the primary concerns of macroeconomics. The most commonly used framework for explaining such fluctuations is derived from Keynesian economics. In the Keynesian view, business cycles reflect the possibility that the economy may reach short-run equilibrium at levels below, or above full employment. If the economy is operating with less than full employment, i.e., with high unemployment above the NAIRU, then in theory monetary policy and fiscal policy can have a positive role to play rather than simply creating booms that necessarily collapse on themselves.

Keynesian models do not necessarily imply intermittent business cycles. However, simple Keynesian models connecting the interface of the Keynesian multiplier and accelerator give rise to cyclical responses to initial shocks. A model designed by Paul Samuelson, named the "oscillator model", is supposed to explain for business cycles thanks to the multiplier and the accelerator. The amplitude of the variations in economic output depends on the level of the investment, for investment determines the level of cumulative output (multiplier), and is determined by demand (accelerator).

Another explanation linked to the Keynesian thought is that of Goodwin, who accounts for cycles in output by the allocation of income between benefits and wages. The fluctuations in wages are the same as in the level of employment, for when the economy is at full-employment, workers are able to demand rises in wages, whereas in unemployment periods, they cannot.

According to Goodwin, when unemployment and the part of benefits rise, the output rises.

Keynesian economist Minski has proposed an explanation of cycles founded on fluctuations in interest rates: in an expansion period, interest rates are low and companies can easily borrow money from banks to invest. They do not hesitate to borrow money, and banks are not reluctant to grant them loans, because they know they would be able to easily pay back the loans thanks to the economic growth and the increase in incomes. But when companies become too indebted, they stop investing, and the economy goes into recession.

Keynesian views have been challenged by real business cycle models which consider fluctuations in supply (technology shocks). This theory is most associated with Finn E. Kydland and Edward C. Prescott, winners of the 2004 Nobel Prize in Economic Sciences. They consider that economic crisis and fluctuations cannot stem from a monetary shock, only from an external shock, such as an innovation.

11.7 Explanation of the recovery

Productive capital used by firms gets worn out over time and require replacements. Spending on capital equipment such as machinery is necessary, which increases aggregate expenditure (AE) and causes the economy to slowly climb. Secondly, the low prices characteristic of a trough phase causes increased demand for them, resulting in inflation which is characteristic of the boom phase. Lower interest rates stimulate increased borrowing. The repayments and interest which need to be paid back contribute to the rise in AE. Governments aim to improve the business cycle so as to provide stability, get re-elected and to ease worries about the state of the economy. They also do this to attract foreign investors and improve their international standing.

11.8 Preventing business cycles

Because the periods of stagnation are painful for many who lose their jobs, pressure arises for politicians to try to smooth out the oscillations. An important goal of all Western nations since the Great Depression has been to limit the dips.

Managing economic strategy to even out the cycle is a difficult task in a society with a composite economy, even when Keynesian theory is applied. According to some theorists, notably nineteenth-century advocates of communism, this difficulty is insurmountable. Karl Marx in particular claimed that the recurrent business cycle crises of capitalism were inevitable results of the system's operations. In this view, all that the government can do is to change the *timing* of economic crises. The crisis could also show up in a different *form*, for example as severe inflation or a steadily increasing government deficit. Worse, by delaying a crisis, government policy is seen as making it *more dramatic* and thus more painful.

Additionally, neoclassical economics plays down the capability of Keynesian policies to manage an economy. Challenging the Phillips Curve since the 1960s, economists like Nobel Laureate Milton Friedman or 2006 Nobel Laureate Edmund Phelps have made ground in their arguments that inflationary expectations negate the Phillips Curve in the long run. The stagflation of the 70's supported their theory by flying in the face of Keynesian predictions. Friedman has gone so far as to argue, that all the Federal Reserve System can do is to avoid making large mistakes, as he believes they did by contracting the money supply very rapidly in the face of the Stock Market Crash of 1929, in which they made what would have been a recession into a great depression.

11.9 Alternative interpretations of business cycles

11.9.1 Politically-based business cycle models

Another set of models tries to derive the business cycle from political decisions.

The partisan business cycle advises that cycles result from the successive elections of administrations with different policy regimes. Regime A adopts expansionary policies, resulting in growth and inflation, but is voted out of office when inflation becomes unacceptably high. The replacement, Regime B, adopts contractionary policies reducing inflation and growth, and the substitute downwards swing of the cycle. It is voted out of office when unemployment is too high, being replaced by Party A.

The political business cycle is shade theory stating that when an administration of any is elected, it initially adopts a contractionary policy to reduce inflation and gain a reputation for economic competence. It then adopts an expansionary policy in the lead up to the next election, hoping to achieve concurrently low inflation and unemployment on election day.

11.9.2 Marxist

Michal Kalecki's Marxian-influenced "political business cycle" theory blames the government. He argued that no democratic government under capitalism would allow the persistence of full employment, so that recessions would be caused by *political* decisions: importunate full employment would mean increasing workers' bargaining power to raise wages and to avoid doing unpaid labor, potentially sting profitability. In recent years, proponents of the "electoral business cycle" theory have argued that present politicians encourage prosperity before elections in order to ensure re-election – and make the citizens pay for it with recessions afterwards.

11.9.3 Anarcho-syndicalist

According to anarcho-syndicalism and related anarchist-libertarian socialisteconomic theories, the key to understanding the workings of the business cycle is the workers' corrosion of income as capital investment "pulls" money towards it over time, eventually resulting in a collapse of demand for the goods the system produces.

In this theory, the fact that profit-seeking capitalists plan not with respect of demand at the present instant, but with respect to future demand also drives the cycle. The need to maximise profits results in more and more investment in order to improve the productivity of the workforce (i.e. to increase the amount of surplus value produced). A rise in productivity, however, means that whatever profit is produced is spread over an increasing number of commodities. This profit still needs to be realised on the market but this may prove difficult as capitalists produce not for existing markets but for expected ones. As individual firms cannot predict what their competitors will do, it is rational for them to try to maximise their market share by increasing production (by increasing investment). As the market does not provide the necessary information to co-ordinate their actions, this leads to supply exceeding demand and difficulties realising sufficient profits. In other words, a period of over-production occurs due to the over-accumulation of capital.

Anarcho-syndicalist theory holds that there are means by which capitalism can postpone (but not stop) a general crisis developing as a result of the business cycle. The extension of credit by banks to both investors and consumers is the traditional, and most common, way. Imperialism, by which markets are increased and profits are extracted from less developed countries and used to boost the imperialist countries profits, is another method. Another is state intervention in the economy (such as minimum wages, the incorporation of trades unions into the system, arms production, manipulating interest rates to maintain a "natural" rate of unemployment to keep workers on their toes, etc.). Another is state spending to increase aggregate demand, which can increase consumption and so lessen the dangers of over-production. However, these are considered to have (objective and subjective) limits and can never succeed in stopping depressions from occurring as they ultimately flow from capitalist production and the need to make profits.

11.9.4 Austrian school

The Austrian School of economics rejects the suggestion that the business cycle is an inherent feature of a market economy and argues that it is caused mainly by central government intervention in the money supply. Austrian School economists, following Ludwig von Mises, point to the role of the interest rate as the price of investment capital, guiding investment decisions. In an unregulated (free-market) economy, where there is no central bank, it is posited that the interest rate reflects the actual time preference of lenders and borrowers. Some follow Knut Wicksell to call this the "natural" interest rate.

The government's attempt to gain control over money destroys the natural equilibrium of interest rates between savers and borrowers. Austrian School economists conclude that, if the interest rate is held artificially low by the government or central bank, then the demand for loans will be higher than the actual supply of willing lenders, and if the interest rate is artificially high, the opposite situation will occur. This pricing misinformation leads investors to misallocate capital, borrowing and investing either too much or too little in long-term projects. Periodic recessions, then, are seen as necessary "corrections" following periods of fiat credit expansion, when unprofitable investments are liquidated, freeing capital for new investment.

The Austrian Business Cycle Theory also predicts that the imposition of unnatuarally low interest rates, and the resulting increase in the supply of fiat credit, generates price inflation (often focused in capital or asset markets which employ many people). Once this monetary "boom" is in effect, often governments become fearful of a correction to the "monetary boom" given the negative employment effects of the inevitable correction. This then obliges the central bank to increase the supply of credit yet further to maintain the artificially low interest rate, thus prolonging the "fake" monetary boom and worsening the inevitable "correction" when credit expansion can no longer be sustained. In Austrian theory, depressions and recessions are positive forces in-so-much that they are the market's natural mechanism of undoing the misallocation of resources present during the "boom" or inflationary phase. Austrian School economists point to the dot-com investment frenzy and the U.S. housing bubble as a modern examples of artificially abundant credit subsidizing unsustainable overinvestment.

11.10 Problems of measurement

Some dispute that modern business cycle theory often measures growth by using the flawed measure of the economy's aggregate production, i.e., real gross domestic product, which is not useful for measuring well-being and also generates distortions in the perception of economic growth because the price changes of the various products are disproportional. Accordingly, there may be a mismatch between the state of economic health as perceived by many individuals and that perceived by the bankers and economists, which would drive them apart politically. However it is fluctuations in real GDP that cause changes in employment, unemployment, interest rates, and inflation, i.e. economic issues which are their main concern of business cycle experts.

Business cycle theory has been most effective in microeconomics where it aids in the preparation of risk management scenarios and timing investment, especially in infrastructural capital that must pay for itself over a long period, and which must fund itself by cashflow in late years. When planning such large investments, it is often useful to use the anticipated business cycle as a baseline, so that unreasonable assumptions, e.g. constant exponential growth, are more easily eliminated.

Chapter 12

Material Handling Equipment

12.1 Material handling equipment is all equipment that relates to the movement, storage, control and protection of materials, goods and products throughout the process of manufacturing, distribution, consumption and disposal. Material handling equipment is the mechanical equipment involved in the complete system. Material handling equipment is generally separated into four main categories; Storage and Handling Equipment, Engineered Systems, Industrial Trucks and Bulk Material Handling.

Ways in Which Material Handling Equipment Can Improve Efficiency

Material handling equipment is used to increase throughput, control costs, and maximize productivity. There are several ways to determine if the material handling equipment is achieving peak efficiency. These include capturing all relevant data related to the warehouse's operation (such as SKUs), measuring how many times an item is "touched" from the time it is ordered until it leaves the building, making sure you are using the proper picking technology, and keeping system downtime to a minimum.

12.2 Types of Material Handling Equipment

12.2.1 Storage and Handling Equipment

Storage and handling equipment is a category within the material handling industry. The equipment that falls under this description is usually non-automated storage equipment. Products such as Pallet rack, shelving, carts, etc. belong to storage and handling. Many of these products are often referred to as "catalog" items because they generally have globally accepted standards and are often sold as stock materials out of Material handling catalogs.

12.2.2 Engineered Systems

Engineered systems are typically custom engineered material handling systems. Conveyors, AS/RS, AGV and most other automated material handling systems fall into this category. Engineered systems are often a combination of products integrated to one system. Many distribution centers will optimize storage and picking by utilizing engineered systems such as pick modules and sortation systems.

12.2.3 Industrial Trucks

Industrial trucks usually refer to operator driven motorized warehouse vehicles. Industrial trucks assist the material handling system with versatility; they can go where engineered systems cannot. Forklift trucks are the most common example of industrial trucks but certainly aren't the extent of the category. Tow tractors and stock chasers are additional examples of industrial trucks.

12.2.4 Bulk Material Handling

Bulk material handling equipment is used to move and store bulk materials such as ore, liquids, and cereals. This equipment is often seen on farms, mines, shipyards and refineries. This category is also explained in Bulk material handling.

Pallet (sometimes called a **skid**) is a flat transport structure that supports goods in a stable fashion while being lifted by a forklift, pallet jack, or other jacking device. A pallet is the foundation of a unit load design, which can be as simple as placing the goods on a pallet, and securing them with straps or stretch-wrapped plastic film, or as exotic as a ULD minicontainer.

While the majority of pallets are made of wood, pallets manufactured from plastic, metal, and paper can also be found. Each material has advantages and disadvantages relative to the others.

12.3 Overview

Containerization for transport has spurred the use of pallets because the containers have the clean, level surfaces needed for easy pallet movement. Most pallets can easily carry a load of 1,000 kg (about 2,000 lb). Today, over half a billion pallets are manufactured each year and about two billion pallets are in use across the United States alone.

Pallets make it easy to move heavy stacks. Loads with pallets under them can be hauled by forklift trucks of different sizes, or even by hand-pumped and hand-drawn pallet jacks. Movement is easy on a wide, strong, flat floor: concrete is excellent. A forklift truck can cost the same as a luxury automobile, but a good reconditioned hand-drawn pallet jack costs only a few hundred dollars. The greatest investment is thus in the construction of commercial or industrial buildings where the use of pallets could be economical. Passage through doors and buildings must be possible. To help this issue, some later pallet standards (the europallet and the U.S. Military 35x45.5") are designed to pass through standard doorways.

Organizations using standard pallets for loading and unloading can have much lower costs for handling and storage, with faster material movement than businesses that do not. The exceptions are establishments that move small items such as jewelry or large items such as cars. But even they can be improved. For instance, the distributors of costume jewelry normally use pallets in their warehouses and car manufacturers use pallets to move components and spare parts.

The lack of a single international standard for pallets causes substantial continuing expense in international trade. A single standard is difficult because of the wide variety of needs a standard pallet would have to satisfy: passing doorways, fitting in standard containers, and bringing low labor costs. For example, organizations already handling large pallets often see no reason to pay the higher handling cost of using smaller pallets that can fit through doors.

12.4 History

Development of commercial transport packaging

Pallets stacked for loading onto barges in North London

Skids and pallets were slowly introduced throughout the early 20th century; wooden boxes, crates, barrels and kegs were much more commonly used to unitize, protect, store and transport goods. The predecessor of the modern wooden pallet was a simple skid that consisted only of stringers fastened to a top deck. It first appeared in American factories in conjunction with the low lift truck. A crude low lift hand truck was invented in 1887 and a more durable, all-steel low lift truck design was introduced in 1909.

The high lift fork truck first appeared in 1915. With further modification in 1919, the truck could lift loads several feet high while other improvements included cantilever design and forks. The emergence of forks as well during the same period enabled lift trucks to handle a much greater range of materials.

An additional expansion was the new capability of the mast of the fork lift to tilt both forward and back, independent of the lifting mechanism. These developments, along with the emergence of the double-faced pallet during the same time period, allowed for tiering of unit loads. As early as 1926, the essence of the modern lift truck had been developed. Now, pallets no longer were simply a means of moving materials within the plant. High lift trucks made possible vertical stacking of unit loads and a resulting dramatic improvement of warehouse and plant storage efficiencies.

1. Development of the pallet

The pallet was developed in stages. Spacers were used between loads to allow fork entry, progressing to the placement of boards atop stringers to make skids. Eventually boards were fastened to the bottom to create the pallet. The addition of bottom boards on the skid, which appeared by 1925, resulted in the modern form of the pallet. With the bottom deck, several problems common to the single faced skid were addressed. For example, the bottom boards provided better weight distribution and reduced product damage; they also provided better stacking strength and rigidity. Lift truck manufacturers promoted the idea of using more vertical area of a plant for stock storage.

In size, skids started narrow in order to pass through ordinary doors. As facilities were rebuilt, many organizations optimized their buildings for larger pallets in order to reduce labor costs.

The earliest referenced U.S. patent on a skid is Hallowell's 1924 "Lift Truck Platform. In 1939, Carl Clark patented a recognizably modern pallet, although with steel stringers. In World War II, palleted material handling was rapidly perfected in order to transfer Allied war materials. The patent activity picked up again after the war, as inventors claimed items they improvised for the war effort. The first four direction pallet was claimed in 1945 by Robert Braun. At the end of 1948, Sullivan Stemple claimed the basic idea of a pallet designed to be used with a fork lift; the pallet was to be stamped from steel. During World War II, to reduce the resupply time of warships, the first modern disposable four-way block pallet was developed, and patented in early 1949 by Norman Cahners, a U.S. Navy Supply Officer in the ordnance depot at Hingham, Massachusetts. The first completely modern 2-direction stringer pallet was described in 1949 by Darling Graeme.

2. Impact of pallet on rail transport

Pallets and forklifts also provided much quicker turnaround of rail cars and ships. In 1931, three days were required to unload a boxcar containing 13,000 cases of unpalletized canned goods. When the same amount of goods were loaded into the railway trucks on pallets or skids, the identical task took only four hours. With the entry of the U.S. into World War II, the urgency for material handling reform changed almost overnight. Palletization was regarded as an enormous opportunity to help the U.S. armed forces do more with less. Palletized loads could handle more goods with fewer people, freeing up men for military duty; it also could increase warehouse storage capacity and throughput, reducing the need for additional warehouse capacity. Pallets were used somewhat in the European theater, but they were put to work extensively in the Pacific.

12.5 Standardization and regulation

1. Dimensions

In a pallet quantity the first number is the stringer length and the second is the deck board length. Square or nearly-square pallets help a load resist tipping.

Two-way pallets are designed to lifted by the deckboards. In a warehouse the deckboard side faces the corridor. For optimal cubage in a warehouse, the deckboard dimension should be the shorter. This also helps the deckboards be more rigid.

Four-way pallets, or pallets for heavy loads, or general-purpose systems that might have heavy loads are best lifted by their more rigid stringers. A warehouse has the stringer side facing the corridor. For optimal cubage in a warehouse, the stringer dimension should be the shorter.

Pallet users want pallets to easily pass through buildings, stack and fit in racks, forklifts, pallet jacks and automated warehouses. To avoid shipping air, pallets should also pack tightly inside containers and vans.

No universally accepted standards for pallet dimensions exist. Companies and organizations utilize hundreds of different pallet sizes around the globe. While no single dimensional standard governs pallet production, a few different sizes are widely used._Pallet construction

12.6 Types of pallets

Fig. : Pallets being used in a warehouse in Finland.

Although pallets come in all manner of sizes and configurations, all pallets fall into two very broad categories: "stringer" pallets and "block" pallets. The National Wooden Pallet & Container Association has developed a Pallet Design System PDS© to manufacture pallets. PDS© is a computer program that allows the pallet maker to generate the best suited pallet design for a specific load and generate several options for wood selections to further reduce costs. Cap3d is another program that does the same thing.

1. Stringer pallet

Stringer pallets use a edge of three parallel pieces of timber (called stringers). The top deckboards are then affixed to the stringers to create the pallet structure. Stringer pallets are also known as "two-way" pallets, since a pallet-jack may only lift it from two directions instead of four. Forklifts can lift a stringer pallet from all four directions, though lifting by the stringers is more secure.

2. Block pallet

Block pallets are naturally stronger than stringer pallets. Block pallets use both parallel and perpendicular stringers to better facilitate efficient handling. A block pallet is also known as a "four-way" pallet, since a pallet-jack may be used from any side to move it.

3. Perimeter base pallet

All stringer and some block pallets have "unidirectional bases," i.e. bottom boards oriented in one direction. While automated handling equipment can be designed for this, often it can operate faster and more effectively if the bottom edges of a pallet have bottom boards oriented in both directions. For example, it may not need to turn a pallet to rack it, and operation is less sensitive to pallet orientation.

12.7 Quality improvements

The least expensive way to improve a pallet is usually to specify better nails. With non-wood pallets, a controlled coefficient of friction is often helpful to prevent the pallet from slipping from forks and racks. Stiffer pallets are more durable, and are handled more easily by automated equipment. If a pallet does not need to be lifted from all four sides, two-way pallets with unnotched stringers may be used, with the additional benefits of added rigidity and strength. Specifying tolerances on flatness and water content may help the supplier meet target requirements. Inspection of pallets, whether in person or by a third-party offer additional assurance of quality.

A **forklift** (also called a **lift truck**, a **high/low**, a **stacker-truck**, or a **sideloader**) is a powered industrial truck used to lift and transport materials. The modern forklift was developed in the 1920s by various companies including the transmission manufacturing company Clark and the hoist company Yale & Towne Manufacturing.[1] The forklift has since become an indispensable piece of equipment in manufacturing and warehousing operations.

12.8 History

The middle 19th century through the early 20th century saw the developments that led to today's modern forklifts. The Pennsylvania Railroad in 1906 introduced battery powered platform trucks for moving luggage at their Altoona, Pennsylvania train station. World War I saw the development of different types of material handling equipment in the United Kingdom by Ransomes, Sims and Jeffries of Ipswich. This was in part due to the labor shortages caused by the war. In 1917 Clark in the United States began developing and using powered tractor and powered lift tractors in their factories. In 1919 the Towmotor Company and Yale & Towne Manufacturing in 1920 entered the lift truck market in the United States.

Continuing development and expanded use of the forklift continued through the 1920s and 1930s. World War II, like World War I before, spurred the use of forklift trucks in the war effort. Following the war, more efficient methods for storing products in warehouses were being implemented. Warehouses needed more maneuverable forklift trucks that could reach greater heights. New forklift models were made that filled this need.

12.9 Design types

Forklift Classes and Lift Codes

Class #	Type of Propulsion and Operation	Lift Code	Description	Picture
I	Electric Motor Rider	4	Counterbalanced, sit-down, 3-wheel	
		5	Counterbalanced, sit-down, cushion (solid) tire	
		6	Counterbalanced, sit-down, pneumatic tire	
III	Electric Motor Walkie	2	Low-lift pallet	
		5	High lift reach type	
		7	High lift counterbalanced	
IV	Internal Combustion Engine Rider	3	Counterbalanced, sit-down, cushion (solid) tire	
V	Internal Combustion Engine Rider	4	Counterbalanced, sit-down, pneumatic tire	
VII	Rough Terrain	1	All types	

The following is a list of the more common lift truck types. It is arranged from the smallest type of lift to largest:

- Hand pallet truck
- Walkie low lift truck (powered pallet truck, usually electrically powered)
- Rider low lift truck
- Towing tractor
- Walkie stacker
- Rider stacker
- Reach truck (small forklift, designed for small aisles, usually electrically powered)
- Electric counterbalanced truck
- IC counterbalanced truck
- Sideloader
- Telescopic handler
- Slip Sheet machine
- Walkie Order Picking truck
- Rider Order Picking truck (commonly called an "Order Picker"; like a small forklift, except the operator rides up to the load and transfers it article by article)
- Articulated Very Narrow Aisle Counterbalanced trucks (commonly called "Flexi Truck")
- Guided Very Narrow Aisle truck - 'Man Down' (a type of reach truck designed for aisles less than five feet wide) and 'Man Riser' Combination pickcle Picker/ Stacker truck
- Truck Mounted Forklift / Sod Loader

12.10 Specialty trucks

At the other end of the spectrum from the counterbalanced forklift trucks are more 'high end' specialty trucks:

1. Articulated Counterbalance Trucks

These are, unlike most other lift trucks, front wheel steer, and are a hybrid VNA (Very Narrow Aisle) truck designed to be both able to offload trailers and place the load in narrow aisle racking. Increasingly these trucks are able to compete in terms of pallet storage density, lift heights and pallet throughput with Guided Very Narrow Aisle trucks.

2. Guided Very Narrow Aisle Trucks

These are rail or wide guided and available with lift heights up to 40' non top-tied and 98' top-tied. Two forms are available; 'man-down' and 'man-riser' where the operator elevates with the load for increased visibility or for multilevel 'break bulk' order picking. This type of truck, unlike Articulated Narrow Aišle Trucks, requires a high standard of floor flatness.

3. U.S. Military 10K-AT "Adverse Terrain"

12.11 Counterbalanced forklift components

Image of an electric forklift with component descriptions

12.11.1 A typical counterbalanced forklift contains the following components:

- **The Truck Frame** - is the base of the machine to which the mast, axles, wheels, counterweight, overhead guard and power source are attached. The frame may have fuel and hydraulic fluid tanks constructed as part of the frame assembly.

- **The Counterweight** - is a heavy cast iron mass attached to the rear of the forklift truck frame. The purpose of the counterweight is to counterbalance the load being lifted. In an electric forklift the large lead-acid battery itself may serve as part of the counterweight.
- **The Cab** - is the area that contains a seat for the operator along with the control pedals, steering wheel, levers, switches and a dashboard containing operator readouts. The cab area may be open air or enclosed, but it is covered by the cage-like overhead guard assembly.
- **The Overhead Guard** - is a metal roof supported by posts at each corner of the cab that helps protect the operator from any falling objects. On some forklifts, the overhead guard is part of the frame assembly.
- **The Power Source** - may consist of an internal combustion engine that can be powered by LP gas, CNG gas, gasoline or diesel fuel. Electric forklifts are powered by either a battery or fuel cells that provide power to electric motors. The motors may be either DC or AC types.
- **Tilt Cylinders** - are hydraulic cylinders that are mounted to the truck frame and the mast. The tilt cylinders pivot the mast to assist in engaging a load.
- **The Mast** - is the vertical assembly that does the work of raising and lowering the load. It is made up of interlocking rails that also provide lateral stability. The interlocking rails may either have rollers or bushings as guides. The mast is either hydraulically operated by one or more hydraulic cylinders or it may be chain operated with a hydraulic motor providing motive power. It may be mounted to the front axle or the frame of the forklift.
- **The Carriage** - is the component to which the forks or other attachments mount. It is mounted into and moves up and down the mast rails by means of chains or by being directly attached to the hydraulic cylinder. Like the mast, the carriage may have either rollers or bushings to guide it in the interlocking mast rails.

- **The Load Back Rest** - is a rack-like extension that is either bolted or welded to the carriage in order to prevent the load from shifting backward when the carriage is lifted to full height.
- **Attachments** - may consist of forks or tines that are the L-shaped members that engage the load. A variety of other types of material handling attachments are available. These include sideshifters, slipsheet attachments, carton clamps, multipurpose clamps, rotators, fork positioners, carpet poles, pole handlers, container handlers, roll clamps and many others.

12.11. 2 Below is a list of common forklift attachments:

- **Sideshifter** - is a hydraulic attachment that allows the operator to move the tines (forks) and backrest laterally. This allows easier placement of a load without having to reposition the truck.
- **Rotator** - To aid the handling of skids that may have become excessively tilted and other specialty material handling needs some forklifts are fitted with an attachment that allows the tines to be rotated. This type of attachment may also be used for dumping containers for quick unloading.
- **Fork Positioner** - is a hydraulic attachment that moves the tines (forks) together or apart. This removes the need for the operator to get out of the cab to manually adjust the tines for different sized loads.
- **Roll and Barrel Clamp Attachment** - A mechanical or hydraulic attachment that is used for handling barrels, kegs, or paper rolls. This type of attachment also usually have a rotate function so that a vertically stored paper roll can be inserted into the horizontal intake of a printing press.
- **Pole Attachments** - In some locations, such as carpet warehouses, a long metal pole is used instead of forks to lift carpet rolls. Similar devices, though much larger, are used to pick up metal coils.

- **Carton and Multipurpose Clamp Attachments** - are hydraulic attachments that allow the operator to open and close around a load, squeezing it to pick it up. Products like cartons, boxes and bales can be moved with this type attachment. With these attachments in use, the forklift truck is sometimes referred to as a clamp truck.
- **Slip Sheet Attachment (Push - Pull)** - is a hydraulic attachment that reaches forward, clamps onto a slipsheet and draws the slipsheet onto wide and thin metal forks for transport. The attachment will push the slip sheet and load off the forks for placement.
- **Drum Handler Attachment** - is a mechanical attachment that slides onto the tines (forks). It usually has a spring loaded jaw that grips the top lip edge of a drum for transport. Another type grabs around the drum in a manner similar to the roll or barrel attachments.
- **Man Basket** - a lift platform that slides onto the tines (forks); meant for hoisting workers. The man basket has railings and brackets for attaching safety harnesses.
- **Telescopic Forks** - are hydraulic attachments that allow the operator to operate in warehouse design for "double-deep stacking", which means that two pallet shelves are placed behind each other without any aisle between them.

12.11.3 Forklift control and capabilities

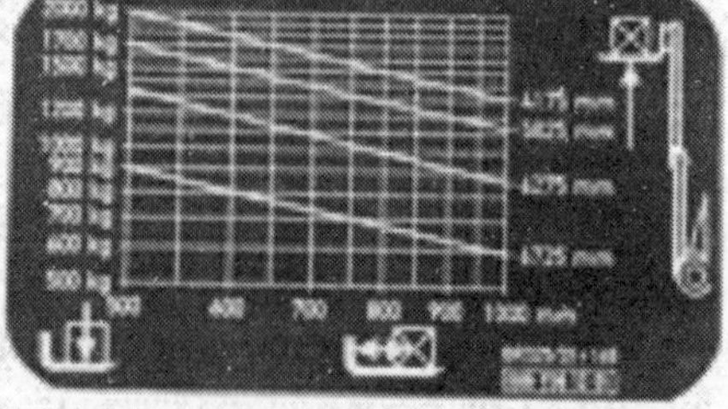

Fig. A typical load capacity chart

Forklift trucks are available in many variations and load capacities. In a typical warehouse setting most forklifts used have load capacities between one to five tons. Larger machines, up to 50 tons lift capacity are used for lifting heavier loads, including loaded shipping containers. In addition to a control to raise and lower the forks (also known as blades or tines), the operator can tilt the mast to compensate for a load's tendency to angle the blades toward the ground and risk slipping off the forks. Tilt also provides a limited ability to operate on non-level ground. Skilled forklift operators annually compete in obstacle and timed challenges at regional forklift rodeos.

12.11.4 General operations

A forklift transporting a pallet of potted plants in Durham, North Carolina.

Forklifts are rated for loads at a specified maximum weight and a specified forward centre of gravity. This information is located on a nameplate provided by the manufacturer, and loads must not exceed these specifications(In Canada it is 24" Load Center). In many jurisdictions it is illegal to remove or tamper with the nameplate without the permission of the forklift manufacturer.

An important aspect of forklift operation is that many have rear-wheel steering. While this increases maneuverability in tight cornering situations, it differs from a driver's traditional experience with other wheeled vehicles. While steering, as there is no caster action, it is unnecessary to apply steering force to maintain a constant rate of turn.

Another critical characteristic of the forklift is its instability. The forklift and load must be considered a unit with a continually varying centre of gravity with every movement of the load. A forklift must never negotiate a turn at speed with a raised load, where centrifugal and gravitational forces may combine to cause a disastrous tip-over accident. The forklift are designed with a load limit for the forks which is decreased with fork elevation and undercutting of the load (i.e. load does not butt against the fork "L"). A loading plate for loading reference is usually located on the forklift. A forklift should not be used as a personnel lift without the fitting of specific safety equipment, such as a "cherry picker" or "cage".

12.11.5 Lift truck associations and organizations

There are many national as well as continental associations related to the industrial truck industry. Some of the major organizations are listed as:

- Industrial Truck Association (ITA) **(North America)**
- Material Handling Equipment Distributors Association (MHEDA) **(North America)**
- Fédération Européenne de la Manutention - European Federation of Materials Handling (FEM)
- British Industrial Truck Association (BITA)
- Japan Industrial Vehicles Association (JIVA)
- **Korean Construction Equipment Manufacturers Association (KOCEMA)** There are many significant contacts among these organizations and they have established joint statistical and engineering programs. One program is the **World Industrial Trucks Statistics (WITS)** which is published every month to the association memberships. The statistics are separated by area (continent), country and class of machine. While the statistics are generic, and do not count production from most of the smaller manufacturers, the information is significant for its depth. These contacts have brought to a common definition of a Class System which all the major manufacturers adhere to.

12.11.6 Forklift safety organizations

1. Standards

Forklift safety is subject to a variety of standards world wide. The most important standard is the ANSI B56—of which stewardship has now been passed from the American National Standards Institute (ANSI) to the Industrial Truck Standards Development Foundation after multi-year negotiations. ITSDF is a non-profit organization whose only purpose is the promulgation and modernization of the B56 standard.

Other standards have been implemented in the United States by the Occupational Safety and Health Administration (OSHA) and in the United Kingdom by the Health and Safety Executive. In many countries forklift truck operators must be trained and certified to operate forklift trucks. Certification may be required for each individual class of lift that an operator would use.

A **belt conveyor** consists of two or more pulleys, with a continuous loop of material - the conveyor belt - that rotates about them. One or both of the pulleys are powered, moving the belt and the material on the belt forward. The powered pulley is called the drive pulley while the unpowered pulley is called the idler. There are two main industrial classes of belt conveyors; Those in general material handling such as those moving boxes along inside a factory and bulk material handling such as those used to transport industrial and agricultural materials, such as grain, coal, ores, etc. generally in outdoor locations. Generally companies providing general material handling type belt conveyors do not provide the conveyors for bulk material handling. In addition there are a number of commercial applications of belt conveyors such as those in grocery stores.

The belt consists of one or more layers of material they can be made out of rubber. Many belts in general material handling have two layers. An under layer of material to provide linear strength and shape called a carcass and an over layer called the cover. The carcass is often a cotton or plastic web or mesh. The cover is often various rubber or plastic compounds specified by use of the belt. Covers can be made from more exotic materials for unusual applications such as silicone for heat or gum rubber when traction is essential.

Material flowing over the belt may be weighed in transit using a beltweigher. Belts with regularly spaced partitions, known as *elevator belts*, are used for transporting loose materials up steep inclines. Belt Conveyors are used in self-unloading bulk freighters and in live bottom trucks. Conveyor technology is also used in conveyor transport such as moving sidewalks or escalators, as well as on many manufacturing assembly lines. Stores often have conveyor belts at the check-out counter to move shopping items. Ski areas also use conveyor belts to transport skiers up the hill. A wide variety of related conveying machines are available, different as regards principle of operation, means and direction of conveyance, including screw conveyors, vibrating conveyors, pneumatic conveyors, the moving floor system, which uses reciprocating slats to move cargo, and roller conveyor system, which uses a series of powered rollers to convey boxes or pallets.

2. Belt Conveyor Systems

Conveyors are used as components in automated distribution and warehousing. In combination with computer controlled pallet handling equipment this allows for more efficient retail, wholesale, and manufacturing distribution. It is considered a labor saving system that allows large volumes to move rapidly through a process, allowing companies to ship or receive higher volumes with smaller storage space and with less labor expense.

Rubber Conveyor Belts are commonly used to convey items with irregular bottom surfaces, small items that would fall in between rollers (e.g. a sushi conveyor bar), or bags of product that would sag between rollers. Belt conveyors are generally fairly similar in construction consisting of a metal frame with rollers at either end of a flat metal bed. The belt is looped around each of the rollers and when one of the rollers is powered (by an electrical motor) the belting slides across the solid metal frame bed, moving the product. In heavy use applications the beds which the belting is pulled over are replaced with rollers. The rollers allow weight to be conveyed as they reduce the amount of friction generated from the heavier loading on the belting. Belt conveyors can now be manufactured with curved sections which use tapered rollers and curved belting to convey products around a corner. These conveyor systems are commonly used inpostal sorting offices and airport baggage handling systems.

Typical Construction of a Conveyor systems Belt Bend

Belt Conveyor systems at a Packing Depot

Baggage Handling Belt Conveyor systems

3. Snake Sandwich Belt Conveyor

A sandwich belt conveyor uses two conveyor belts, face-to-face, to softly smoothly but firmly contain the product being carried, hence making steep incline and even vertical-lift runs easily achievable. The Snake Sandwich Belt Conveyor was created in 1979. The study was conceived by Joseph A. Dos Santos, P.E., President of Dos Santos International, with the help of a grant from the U.S. Bureau of Mines. The study was to develop a means of moving and elevating large quantities of bulk materials, including coarse products such as rocks, aggregate, coal, etc. at the steepest possible inclines. The intent was to use only existing and generally available hardware in order to achieve the most economically feasible and easily maintained steep-angle conveyor design. Snake Conveyors are available in widely ranging profiles of C and S Shape. In any case, a long bottom belt approach is possible to the sandwich entrance, and discharge may be on the high incline or may be after the extension of the carrying belt beyond the mouth of the sandwich. Snake Sandwich conveyors offer several advantages. First unlimited conveying capacity, a system suitable for the most rugged mine applications and gentle on sensitive and friable materials, high availability and low operating and maintenance costs, smooth surfaced belts allowing continuous belt cleaning by scrapers and plows. This also facilitates intermediate material discharge by belt plows, as appropriate, before and/or beyond the sandwiched part of the Snake profile. All conventional conveyor hardware insures economy and fast delivery of replacement parts.

4. Long belt conveyors

The longest belt conveyor system in the world is in Western Sahara. It is 100 km long, from the phosphate mines of Bu Craa to the coast south of El-Aaiun.

The longest single belt conveyor runs from Meghalaya in India to Sylhet in Bangladesh. It is about 17 km long and conveys limestone and shale at 960 tons/hr, from the quarry in India (25°11′12?N 91°37′15?E25.186729, 91.620797) to a cement factory in Bangladesh (25°02′01?N 91°39′03?E25.033474, 91.650953) (7 km long in India and 10 km long in Bangladesh). The conveyor was engineered by AUMUND France and Larsen & Toubro. The conveyor is actuated by 3 synchronized drive units for a total power of about 1.8 MW (2 drives at the head end in Bangladesh and 1 drive at the tail end in India). The conveyor belt was manufactured in 300-meter lengths on the Indian side and 500-meter lengths on the Bangladesh side, and was installed onsite. The idlers, or rollers, of the system are unique in that they are designed to accommodate both horizontal and vertical curves along the terrain. Dedicated vehicles were designed for the maintenance of the conveyor, which is always at a minimum height of 5 meters above the ground to avoid being flooded during monsoon periods.

12.12 Carton flow

Carton Flow is a form of shelving that uses a gravity-feed rear load design. Each unit consists of one or more inclined runways. Merchandise is loaded in the rear of each runway. As an item is removed from the front, the item directly behind it slides forward in place of the previous.

Put simply, the main advantage of carton flow rack over static rack or shelving systems is that merchandise remains better organized and easier to find/pick. With carton flow rack, the product is automatically rotated on a first in first out basis. Merchandise is stocked in the rear of the carton flow rack and moves toward the picking station in front on an inclined shelf equipped with specially designed roller track. When a carton is removed from the picking station, the next one in line rolls to the front. Carton flow always keeps items within reach. Inventory is easier to monitor and control since products are fully visible at all times.

Restocking and picking typically offer the greatest opportunity for improving efficiency within order picking operations. With carton flow rack systems labor savings of up to 75% can be realized almost immediately. Because items are picked from the front and stocked from the rear, both functions can be performed without interference and with minimized travel.

In a static storage system such as standard shelving, the stockers and pickers are often doing a lot of unnecessary travel.

Chapter 13

Supply Chain Management

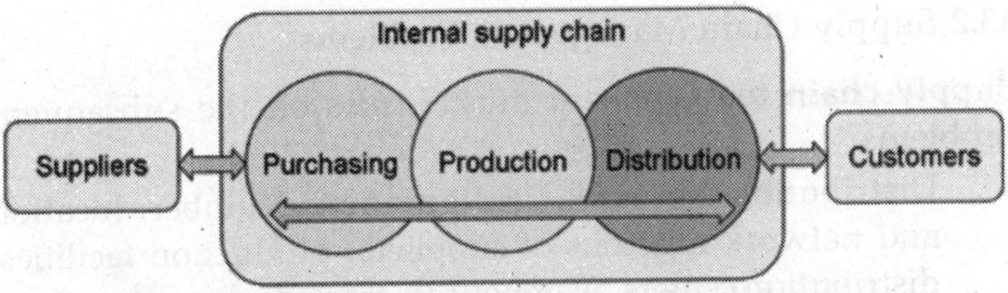

Fig: An illustration of a company's supply chain; the arrows stand for supplier-relationship management, internal SCM and customer-relationship management (cf. Chen/Paulraj, 2004)

13.1 Supply chain management (SCM) is the supervision of a system of interrelated businesses concerned in the decisive condition of product and service packages required by end customers. Supply Chain Management spans all development and storage of raw materials, work-in-process inventory, and finished goods from point-of-origin to point-of-consumption.

One American professional association put forwards is that Supply Chain Management encompasses the planning and management of all actions concerned with sourcing, procurement, conversion, and logistics management activities. Importantly, it also relates with coordination and collaboration with channel partners, which can be suppliers, intermediaries, third-party service providers, and customers. The real meaning, Supply Chain Management integrates supply and demand management within and across the organization. More recenly, the loosely coupled, self-organizing network of businesses that cooperates to provide product and service offerings has been called the *Extended Enterprise*.

Supply Chain Management can also refer to Supply chain management software which is apparatus or modules used in executing supply chain transactions, managing supplier relationships and controlling associated business processes.

Supply chain event management is a reflection of all possible going on events and factors that can cause a disturbance in a supply chain. With SCEM possible scenarios can be created and solutions can be designed.

13.2 Supply Chain Management Problems

Supply chain management must focuss on the subsequent problems:

- Distribution Network Configuration: Number, location and network missions of suppliers, production facilities, distribution centers, warehouses, cross-docks and customers.
- Distribution Strategy: Including questions of operating control (centralized, decentralized or shared); delivery scheme (e.g., direct shipment, pool point shipping, Cross docking, DSD (direct store delivery), closed loop shipping); mode of transportation (e.g., motor carrier, including truckload, LTL, parcel; railroad; intermodal, including TOFC and COFC; ocean freight; airfreight); replenishment strategy (e.g., pull, push or hybrid); and transportation control (e.g., owner-operated, private carrier, common carrier, contract carrier, or 3PL). Trade-Offs in Logistical Activities

The above actions must be synchromised well together in order to achieve the least total logistics cost. Trade-offs exist that increase the total cost if only one of the activities is optimized. For example, full truckload (FTL) rates are more economical on a cost per pallet basis than less than truckload (LTL) shipments. If, however, a full truckload of a product is ordered to reduce transportation costs there will be an increase in inventory holding costs which may increase total logistics costs. It is therefore imperative to take a systems approach when planning logistical activities. These trades-offs are key to developing the most efficient and effective Logistics and SCM strategy.

- Information: Integration of and other processes through the supply chain to share valuable information, including demand signals, forecasts, inventory, transportation, and potential collaboration etc.
- Inventory Management: Quantity and location of inventory including raw materials, work-in-progress (WIP) and finished goods.
- Cash-Flow: Arranging the payment terms and the methodologies for exchanging funds across entities within the supply chain.

Supply chain execution is managing and coordinating the movement of materials, information and funds across the supply chain. The flow is bi-directional.

13.3 Activities/functions of Supply Chain Management

Supply chain management is a cross-functional approach to manage the movement of raw materials into an organization, certain aspects of the internal processing of materials into finished goods, and then the movement of finished goods out of the organization toward the end-consumer. As organizations strive to focus on core competencies and becoming more flexible, they have reduced their ownership of raw materials sources and distribution channels. These functions are increasingly being outsourced to other entities that can perform the activities better or more cost effectively. The effect is to increase the number of organizations involved in satisfying customer demand, while reducing management control of daily logistics operations. Less control and more supply chain partners led to the creation of supply chain management concepts. The purpose of supply chain management is to improve trust and collaboration among supply chain partners, thus improving inventory visibility and improving inventory velocity.

Several models have been proposed for understanding the activities required to manage material movements across organizational and functional boundaries. SCOR is a supply chain management model promoted by the Supply Chain Management Council. Another model is the SCM Model proposed by the Global Supply Chain Forum (GSCF). Supply chain activities can be grouped into strategic, tactical, and operational levels of activities.

13.4 Strategies of SCM

- Strategies network optimization, including the number, location, and size of warehouses, distribution centers and facilities.
- Strategies partnership with suppliers, distributors, and customers, creating communication channels for critical information and operational improvements such as cross docking, direct shipping, and third-party logistics.
- Product design coordination, so that new and existing products can be optimally integrated into the supply chain, load management
- Information Technology infrastructure, to support supply chain operations.
- Where-to-make and what-to-make-or-buy decisions
- Aligning overall organizational strategy with supply strategy.

13.5 Tactics of SCM

- Sourcing contracts and other purchasing decisions.
- Production decisions, including contracting, scheduling, and planning process definition.
- Inventory decisions, including quantity, location, and quality of inventory.
- Transportation strategy, including frequency, routes, and contracting.
- Milestone payments
- Focus on customer demand.
- Benchmarking of all operations against competitors and implementation of best practices throughout the enterprise.

13.6 Operational Strategies of SCM

- Daily production and distribution planning, including all nodes in the supply chain.
- Production scheduling for each manufacturing facility in the supply chain (minute by minute).
- Demand planning and forecasting, coordinating the demand forecast of all customers and sharing the forecast with all suppliers.
- Sourcing planning, including current inventory and forecast demand, in collaboration with all suppliers.
- Inbound operations, including transportation from suppliers and receiving inventory.
- Production operations, including the consumption of materials and flow of finished goods.
- Outbound operations, including all fulfillment activities and transportation to customers.
- Order promising, accounting for all constraints in the supply chain, including all suppliers, manufacturing facilities, distribution centers, and other customers...

13.7 Supply chain management

Organizations increasingly find that they must rely on effective supply chains, or networks, to successfully compete in the global market and networked economy. In Peter Drucker's (1998) management's new paradigms, this concept of business relationships extends beyond traditional enterprise boundaries and seeks to organize entire business processes throughout a value chain of multiple companies.

During the past decades, globalization, outsourcing and information technology have enabled many organizations, such as Dell and Hewlett Packard, to successfully operate solid collaborative supply networks in which each specialized business partner focuses on only a few key strategic actions. This inter-organizational supply network can be acknowledged as a new form of organization. However, with the complicated interactions among the players, the network structure fits neither "market" nor "hierarchy" categories (Powell, 1990). It is not clear what kind of performance impacts that different supply network structures could have on firms, and little is known about the coordination conditions and trade-offs that may exist among the players. From a system's point of view, a complex network structure can be decomposed into individual component firms (Zhang and Dilts, 2004). Traditionally, companies in a supply network concentrate on the inputs and outputs of the processes, with little concern for the internal management working of other individual players. Therefore, the choice of an internal management control structure is known to impact local firm performance.

In the 21st century, there have been a few changes in business environment that have contributed to the development of supply chain networks. First, as an outcome of globalization and the proliferation of multi-national companies, joint ventures, strategic alliances and business partnerships, there were found to be significant success factors, following the earlier "Just-In-Time", "Lean Management" and "Agile Manufacturing" practices. Second, technological changes, particularly the dramatic fall in information communication costs, which are a paramount component of transaction costs, have led to changes in coordination among the members of the supply chain network.

Many researchers have recognized these kinds of supply network structures as a new organization form, using terms such as "Keiretsu", "Extended Enterprise", "Virtual Corporation", "Global Production Network", and "Next Generation Manufacturing System".In general, such a structure can be defined as "a group of semi-independent organizations, each with their capabilities, which collaborate in ever-changing constellations to serve one or more markets in order to achieve some business goal specific to that collaboration".

13.8 Developments in Supply Chain Management

Six major movements can be observed in the evolution of supply chain management studies: Creation, Integration, and

Globalization (Lavassani et al., 2008[a]), Specialization Phases One and Two, and SCM 2.0.

1. Creation Period

The word supply chain management was first coined by an American industry consultant in the early 1980s. However the concept of supply chain in management, was of great importance long before in the early 20th century, especially by the creation of the assembly line. The characteristics of this era of supply chain management include the need for large scale changes, reengineering, downsizing driven by cost reduction programs, and widespread attention to the Japanese practice of management.

2. Integration Period

This era of supply chain management studies was highlighted with the development of Electronic Data Interchange (EDI) systems in the 1960s and developed through the 1990s by the introduction of Enterprise Resource Planning (ERP) systems. This era has continued to develop into the 21st century with the expansion of internet-based collaborative systems. This era of SC evolution is characterized by both increasing value-added and cost reduction through integration.

3. Globalization Period

The third movement of supply chain management development, globalization era, can be characterized by the attention towards global systems of supplier relations and the expansion of supply chain over national boundaries and into other continents. Although the use of global sources in the supply chain of organizations can be traced back to several decades ago (e.g. the oil industry), it was not until the late 1980s that a considerable number of organizations started to integrate global sources into their core business. This era is characterized by the globalization of supply chain management in organizations with the goal of increasing competitive advantage, creating more value-added, and reducing costs through global sourcing.

4. Specialization Period – Phase One – Outsourced Manufacturing and Distribution

In the 1990s industries began to focus on "core competencies" and adopted a specialization model. Companies abandoned vertical integration, sold off non-core operations, and outsourced those functions to other companies. This changed management requirements by extending the supply chain well beyond the four walls and distributing management across specialized supply chain partnerships.

This transition also refocused the fundamental perspectives of each respective organization. OEMs became brand owners that needed deep visibility into their supply base. They had to control the entire supply chain from above instead of from within. Contract manufacturers had to manage bills of material with different part numbering schemes from multiple OEMs and support customer requests for work -in-process visibility and vendor-managed inventory (VMI).

The specialization model creates manufacturing and distribution networks composed of multiple, individual supply chains specific to products, suppliers, and customers, who work together to design, manufacture, distribute, market, sell, and service a product. The set of partners may change according to a given market, region, or channel, resulting in a proliferation of trading partner environments, each with its own unique characteristics and demands.

5. Specialization Period – Phase Two – Supply Chain Management as a Service

Specialization within the supply chain began in the 1980s with the inception of transportation brokerages, warehouse management, and non asset based carriers and has matured beyond transportation and logistics into aspects of supply planning, collaboration, execution and performance management.

At any given moment, market forces could demand changes within suppliers, logistics providers, locations, customers and any number of these specialized participants within supply chain networks. This variability has significant effect on the supply chain infrastructure, from the foundation layers of establishing and managing the electronic communication between the trading partners to the more-complex requirements, including the configuration of the processes and work flows that are essential to the management of the network itself.

Supply chain specialization enables companies to improve their overall competencies in the same way that outsourced manufacturing and distribution has done; it allows them to focus on their core competencies and assemble networks of best in class domain specific partners to contribute to the overall value chain itself – thus increasing overall performance and efficiency. The ability to quickly obtain and deploy this domain specific supply chain expertise without developing and maintaining an entirely unique and complex competency in house is the leading reason why supply chain specialization is gaining popularity.

Outsourced technology hosting for supply chain solutions debuted in the late 1990s and has taken root in transportation and collaboration categories most dominantly. This has progressed from the Application Service Provider (ASP) model from approximately 1998 through 2003 to the On-Demand model from approximately 2003-2006 to the Software as a Service (SaaS) model we are currently focused on today.

6. Supply Chain Management 2.0 (SCM 2.0)

Building off of globalization and specialization, SCM 2.0 has been coined to describe both the changes within the supply chain itself as well as the evolution of the processes, methods and tools that manage it in this new "era".

Web 2.0 is defined as a trend in the use of the World Wide Web that is meant to increase creativity, information sharing, and collaboration among users. At its core, the common attribute that Web 2.0 brings is it helps us navigate the vast amount of information available on the web to find what we are looking for. It is the notion of a usable pathway. SCM 2.0 follows this notion into supply chain operations. It is the pathway to SCM results – the combination of the processes, methodologies, tools and delivery options to guidecompanies to their results quickly as the complexity and speed of the supply chain increase due to the effects of global competition, rapid price flucuations, surging oil prices, short product life cycles, expanded specialization, near/far and off shoring, and talent scarcity.

SCM 2.0 leverages proven solutions designed to rapidly deliver results with the agility to quickly manage future change for continuous flexibility, value and success. This is delivered through competency networks composed of best of breed supply chain domain expertise to understand which elements, both operationally and organizationally, are the critical few that deliver the results as well as the intimate understanding of how to manage these elements to achieve desired results, finally the solutions are delivered in a variety of options as no-touch via business process outsourcing, mid-touch via managed services and software as a service (SaaS), or high touch in the traditional software deployment model.

13.9 Supply chain business process integration

Successful SCM requires a change from managing individual functions to integrating activities into key supply chain processes. An example scenario: the purchasing department places orders as requirements become appropriate. Marketing, responding to customer demand, communicates with several distributors and retailers as it attempts to satisfy this demand. Shared information between supply chain partners can only be fully leveraged through process integration.

Supply chain business process integration involves collaborative work between buyers and suppliers, joint product development, common systems and shared information. According to Lambert and Cooper (2000) operating an integrated supply chain requires continuous information flow. However, in many companies, management has reached the conclusion that optimizing the product flows cannot be accomplished without implementing a process approach to the business. The key supply chain processes stated by Lambert (2004) are:

- Customer relationship management
- Customer service management
- Demand management
- Order fulfillment
- Manufacturing flow management
- Supplier relationship management
- Product development and commercialization
- Returns management

One could suggest other key critical supply business processes combining these processes stated by Lambert such as:

a. Customer service management
b. Procurement
c. Product development and commercialization
d. Manufacturing flow management/support
e. Physical distribution
f. Outsourcing/partnerships
g. Performance measurement

a) Customer service management process

Customer Relationship Management concerns the relationship between the organization and its customers. Customer service provides the source of customer information. It also provides the customer with real-time information on promising dates and product availability through interfaces with the company's production and distribution operations. Successful organizations use following steps to build customer relationships:

- determine mutually satisfying goals between organization and customers.
- establish and maintain customer rapport.
- produce positive feelings in the organization and the customers.

b) Procurement process

Strategies plans are developed with suppliers to support the manufacturing flow management process and development of new products. In firms where operations extend globally, sourcing should be managed on a global basis. The desired outcome is a win-win relationship, where both parties benefit, and reduction times in the design cycle and product development are achieved. Also, the purchasing function develops rapid communication systems, such as electronic data interchange (EDI) and Internet linkages to transfer possible requirements more rapidly. Activities related to obtaining products and materials from outside suppliers requires performing resource planning, supply sourcing, negotiation, order placement, inbound transportation, storage, handling and quality assurance, many of which include the responsibility to coordinate with suppliers in scheduling, supply continuity, hedging, and research into new sources or programmes.

c) Product development and commercialization

Here, customers and suppliers must be united into the product development process, thus to reduce time to market. As product life cycles shorten, the appropriate products must be developed and successfully launched in ever shorter time-schedules to remain competitive. According to Lambert and Cooper (2000), managers of the product development and commercialization process must:

1. coordinate with customer relationship management to identify customer-articulated needs;
2. select materials and suppliers in conjunction with procurement, and
3. develop production technology in manufacturing flow to manufacture and integrate into the best supply chain flow for the product/market combination.

d) Manufacturing flow management process

The manufacturing process is produced and supplies products to the distribution channels based on past forecasts. Manufacturing processes must be flexible to respond to market changes, and must accommodate mass customization. Orders are processes operating on a just-in-time (JIT) basis in minimum lot sizes. Also, changes in the manufacturing flow process lead to shorter cycle times, meaning improved responsiveness and efficiency of demand to customers. Activities related to planning, scheduling and supporting manufacturing operations, such as work-in-process storage, handling, transportation, and time phasing of components, inventory at manufacturing sites and maximum flexibility in the coordination of geographic and final assemblies postponement of physical distribution operations.

e) Physical distribution

This concerns movement of a finished product/service to customers. In physical distribution, the customer is the final destination of a marketing channel, and the availability of the product/service is a vital part of each channel participant's marketing effort. It is also through the physical distribution process that the time and space of customer service become an integral part of marketing, thus it links a marketing channel with its customers (e.g. links manufacturers, wholesalers, retailers).

f) Outsourcing/partnerships

This is not just outsourcing the procurement of materials and components, but also outsourcing of services that traditionally have been provided in-house. The logic of this trend is that the company will increasingly focus on those activities in the value chain where it has a distinctive advantage and everything else it will outsource. This movement has been particularly evident in logistics where the provision of transport, warehousing and inventory control is increasingly subcontracted to specialists or logistics partners. Also, to manage and control this network of partners and suppliers requires a blend of both central and local involvement. Hence, strategic decisions need to be taken centrally with the monitoring and control of supplier performance and day-to-day liaison with logistics partners being best managed at a local level.

g) Performance measurement

Experts found a strong relationship from the largest arcs of supplier and customer integration to market share and profitability. By taking advantage of supplier capabilities and emphasizing a long-term supply chain perspective in customer relationships can be both correlated with firm performance. As logistics competency becomes a more critical factor in creating and maintaining competitive advantage, logistics measurement becomes increasingly important becausethe difference between profitable and unprofitable operations becomes more narrow. A.T. Kearney Consultants (1985) noted that firms engaging in comprehensive performance measurement realized improvements in overall productivity. According to experts internal measures are generally collected and analyzed by the firm including

1. Cost,
2. Customer Service,
3. Productivity measures,
4. Asset measurement, and
5. Quality.

External performance measurement is examined through customer perception measures and "best practice" benchmarking, and includes 1) customer perception measurement, and 2) best practice benchmarking. Components of Supply Chain Management are 1. Standardization 2. Postponement 3. Customization

13.10 Theories of Supply Chain Management

Currently there exists a gap in the literature available in the area of supply chain management studies, on providing theoretical support for explaining the existence and the boundaries of supply chain management. Few authors such as Halldorsson, et al. (2003), Ketchen and Hult (2006) and Lavassani, et al. (2008[b]) had tried to provide theoretical foundations for different areas related to supply chain with employing organizational theories. These theories include:

- Resource-based view (RBV)
- Transaction Cost Analysis (TCA)
- Knowledge-based view (KBV)
- Strategic Choice Theory (SCT)
- Agency theory (AT)
- Institutional theory (InT)
- Systems Theory (ST)
- Network Perspective (NP)

13.11 Components of Supply Chain Management Integration

13.11.1 The management components of SCM

The SCM components are the third element of the four-square circulation framework. The level of integration and management of a business process link is a function of the number and level, ranging from low to high, of components added to the link (Ellram and Cooper, 1990; Houlihan, 1985). Consequently, adding more management components or increasing the level of each component can increase the level of integration of the business process link. The literature on business process reengineering, buyer-supplier relationships, and SCM suggests various possible components that must receive managerial attention when managing supply relationships. Lambert and Cooper (2000) identified the following components which are:

- Planning and control
- Work structure
- Organization structure
- Product flow facility structure
- Information flow facility structure
- Management methods
- Power and leadership structure
- Risk and reward structure
- Culture and attitude

However, a more careful examination of the existing literature will lead us to a more comprehensive structure of what should be the key critical supply chain components, the "branches" of the previous identified supply chain business processes, that is, what kind of relationship the components may have that are related with suppliers and customers accordingly. Bowersox and Closs states that the emphasis on cooperation represents the synergism leading to the highest level of joint achievement (Bowersox and Closs, 1996). A primary level channel participant is a business that is willing to participate in the inventory ownership responsibility or assume other aspects of financial risk, thus including primary level components. A secondary level participant (specialized), is a business that participates in channel relationships by performing essential services for primary participants, thus including secondary level components, which are in support of primary participants. Third level channel participants and components that will support the primary level channel participants, and which are the fundamental branches of the secondary level components, may also be included.

Consequently, Lambert and Cooper's framework of supply chain components does not lead us to the conclusion about what are the primary or secondary (specialized) level supply chain components. That is, what supply chain components should be viewed as primary or secondary, how these components should be structured in order to have a more comprehensive supply chain structure, and to examine the supply chain as an integrative one.

13.12 Reverse Supply Chain Reverse logistics is the process of planning, implementing and controlling the efficient, effective inbound flow and storage of secondary goods and related information opposite to the traditional supply chain direction for the purpose of recovering value or proper disposal. Reverse logistics is also referred to as "Aftermarket Customer Services". In other words, anytime money is taken from a company's Warranty Reserve or Service Logistics budget, that is a Reverse Logistics operation.

Chapter 14

Automation

14.1 Automation (ancient Greek: = *self dictated*), **roboticization** or industrial automation or numerical control is the use of control systems such as computers to control industrial machinery and processes, reducing the need for human intervention.[1] In the scope of industrialization, automation is a step beyond mechanization. Whereas *mechanization* provided human operators with machinery to assist them with the *physical* requirements of work, *automation* greatly reduces the need for human *sensory* and *mental* requirements as well. Processes and systems can also be automated.

Automation plays an increasingly important role in the global economy and in daily experience. Engineers strive to combine automated devices with mathematical and organizational tools to create complex systems for a rapidly expanding range of applications and human activities.

Many roles for humans in industrial processes presently lie beyond the scope of automation. Human-level pattern recognition, language recognition, and language production ability are well beyond the capabilities of modern mechanical and computer systems. Tasks requiring subjective assessment or synthesis of complex sensory data, such as scents and sounds, as well as high-level tasks such as strategic planning, currently require human expertise. In many cases, the use of humans is more cost-effective than mechanical approaches even where automation of industrial tasks is possible.

Specialised hardened computers, referred to as programmable logic controllers (PLCs), are frequently used to synchronize the flow of inputs from (physical) sensors and events with the flow of outputs to actuators and events. This leads to precisely controlled actions that permit a tight control of almost any industrial process.

Human-machine interfaces (HMI) or computer human interfaces (CHI), formerly known as *man-machine interfaces,* are usually employed to communicate with PLCs and other computers, such as entering and monitoring temperatures or pressures for further automated control or emergency response. Service personnel who monitor and control these interfaces are often referred to as stationary engineers.

14.2 Impact of Automotion

Automation has had a notable impact in a wide range of highly visible industries beyond manufacturing. Once-ubiquitous telephone operators have been replaced largely by automated telephone switchboards and answering machines. Medical processes such as primary screening in electrocardiography or radiography and laboratory analysis of human genes, sera, cells, and tissues are carried out at much greater speed and accuracy by automated systems. Automated teller machines have reduced the need for bank visits to obtain cash and carry out transactions. In general, automation has been responsible for the shift in the world economy from agrarian to industrial in the 19th century and from industrial to services in the 20th century.

The widespread impact of industrial automation raises social issues, among them its impact on employment. Historical concerns about the effects of automation date back to the beginning of the industrial revolution, when a social movement of English textile machine operators in the early 1800s known as the Luddites protested against Jacquard's automated weaving looms[4] – often by destroying such textile machines– that they felt threatened their jobs. One author made the following case. When automation was first introduced, it caused widespread fear. It was thought that the displacement of human operators by computerized systems would lead to severe unemployment. Critics of automation contend that increased industrial automation causes increased unemployment; this was a pressing concern during the 1980s. One argument claims that this has happened invisibly in recent years, as the fact that many manufacturing jobs left the United States during the early 1990s was offset by a one-time massive increase in IT jobs at the same time. Some authors argue that the opposite has often been true, and that automation has led to *higher* employment. Under this point of view, the freeing up of the labour force has allowed more people to enter higher skilled managerial as well as specialised consultant/contractor jobs (like cryptographers), which are typically higher paying. One odd side effect of this shift is that "unskilled labour" is in higher demand in many first-world nations, because fewer people are available to fill such jobs.

At first glance, automation might appear to devalue labor through its replacement with less-expensive machines; however, the overall effect of this on the workforce as a whole remains unclear. Today automation of the workforce is quite advanced, and continues to advance increasingly more rapidly throughout the world and is encroaching on ever more skilled jobs, yet during the same period the general well-being and quality of life of most people in the world (where political factors have not muddied the picture) have improved dramatically. What role automation has played in these changes has not been well studied.

14.3 Current emphasis

Currently, for manufacturing companies, the purpose of automation has shifted from increasing productivity and reducing costs, to broader issues, such as increasing quality and flexibility in the manufacturing process.

The old focus on using automation simply to increase productivity and reduce costs was seen to be short-sighted, because it is also necessary to provide a skilled workforce who can make repairs and manage the machinery. Moreover, the initial costs of automation were high and often could not be recovered by the time entirely new manufacturing processes replaced the old.

Automation is now often applied primarily to increase quality in the manufacturing process, where automation can increase quality substantially. For example, automobile and truck pistons used to be installed into engines manually. This is rapidly being transitioned to automated machine installation, because the error rate for manual installment was around 1-1.5%, but has been reduced to 0.00001% with automation. Hazardous operations, such as oil refining, the manufacturing of industrial chemicals, and all forms of metal working, were always early contenders for automation.

Another major shift in automation is the increased emphasis on flexibility and convertibility in the manufacturing process. Manufacturers are increasingly demanding the ability to easily switch from manufacturing Product A to manufacturing Product B without having to completely rebuild the production lines. Flexibility and distributed processes have led to the introduction of Automated Guided Vehicles with Natural Features Navigation.

14.4 Automation tools

Different types of automation tools exist:

- ANN - Artificial neural network
- DCS - Distributed Control System
- HMI - Human Machine Interface
- SCADA - Supervisory Control and Data Acquisition
- PLC - Programmable Logic Controller

14.5 Artificial neural network

An **artificial neural network (ANN)**, often just called a "neural network" (NN), is a mathematical model or computational model based on biological neural networks. It consists of an interconnected group of artificial neurons and processes information using a connectionist approach to computation. In most cases an ANN is an adaptive system that changes its structure based on external or internal information that flows through the network during the learning phase.

In more practical terms neural networks are non-linear statistical data modeling tools. They can be used to model complex relationships between inputs and outputs or to find patterns in data.

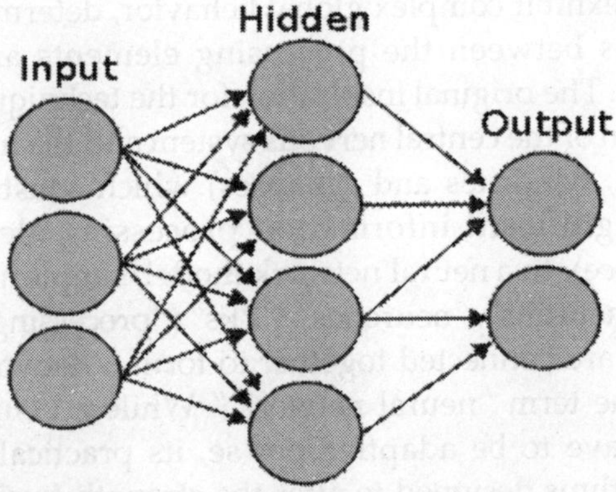

A neural network is an interconnected group of nodes, akin to the vast network of neurons in the human brain.

14.5.1 Background

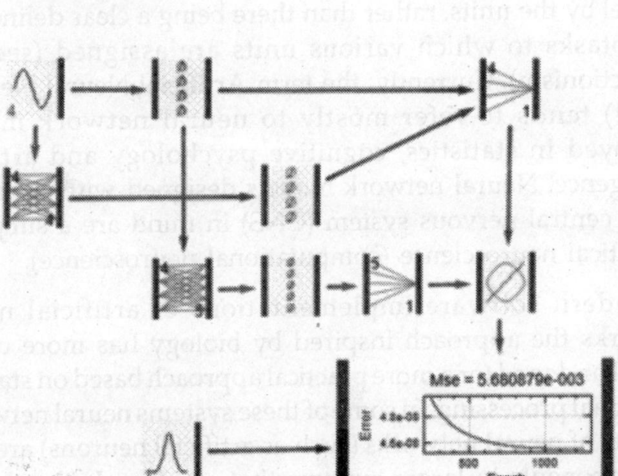

Component based representation of a neural network. This kind of more general representation is used by some neural network software.

There is no precise agreed-upon definition among researchers as to what a neural network is, but most would agree that it involves a network of simple processing elements (neurons), which can exhibit complex global behavior, determined by the connections between the processing elements and element parameters. The original inspiration for the technique was from examination of the central nervous system and the neurons (and their axons, dendrites and synapses) which constitute one of its most significant information processing elements (see Neuroscience). In a neural network model, simple nodes (called variously "neurons", "neurodes", "PEs" ("processing elements") or "units") are connected together to form a network of nodes — hence the term "neural network." While a neural network does not have to be adaptive per se, its practical use comes with algorithms designed to alter the strength (weights) of the connections in the network to produce a desired signal flow.

These networks are also similar to the biological neural networks in the sense that functions are performed collectively and in parallel by the units, rather than there being a clear delineation of subtasks to which various units are assigned (see also connectionism). Currently, the term Artificial Neural Network (ANN) tends to refer mostly to neural network models employed in statistics, cognitive psychology and artificial intelligence. Neural network models designed with emulation of the central nervous system (CNS) in mind are a subject of theoretical neuroscience (computational neuroscience).

In modern software implementations of artificial neural networks the approach inspired by biology has more or less been abandoned for a more practical approach based on statistics and signal processing. In some of these systems neural networks, or parts of neural networks (such as artificial neurons) are used as components in larger systems that combine both adaptive and non-adaptive elements. While the more general approach of such adaptive systems is more suitable for real-world problem solving, it has far less to do with the traditional artificial intelligence connectionist models. What they do, however, have in common is the principle of non-linear, distributed, parallel and local processing and adaptation.

14.5.2 Neural Network Models

Neural network models in artificial intelligence are usually referred to as artificial neural networks (ANNs); these are essentially simple mathematical models defining a function $f : X \rightarrow Y$. Each type of ANN model corresponds to a *class* of such functions.

The *network* in *artificial neural network*

The word *network* in the term 'artificial neural network' arises because the function $f(x)$ is defined as a composition of other functions $g_i(x)$, which can further be defined as a composition of other functions. This can be conveniently represented as a network structure, with arrows depicting the dependencies between variables. A widely used type of composition is the *nonlinear weighted sum*, where, where K is some predefined function, such as the hyperbolic tangent. It will be convenient for the following to refer to a collection of functions g_i as simply a vector $(g_1, g_2 \ldots\ldots, g_n)$.

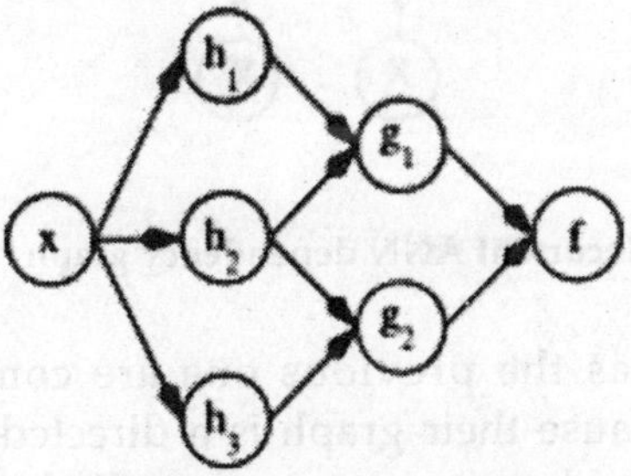

ANN dependency graph

This figure depicts such a decomposition of *f*, with dependencies between variables indicated by arrows. These can be interpreted in two ways.

The first view is the functional view: the input x is transformed into a 3-dimensional vector h, which is then transformed into a 2-dimensional vector g, which is finally transformed into f. This view is most commonly encountered in the context of optimization.

The second view is the probabilistic view: the random variable $F = f(G)$ depends upon the random variable $G = g(H)$, which depends upon $H = h(X)$, which depends upon the random variable X. This view is most commonly encountered in the context of graphical models.

The two views are largely equivalent. In either case, for this particular network architecture, the components of individual layers are independent of each other (e.g., the components of g are independent of each other given their input h). This naturally enables a degree of parallelism in the implementation.

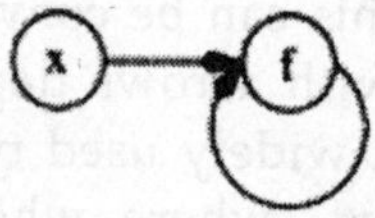

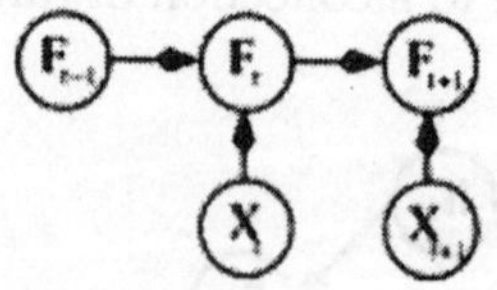

Recurrent ANN dependency graph

Networks such as the previous one are commonly called feedforward, because their graph is a directed acyclic graph. Networks with cycles are commonly called recurrent. Such networks are commonly depicted in the manner shown at the top of the figure, where f is shown as being dependent upon itself. However, there is an implied temporal dependence which is not shown.

14.5.3 Neural Network Learning

However interesting such functions may be in themselves, what has attracted the most interest in neural networks is the possibility of *learning*, which in practice means the following:

Given a specific *task* to solve, and a *class* of functions F, learning means using a set of *observations*, in order to find $f^* \in F$ which solves the task in an *optimal sense*.

This entails defining a cost function $C : F \rightarrow R$ such that, for the optimal solution f^*, $(f^*) \leq C(f) \quad f \in F$ (no solution has a cost less than the cost of the optimal solution).

The cost function C is an important concept in learning, as it is a measure of how far away we are from an optimal solution to the problem that we want to solve. Learning algorithms search through the solution space in order to find a function that has the smallest possible cost.

For applications where the solution is dependent on some data, the cost must necessarily be a *function of the observations*, otherwise we would not be modelling anything related to the data. It is frequently defined as a statistic to which only approximations can be made. As a simple example consider the problem of finding the model f which minimizes, $C = E\,[\{f(x)-y\}^2]$, for data pairs (x,y) drawn from some distribution D. In practical situations we would only have N samples from D and thus, for the above example, we would only minimize $C = \frac{1}{N}\sum_{i=1}^{N}(f(x_i) - y_i)^2$. Thus, the cost is minimized over a sample of the data rather than the true data distribution.

When $N \rightarrow \infty$ some form of online learning must be used, where the cost is partially minimized as each new example is seen. While online learning is often used when is fixed, it is most useful in the case where the distribution changes slowly over time. In neural network methods, some form of online learning is frequently also used for finite datasets.

1. Choosing a cost function

While it is possible to arbitrarily define some ad hoc cost function, frequently a particular cost will be used either because it has desirable properties (such as convexity) or because it arises naturally from a particular formulation of the problem (i.e., In a probabilistic formulation the posterior probability of the model can be used as an inverse cost). **Ultimately, the cost function will depend on the task we wish to perform**. The three main categories of learning tasks are overviewed below.

2. Learning paradigms

There are three major learning paradigms, each corresponding to a particular abstract learning task. These are supervised learning, unsupervised learning and reinforcement learning. Usually any given type of network architecture can be employed in any of those tasks.

3. Supervised learning

In supervised learning, we are given a set of example pairs (x, y), xεX, yεY and the aim is to find a function f : x → Yin the allowed class of functions that matches the examples. In other words, we wish to *infer* the mapping implied by the data; the cost function is related to the mismatch between our mapping and the data and it implicitly contains prior knowledge about the problem domain.

A commonly used cost is the mean-squared error which tries to minimize the average squared error between the network's output, f(x), and the target value y over all the example pairs. When one tries to minimise this cost using gradient descent for the class of neural networks called Multi-Layer Perceptrons, one obtains the common and well-known backpropagation algorithm for training neural networks.

Tasks that fall within the paradigm of supervised learning are pattern recognition (also known as classification) and regression (also known as function approximation). The supervised learning paradigm is also applicable to sequential data (e.g., for speech and gesture recognition). This can be thought of as learning with a "teacher," in the form of a function that provides continuous feedback on the quality of solutions obtained thus far.

4. Unsupervised learning

In unsupervised learning we are given some data x, and the cost function to be minimized can be any function of the data x and the network's output, f.

The cost function is dependent on the task (what we are trying to model) and our *a priori* assumptions (the implicit properties of our model, its parameters and the observed variables).

As a trivial example, consider the model $f(x) = a$, where a is a constant and the cost $C = E[(x - f(x))^2]$. Minimizing this cost will give us a value of a that is equal to the mean of the data. The cost function can be much more complicated. Its form depends on the application: For example in compression it could be related to the mutual information between x and y. In statistical modelling, it could be related to the posterior probability of the model given the data. (Note that in both of those examples those quantities would be maximized rather than minimised).

Tasks that fall within the paradigm of unsupervised learning are in general estimation problems; the applications include clustering, the estimation of statistical distributions, compression and filtering.

5. Reinforcement learning

In reinforcement learning, data x is usually not given, but generated by an agent's interactions with the environment. At each point in time t, the agent performs an action y_t and the environment generates an observation x_t and an instantaneous cost c_t, according to some (usually unknown) dynamics. The aim is to discover a *policy* for selecting actions that minimizes some measure of a long-term cost, i.e. the expected cumulative cost. The environment's dynamics and the long-term cost for each policy are usually unknown, but can be estimated.

More formally, the environment is modeled as a Markov decision process (MDP) with states $S_1,..., S_n$ ε_S and actions $a_1,..., a_m$ ε A with the following probability distributions: the instantaneous cost distribution $P(c_t \mid s_t)$, the observation distribution $P(x_t \mid s_t)$ and the transition $P(s_{t+1} \mid s_t, a_t)$, while a policy is defined as conditional distribution over actions given the observations. Taken together, the two define a Markov chain (MC). The aim is to discover the policy that minimizes the cost, i.e. the MC for which the cost is minimal.

ANNs are frequently used in reinforcement learning as part of the overall algorithm.

Tasks that fall within the paradigm of reinforcement learning are control problems, games and other sequential decision making tasks.

6. Learning algorithms

Training a neural network model essentially means selecting one model from the set of allowed models (or, in a Bayesian framework, determining a distribution over the set of allowed models) that minimises the cost criterion. There are numerous algorithms available for training neural network models; most of them can be viewed as a straightforward application of optimization theory and statistical estimation.

Most of the algorithms used in training artificial neural networks are employing some form of gradient descent. This is done by simply taking the derivative of the cost function with respect to the network parameters and then changing those parameters in a gradient-related direction.

Evolutionary methods, simulated annealing, and expectation-maximization and non-parametric methods are among other commonly used methods for training neural networks. See also machine learning.

Temporal perceptual learning relies on finding temporal relationships in sensory signal streams. In an environment, statistically salient temporal correlations can be found by monitoring the arrival times of sensory signals. This is done by the perceptual network.

7. Employing artificial neural networks

Perhaps the greatest advantage of ANNs is their ability to be used as an arbitrary function approximation mechanism which 'learns' from observed data. However, using them is not so straightforward and a relatively good understanding of the underlying theory is essential.

- Choice of model: This will depend on the data representation and the application. Overly complex models tend to lead to problems with learning.
- Learning algorithm: There are numerous tradeoffs between learning algorithms. Almost any algorithm will work well with the *correct hyperparameters* for training on a particular fixed dataset. However selecting and tuning an algorithm for training on unseen data requires a significant amount of experimentation.
- Robustness: If the model, cost function and learning algorithm are selected appropriately the resulting ANN can be extremely robust.

With the correct implementation ANNs can be used naturally in online learning and large dataset applications. Their simple implementation and the existence of mostly local dependencies exhibited in the structure allows for fast, parallel implementations in hardware.

8. Applications

The utility of artificial neural network models lies in the fact that they can be used to infer a function from observations. This is particularly useful in applications where the complexity of the data or task makes the design of such a function by hand impractical.

14.6 Real life applications

The tasks to which artificial neural networks are applied tend to fall within the following broad categories:

- Function approximation, or regression analysis, including time series prediction and modelling.

- Classification, including pattern and sequence recognition, novelty detection and sequential decision making.
- Data processing, including filtering, clustering, blind source separation and compression.

Application areas include system identification and control (vehicle control, process control), game-playing and decision making (backgammon, chess, racing), pattern recognition (radar systems, face identification, object recognition and more), sequence recognition (gesture, speech, handwritten text recognition), medical diagnosis, financial applications (automated trading systems), data mining (or knowledge discovery in databases, "KDD"), visualization and e-mail spam filtering.

14.7 Neural network software

Neural network software is used to simulate, research, develop and apply artificial neural networks, biological neural networks and in some cases a wider array of adaptive systems. See also logistic regression.

14.8 Types of neural networks

1. Feed forward neural network

The feedforward neural network was the first and arguably simplest type of artificial neural network devised. In this network, the information moves in only one direction, forward, from the input nodes, through the hidden nodes (if any) and to the output nodes. There are no cycles or loops in the network.

2. Radial basis function (RBF) network

Radial Basis Functions are powerful techniques for interpolation in multidimensional space. A RBF is a function which has built into a distance criterion with respect to a centre. Radial basis functions have been applied in the area of neural networks where they may be used as a replacement for the sigmoidal hidden layer transfer characteristic in Multi-Layer Perceptrons. RBF networks have two layers of processing: In the first, input is mapped onto each RBF in the 'hidden' layer. The RBF chosen is usually a Gaussian. In regression problems the output layer is then a linear combination of hidden layer values representing mean predicted output. The interpretation of this output layer value is the same as a regression model in statistics. In classification problems the output layer is typically a sigmoid function of a linear combination of hidden layer values, representing a posterior probability. Performance in both cases is often improved by shrinkage techniques, known as ridge regression in classical statistics and known to correspond to a prior belief in small parameter values (and therefore smooth output functions) in a Bayesian framework.

RBF networks have the advantage of not suffering from local minima in the same way as Multi-Layer Perceptrons. This is because the only parameters that are adjusted in the learning process are the linear mapping from hidden layer to output layer. Linearity ensures that the error surface is quadratic and therefore has a single easily found minimum. In regression problems this can be found in one matrix operation. In classification problems the fixed non-linearity introduced by the sigmoid output function is most efficiently dealt with using iteratively re-weighted least squares.

RBF networks have the disadvantage of requiring good coverage of the input space by radial basis functions. RBF centres are determined with reference to the distribution of the input data, but without reference to the prediction task. As a result, representational resources may be wasted on areas of the input space that are irrelevant to the learning task. A common solution is to associate each data point with its own centre, although this can make the linear system to be solved in the final layer rather large, and requires shrinkage techniques to avoid overfitting.

Associating each input datum with an RBF leads naturally to kernel methods such as Support Vector Machines and Gaussian Processes (the RBF is the kernel function). All three approaches use a non-linear kernel function to project the input data into a space where the learning problem can be solved using a linear model. Like Gaussian Processes, and unlike SVMs, RBF networks are typically trained in a Maximum Likelihood framework by maximizing the probability (minimizing the error) of the data under the model. SVMs take a different approach to avoiding overfitting by maximizing instead a margin. RBF networks are outperformed in most classification applications by SVMs. In regression applications they can be competitive when the dimensionality of the input space is relatively small.

3. Kohonen self-organizing network

The self-organizing map (SOM) invented by Teuvo Kohonen performs a form of unsupervised learning. A set of artificial neurons learn to map points in an input space to coordinates in an output space. The input space can have different dimensions and topology from the output space, and the SOM will attempt to preserve these.

4. Recurrent network

Contrary to feedforward networks, recurrent neural networks (RNs) are models with bi-directional data flow. While a feedforward network propagates data linearly from input to output, RNs also propagate data from later processing stages to earlier stages.

5. Simple recurrent network

A *simple recurrent network* (SRN) is a variation on the Multi-Layer Perceptron, sometimes called an "Elman network" due to its invention by Jeff Elman. A three-layer network is used, with the addition of a set of "context units" in the input layer. There are connections from the middle (hidden) layer to these context units fixed with a weight of one. At each time step, the input is propagated in a standard feed-forward fashion, and then a learning rule (usually back-propagation) is applied. The fixed back connections result in the context units always maintaining a copy of the previous values of the hidden units (since they propagate over the connections before the learning rule is applied). Thus the network can maintain a sort of state, allowing it to perform such tasks as sequence-prediction that are beyond the power of a standard Multi-Layer Perceptron.

In a *fully recurrent network,* every neuron receives inputs from every other neuron in the network. These networks are not arranged in layers. Usually only a subset of the neurons receive external inputs in addition to the inputs from all the other neurons, and another disjunct subset of neurons report their output externally as well as sending it to all the neurons. These distinctive inputs and outputs perform the function of the input and output layers of a feed-forward or simple recurrent network, and also join all the other neurons in the recurrent processing.

6. Hopfield network

The Hopfield network is a recurrent neural network in which all connections are symmetric. Invented by John Hopfield in 1982, this network guarantees that its dynamics will converge. If the connections are trained using Hebbian learning then the Hopfield network can perform as robust content-addressable (or associative) memory, resistant to connection alteration.

7. Echo state network

The echo state network (ESN) is a recurrent neural network with a sparsely connected random hidden layer. The weights of output neurons are the only part of the network that can change and be learned. ESN are good to (re)produce temporal patterns.

8. Long short term memory network

The Long short term memoryis an artificial neural net structure that unlike traditional RNNs doesn't have the problem of vanishing gradients. It can therefore use long delays and can handle signals that have a mix of low and high frequency components.

9. Stochastic neural networks

A stochastic neural network differs from a typical neural

network because it introduces random variations into the network. In a probabilistic view of neural networks, such random variations can be viewed as a form of statistical sampling, such as Monte Carlo sampling.

10. Boltzmann machine

The Boltzmann machine can be thought of as a noisy Hopfield network. Invented by Geoff Hinton and Terry Sejnowski in 1985, the Boltzmann machine is important because it is one of the first neural networks to demonstrate learning of latent variables (hidden units). Boltzmann machine learning was at first slow to simulate, but the contrastive divergence algorithm of Geoff Hinton (circa 2000) allows models such as Boltzmann machines and *products of experts* to be trained much faster.

11. Modular neural networks

Biological studies have shown that the human brain functions not as a single massive network, but as a collection of small networks. This realization gave birth to the concept of modular neural networks, in which several small networks cooperate or compete to solve problems.

12. Committee of machines

A committee of machines (CoM) is a collection of different neural networks that together "vote" on a given example. This generally gives a much better result compared to other neural network models. Because neural networks suffer from local minima, starting with the same architecture and training but using different initial random weights often gives vastly different networks. A CoM tends to stabilize the result.

The CoM is similar to the general machine learning *bagging* method, except that the necessary variety of machines in the committee is obtained by training from different random starting weights rather than training on different randomly selected subsets of the training data.

13. Associative neural network (ASNN)

The ASNN is an extension of the *committee of machines* that goes beyond a simple/weighted average of different models. ASNN represents a combination of an ensemble of feed-forward neural networks and the k-nearest neighbor technique (kNN). It uses the correlation between ensemble responses as a measure of **distance** amid the analyzed cases for the kNN. This corrects the bias of the neural network ensemble. An associative neural network has a memory that can coincide with the training set. If new data becomes available, the network instantly improves its predictive ability and provides data approximation (self-learn the data) without a need to retrain the ensemble. Another important feature of ASNN is the possibility to interpret neural network results by analysis of correlations between data cases in the space of models

14.9 Distributed control system

A **distributed control system** (DCS) refers to a control system usually of a manufacturing system, process or any kind of dynamic system, in which the controller elements are not central in location (like the brain) but are distributed throughout the system with each component sub-system controlled by one or more controllers. The entire system of controllers are connected by networks for communication and monitoring.

DCS is a very broad term used in a variety of industries, to monitor and control distributed equipment.

- Electrical power grids and electrical generation plants
- Environmental control systems
- Traffic signals
- Water management systems
- Oil refining plants
- Chemical plants
- Pharmaceutical manufacturing
- Sensor networks
- Dry cargo and bulk oil carrier ships

1. Elements

A DCS typically uses custom designed processors as controllers and uses both proprietary interconnections and Communications protocol for communication. Input & output modules form component parts of the DCS. The processor receives information from input modules and sends information to output modules. The input modules receive information from input instruments in the process (a.k.a. field) and transmit instructions to the output instruments in the field. Computer buses or electrical buses connect the processor and modules through multiplexer or demultiplexers. Buses also connect the distributed controllers with the central controller and finally to the Human-Machine Interface (HMI) or control consoles. See Process Automation System.

Elements of a distributed control system may directly connect to physical equipment such as switches, pumps and valves or may work through an intermediate system such as a SCADA system.

2. Applications

Distributed Control Systems (DCSs) are dedicated systems used to control manufacturing processes that are continuous or batch-oriented, such as oil refining, petrochemicals, central station power generation, pharmaceuticals, food & beverage manufacturing, cement production, steelmaking, and papermaking. DCSs are connected to sensors and actuators and use setpoint control to control the flow of material through the plant. The most common example is a setpoint control loop consisting of a pressure sensor, controller, and control valve. Pressure or flow measurements are transmitted to the controller, usually through the aid of a signal conditioning Input/Output (I/O) device. When the measured variable reaches a certain point, the controller instructs a valve or actuation device to open or close until the fluidic flow process reaches the desired setpoint. Large oil refineries have many thousands of I/O points and employ very large DCSs. Processes are not limited to fluidic flow through pipes, however, and can also include things like paper machines and their associated variable speed drives and motor control centers, cement kilns, mining operations, ore processing facilities, and many others.

A typical DCS consists of functionally and/or geographically distributed digital controllers capable of executing from 1 to 256 or more regulatory control loops in one control box. The input/output devices (I/O) can be integral with the controller or located remotely via a field network. Today's controllers have extensive computational capabilities and, in addition to proportional, integral, and derivative (PID) control, can generally perform logic and sequential control.

DCSs may employ one or several workstations and can be configured at the workstation or by an off-line personal computer. Local communication is handled by a control network with transmission over twisted pair, coaxial, or fiber optic cable. A server and/or applications processor may be included in the system for extra computational, data collection, and reporting capability.

3. History

Early minicomputers were used in the control of industrial processes since the beginning of the 1960s. The IBM 1800, for example, was an early computer that had input/output hardware to gather process signals in a plant for conversion from field contact levels (for digital points) and analog signals to the digital domain.

The DCS was introduced in 1975. Both Honeywell and Japanese electrical engineering firm Yokogawa introduced their own independently produced DCSs at roughly the same time, with the TDC 2000 and CENTUM[1] systems, respectively. US-based Bristol also introduced their UCS 3000 universal controller in 1975. In 1980, Bailey (now part of ABB[2]) introduced the NETWORK 90 system. Also in 1980, Fischer & Porter Company (now also part of ABB[3]) introducted DCI-4000 (DCI stands for Distributed Control Instrumentation).

The DCS largely came about due to the increased availability of microcomputers and the proliferation of microprocessors in the world of process control. Computers had already been applied to process automation for some time in the form of both Direct Digital Control (DDC) and Set Point Control. In the early 1970s Taylor Instrument Company, (now part of ABB) developed the 1010 system, Foxboro the FOX1 system and Bailey Controls the 1055 systems. All of these were DDC applications implemented within mini-computers (DEC PDP 11, Varian Data Machines, MODCOMP etc) and connected to proprietary Input/Output hardware. Sophisticated (for the time) continuous as well as batch control was implemented in this way. A more conservative approach was Set Point Control , where process computers supervised clusters of analog process controllers. A CRT-based workstation provided visibility into the process using text and crude character graphics. Availability of a fully functional graphical user interface was a way away.

Central to the DCS model was the inclusion of control function blocks. Function blocks evolved from early, more primitive DDC concepts of "Table Driven" software. One of the first embodiments of object-oriented software, function blocks were self contained "blocks" of code that emulated analog hardware control components and performed tasks that were essential to process control, such as execution of PID algorithms. Function blocks continue to endure as the predominant method of control for DCS suppliers, and are supported by key technologies such as Foundation Fieldbus today.

Digital communication between distributed controllers, workstations and other computing elements (peer to peer access) was one of the primary advantages of the DCS. Attention was duly focused on the networks, which provided the all-important lines of communication that, for process applications, had to incorporate specific functions such as determinism and redundancy. As a result, many suppliers embraced the IEEE 802.4 networking standard. This decision set the stage for the wave of migrations necessary when information technology moved into process automation and IEEE 802.3 rather than IEEE 802.4 prevailed as the control LAN.

The Network Centric Era of the 1980s

The DCS brought distributed intelligence to the plant and established the presence of computers and microprocessors in process control, but it still did not provide the reach and openness necessary to unify plant resource requirements. In many cases, the DCS was merely a digital replacement of the same functionality provided by analog controllers and a panelboard display. This was embodied in The Purdue Reference Model (PRM) that was developed to define Manufacturing Operations Management relationships. PRM later formed the basis for ISA95 standards activities today.

In the 1980s, users began to look at DCSs as more than just basic process control. A very early example of a Direct Digital Control DCS was completed by the Australian business Midac in 1981-1982 using R-Tec Australian designed hardware. The system installed at the University of Melbourne used a serial communications network, connecting campusbuildings back to a control room "front end". Each remote unit ran 2 Z80 microprocessors whilst the front end ran 11 in a Parallel Processing configuration with paged common memory to share tasks and could run up to 20,000 concurrent controls objects.

It was believed that if openness could be achieved and greater amounts of data could be shared throughout the enterprise that even greater things could be achieved. The first attempts to increase the openness of DCSs resulted in the adoption of the predominant operating system of the day: *UNIX*. UNIX and its companion networking technology TCP-IP were developed by the Department of Defense for openness, which was precisely the issue the process industries were looking to resolve.

As a result suppliers also began to adopt Ethernet-based networks with their own proprietary protocol layers. The full TCP/IP standard was not implemented, but the use of Ethernet made it possible to implement the first instances of object management and global data access technology. The 1980s also witnessed the first PLCs integrated into the DCS infrastructure. Plant-wide historians also emerged to capitalize on the extended reach of automation systems. The first DCS supplier to adopt UNIX and Ethernet networking technologies was Foxboro, who introduced the I/A Series system in 1987.

The Application Centric Era of the 1990s

The drive toward openness in the 1980s gained momentum through the 1990s with the increased adoption of Commercial-Off-The-Shelf (COTS) components and IT standards. Probably the biggest transition undertaken during this time was the move from the UNIX operating system to the Windows environment. While the realm of the real time operating system (RTOS) for control applications remains dominated by real time commercial variants of UNIX or proprietary operating systems, everything above real-time control has made the transition to Windows.

The invasion of Microsoft at the desktop and server layers resulted in the development of technologies such as OLE for Process Control (OPC), which is now a de facto industry connectivity standard. Internet technology also began to make its mark in automation and the DCS world, with most DCS HMI supporting Internet connectivity. The '90s were also known for the "Fieldbus Wars", where rival organizations competed to define what would become the IEC fieldbus standard for digital communication with field instrumentation instead of 4-20 milliamp analog communications. The first fieldbus installations occurred in the 1990s. Towards the end of the decade, the technology began to develop significant momentum, with the market consolidated around Foundation Fieldbus and Profibus PA for process automation applications. Some suppliers built new systems from the ground up to maximize functionality with fieldbus, such as ABB with System 800xA, **Emerson Process Management** with the DeltaV control system, **Siemens**[with the Simatic PCS7 and **azbil**from Yamatake with the Harmonas-DEO system.

The impact of COTS, however, was most pronounced at the hardware layer. For years, the primary business of DCS suppliers had been the supply of large amounts of hardware, particularly I/O and controllers. The initial proliferation of DCSs required the installation of prodigious amounts of this hardware, most of it manufactured from the bottom up by DCS suppliers. Standard computer components from manufacturers such as Intel and Motorola, however, made it cost prohibitive for DCS suppliers to continue making their own components, workstations, and networking hardware.

As the suppliers made the transition to COTS components, they also discovered that the hardware market was shrinking fast. COTS not only resulted in lower manufacturing costs for the supplier, but also steadily decreasing prices for the end users, who were also becoming increasingly vocal over what they perceived to be unduly high hardware costs. Some suppliers that were previously stronger in the PLC business, such as Rockwell Automation, Schnieder and Siemens, were able to leverage their expertise in manufacturing control hardware to enter the DCS marketplace with cost effective offerings. The traditional DCS suppliers introduced new generation DCS System based on the latest Communication and IEC Standards, which resulting in a trend of combining the traditional concepts/ functionalities for PLC and DCS into a one for all solution – named "Process Automation System/Controller".

To compound the issue, suppliers were also realizing that the hardware market was becoming saturated. The lifecycle of hardware components such as I/O and wiring is also typically in the range of 15 to over 20 years, making for a challenging replacement market. Many of the older systems that were installed in the 1970s and 1980s are still in use today, and there is a considerable installed base of systems in the market that are approaching the end of their useful life. Developed industrial economies in North America, Europe, and Japan already had many thousands of DCSs installed, and with few if any new plants being built, the market for new hardware was shifting rapidly to smaller, albeit faster growing regions such as China, Latin America, and Eastern Europe.

Because of the shrinking hardware business, suppliers began to make the challenging transition from a hardware-based business model to one based on software and value-added services. It is a transition that is still being made today. The applications portfolio offered by suppliers expanded considerably in the '90s to include areas such as production management, model-based control, real-time optimization, Plant Asset Management (PAM), Real Time Performance Management (RPM) tools, alarm management, and many others. To obtain the true value from these applications, however, often requires a considerable service content, which the suppliers also provide. DCS supplier such as azbil known as Yamatake services have also expanded in scope to the point where many suppliers can act as Main Automation Contractors (MACs), providing a single point of responsibility for all automation-related facets of a project.

14.10 Human-Machine Interface (HMI) / User interface

The **user interface** (also known as *Human Computer Interface* or *Man-Machine Interface* (MMI)) is the aggregate of means by which people – *the users* – interact with *the system* – a particular machine, device, computer program or other complex tool. The user interface provides means of:

- Input, allowing the users to manipulate a system
- Output, allowing the system to indicate the effects of the users' manipulation.

1. Introduction

To work with a system, users have to be able to control the system and assess the state of the system. For example, when driving an automobile, the driver uses the steering wheel to control the direction of the vehicle, and the accelerator pedal, brake pedal and gearstick to control the speed of the vehicle. The driver perceives the position of the vehicle by looking through the windscreen and exact speed of the vehicle by reading the speedometer. The *user interface of the automobile* is on the whole composed of the instruments the driver can use to accomplish the tasks of driving and maintaining the automobile.

The term *user interface* is often used in the context of computer systems and electronic devices. The user interface of a mechanical system, a vehicle or an industrial installation is sometimes referred to as the **Human-Machine Interface** (**HMI**). HMI is a modification of the original term MMI (Man-Machine Interface). In practice, the abbreviation MMI is still frequently used although some may claim that MMI stands for something different now. Another abbreviation is HCI, but is more commonly used for Human-computer *interaction* than Human-computer *interface*. Other terms used are Operator Interface Console (OIC) and Operator Interface Terminal (OIT).

However it is abbreviated, the terms refer to the 'layer' that separates a human that is operating a machine from the machine itself.

In science fiction, HMI is sometimes used to refer to what is better described as direct neural interface. However, this latter usage is seeing increasing application in the real-life use of (medical) prostheses – the artificial extension that replaces a missing body part (e.g., cochlear implants).

The system may expose several user interfaces to serve different kinds of users. For example, a computerized library database might provide two user interfaces, one for library patrons (limited set of functions, optimized for ease of use) and the other for library personnel (wide set of functions, optimized for efficiency).

In some circumstance computers might observe the user, and react according to their actions without specific commands. A means of tracking parts of the body is required, and sensors noting the position of the head, direction of gaze and so on have been used experimentally. This is particularly relevant to immersive interfaces.

2. Usability

The design of a user interface affects the amount of effort the user must expend to provide input for the system and to interpret the output of the system, and how much effort it takes to learn how to do this. Usability is the degree to which the design of a particular user interface takes into account the human psychology and physiology of the users, and makes the process of using the system effective, efficient and satisfying.

Usability is mainly a characteristic of the user interface, but is also associated with the functionalities of the product and the process to design it. It describes how well a product can be used for its intended purpose by its target users with efficiency, effectiveness, and satisfaction, also taking into account the requirements from its context of use.

3. User interfaces in computing

In computer science and human-computer interaction, the *user interface (of a computer program)* refers to the graphical, textual and auditory information the program presents to the user, and the control sequences (such as keystrokes with the computer keyboard, movements of the computer mouse, and selections with the touchscreen) the user employs to control the program.

14.10.1 Types

Currently (as of 2009) the following types of user interface are the most common:

- **Graphical user interfaces** (GUI) accept input via devices such as computer keyboard and mouse and provide articulated graphical output on the computer monitor. There are at least two different principles widely used in GUI design: Object-oriented user interfaces (OOUIs) and application oriented interfaces.

- **Web-based user interfaces** or **web user interfaces** (WUI) accept input and provide output by generating web pages which are transmitted via the Internet and viewed by the user using a web browser program. Newer implementations utilize Java, AJAX, Adobe Flex, Microsoft .NET, or similar technologies to provide realtime control in a separate program, eliminating the need to refresh a traditional HTML based web browser. Administrative web interfaces for web-servers, servers and networked computers are called Control panel.

User interfaces that are common in various fields outside desktop computing:

- **Command line interfaces**, where the user provides the input by typing a command string with the computer keyboard and the system provides output by printing text on the computer monitor. Used for system administration tasks etc.
- **Tactile interfaces** supplement or replace other forms of output with haptic feedback methods. Used in computerized simulators etc.
- **Touch interfaces** are graphical user interfaces using a touchscreen display as a combined input and output device. Used in many types of point of sale, industrial processes and machines, self-service machines etc.

Other types of user interfaces:

- **Attentive user interfaces** manage the user attention deciding when to interrupt the user, the kind of warnings, and the level of detail of the messages presented to the user.
- **Batch interfaces** are non-interactive user interfaces, where the user specifies all the details of the *batch job* in advance to batch processing, and receives the output when all the processing is done. The computer does not prompt for further input after the processing has started.
- **Conversational Interface Agents** attempt to personify the computer interface in the form of an animated person, robot, or other character (such as Microsoft's Clippy the paperclip), and present interactions in a conversational form.
- **Crossing-based interfaces** are graphical user interfaces in which the primary task consists in crossing boundaries instead of pointing.
- **Gesture interfaces** are graphical user interfaces which accept input in a form of hand gestures, or mouse gestures sketched with a computer mouse or a stylus.
- **Intelligent user interfaces** are human-machine interfaces

that aim to improve the efficiency, effectiveness, and naturalness of human-machine interaction by representing, reasoning, and acting on models of the user, domain, task, discourse, and media (e.g., graphics, natural language, gesture).

- **Multi-screen interfaces,** employ multiple displays to provide a more flexible interaction. This is often employed in computer game interaction in both the commercial arcades and more recently the handheld markets.
- **Noncommand user interfaces,** which observe the user to infer his / her needs and intentions, without requiring that he / she formulate explicit commands.
- Object-oriented User Interface (OOUI)
- **Reflexive user interfaces** where the users control and redefine the entire system via the user interface alone, for instance to change its command verbs. Typically this is only possible with very rich graphic user interfaces.
- **Tangible user interfaces**, which place a greater emphasis on touch and physical environment or its element.
- **Text user interfaces** are user interfaces which output text, but accept other form of input in addition to or in place of typed command strings.
- **Voice user interfaces,** which accept input and provide output by generating voice prompts which are transmitted via a telephone network and heard by the user using a telephone. The user input is made by pressing telephone keys.
- **Natural-Language interfaces** - Used for search engines and on webpages. User types in a question and waits for a response.
- **Zero-Input interfaces** get inputs from a set of sensors instead of querying the user with input dialogs.
- **Zooming user interfaces** are graphical user interfaces in which information objects are represented at different levels of scale and detail, and where the user can change the scale of the viewed area in order to show more detail.

History

The history of user interfaces can be divided into the following phases according to the dominant type of user interface:

- Batch interface, 1945-1968
- Command-line user interface, 1969 to present
- Graphical user interface, 1981 to present – see History of the GUI for a detailed look
- Tangible interfaces / Ubicomp
- Touch User Interface (TUI), e.g. point of sale devices, iPhone

Modalities and modes

A **modality** is a path of communication employed by

the user interface to carry input and output. Examples of modalities:

- Input – computer keyboard allows the user to enter typed text, digitizing tablet allows the user to create free-form drawing
- Output – computer monitor allows the system to display text and graphics (*vision modality*), loudspeaker allows the system to produce sound (*auditory modality*)

The user interface may employ several redundant input modalities and output modalities, allowing the user to choose which ones to use for interaction.

A **mode** is a distinct method of operation within a computer program, in which the same input can produce different perceived results depending of the state of the computer program. Heavy use of modes often reduces the usability of a user interface, as the user must expend effort to remember current mode states, and switch between mode states as necessary.

Standardization

This year ISO has published its standard of ISO/IEC 24752 to specify the technical requirement of IT system.

Supervisory Control and Data Acquisition SCADA

14.11 SCADA stands for *Supervisory Control And Data Acquisition.* It generally refers to an industrial control system: a computer system monitoring and controlling a process. The process can be industrial, infrastructure or facility based as described below:

- Industrial processes include those of manufacturing, production, power generation, fabrication, and refining, and may run in continuous, batch, repetitive, or discrete modes.
- Infrastructure processes may be public or private, and include water treatment and distribution, wastewater collection and treatment, oil and gas pipelines, electrical power transmission and distribution, and large communication systems.
- Facility processes occur both in public facilities and private ones, including buildings, airports, ships, and space stations. They monitor and control HVAC, access, and energy consumption.

14.11.1 A SCADA System usually consists of the following subsystems:

- A Human-Machine Interface or HMI is the apparatus which presents process data to a human operator, and through this, the human operator, monitors and controls the process.
- A supervisory (computer) system, gathering (acquiring) data on the process and sending commands (control) to the process.
- Remote Terminal Units (RTUs) connecting to sensors in the process, converting sensor signals to digital data and sending digital data to the supervisory system.
- Communication infrastructure connecting the supervisory system to the Remote Terminal Units

There is, in several industries, considerable confusion over the differences between SCADA systems and Distributed control systems (DCS). Generally speaking, a SCADA system usually refers to a system that **coordinates**, but does not **control** processes in real time. The discussion on real-time control is muddied somewhat by newer telecommunications technology, enabling reliable, low latency, high speed communications over wide areas. Most differences between SCADA and Distributed control system DCS are culturally determined and can usually be ignored. As communication infrastructures with higher capacity become available, the difference between SCADA and DCS will fade.

1. Systems concepts

The term SCADA usually refers to centralized systems which monitor and control entire sites, or complexes of systems spread out over large areas (anything between an industrial plant and a country). Most control actions are performed automatically by remote terminal units ("RTUs") or by programmable logic controllers ("PLCs"). Host control functions are usually restricted to basic overriding or *supervisory* level intervention. For example, a PLC may control the flow of cooling water through part of an industrial process, but the SCADA system may allow operators to change the set points for the flow, and enable alarm conditions, such as loss of flow and high temperature, to be displayed and recorded. The feedback control loop passes through the RTU or PLC, while the SCADA system monitors the overall performance of the loop.

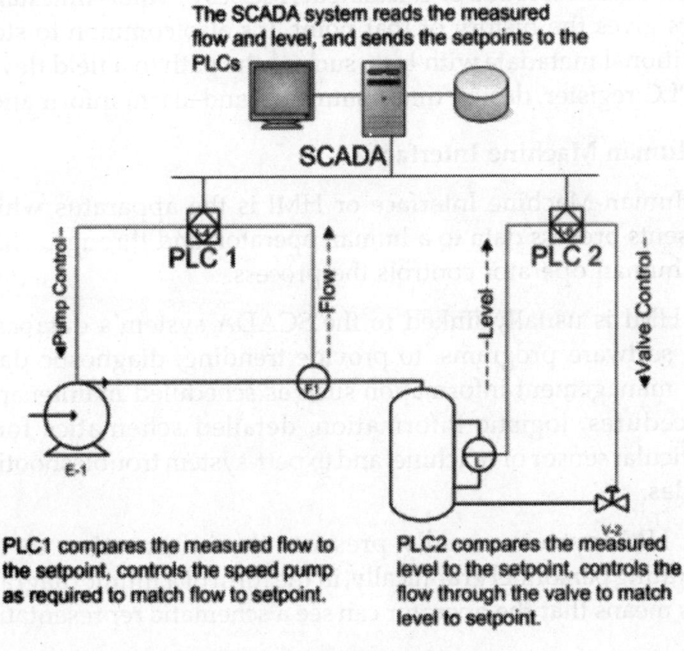

Data acquisition begins at the RTU or PLC level and includes meter readings and equipment status reports that are communicated to SCADA as required. Data is then compiled and formatted in such a way that a control room operator using the HMI can make supervisory decisions to adjust or override normal RTU (PLC) controls. Data may also be fed to a Historian, often built on a commodity Database Management System, to allow trending and other analytical auditing.

SCADA systems typically implement a distributed database, commonly referred to as a *tag database*, which contains data elements called *tags* or *points*. A point represents a single input or output value monitored or controlled by the system. Points can be either "hard" or "soft". A hard point represents an actual input or output within the system, while a soft point results from logic and math operations applied to other points. (Most implementations conceptually remove the distinction by making every property a "soft" point expression, which may, in the simplest case, equal a single hard point.) Points are normally stored as value-timestamp pairs: a value, and the timestamp when it was recorded or calculated. A series of value-timestamp pairs gives the history of that point. It's also common to store additional metadata with tags, such as the path to a field device or PLC register, design time comments, and alarm information.

2. Human Machine Interface

A Human-Machine Interface or HMI is the apparatus which presents process data to a human operator, and through which the human operator controls the process.

An HMI is usually linked to the SCADA system's databases and software programs, to provide trending, diagnostic data, and management information such as scheduled maintenance procedures, logistic information, detailed schematics for a particular sensor or machine, and expert-system troubleshooting guides.

The HMI system usually presents the information to the operating personnel graphically, in the form of a mimic diagram. This means that the operator can see a schematic representation of the plant being controlled. For example, a picture of a pump connected to a pipe can show the operator that the pump is running and how much fluid it is pumping through the pipe at the moment. The operator can then switch the pump off. The HMI software will show the flow rate of the fluid in the pipe decrease in real time. Mimic diagrams may consist of line graphics and schematic symbols to represent process elements, or may consist of digital photographs of the process equipment overlain with animated symbols.

The HMI package for the SCADA system typically includes a drawing program that the operators or system maintenance personnel use to change the way these points are represented in the interface. These representations can be as simple as an on-screen traffic light, which represents the state of an actual traffic light in the field, or as complex as a multi-projector display representing the position of all of the elevators in a skyscraper or all of the trains on a railway.

An important part of most SCADA implementations are alarms. An alarm is a digital status point that has either the value NORMAL or ALARM. Alarms can be created in such a way that when their requirements are met, they are activated. An example of an alarm is the "fuel tank empty" light in a car. The SCADA operator's attention is drawn to the part of the system requiring attention by the alarm. Emails and text messages are often sent along with an alarm activation alerting managers along with the SCADA operator.

3. Hardware solutions

SCADA solutions often have Distributed Control System (DCS) components. Use of "smart" RTUs or PLCs, which are capable of autonomously executing simple logic processes without involving the master computer, is increasing. A functional block programming language, IEC 61131-3 (Ladder Logic), is frequently used to create programs which run on these RTUs and PLCs. Unlike a procedural language such as the C programming language or FORTRAN, IEC 61131-3 has minimal training requirements by virtue of resembling historic physical control arrays. This allows SCADA system engineers to perform both the design and implementation of a program to be executed on an RTU or PLC. Since about 1998, virtually all major PLC manufacturers have offered integrated HMI/SCADA systems, many of them using open and non-proprietary communications protocols. Numerous specialized third-party HMI/SCADA packages, offering built-in compatibility with most major PLCs, have also entered the market, allowing mechanical engineers, electrical engineers and technicians to configure HMIs themselves, without the need for a custom-made program written by a software developer.

4. Remote Terminal Unit (RTU)

The RTU connects to physical equipment. Typically, an RTU converts the electrical signals from the equipment to digital values such as the open/closed status from a switch or a valve, or measurements such as pressure, flow, voltage or current. By converting and sending these electrical signals out to equipment the RTU can control equipment, such as opening or closing a switch or a valve, or setting the speed of a pump.

Quality SCADA RTUs have these characteristics

5. Supervisory Station

The term "Supervisory Station" refers to the servers and software responsible for communicating with the field equipment (RTUs, PLCs, etc), and then to the HMI software running on workstations in the control room, or elsewhere. In smaller SCADA systems, the master station may be composed of a single PC. In larger SCADA systems, the master station may include multiple servers, distributed software applications, and disaster recovery sites. To increase the integrity of the system the multiple servers will often be configured in a dual-redundant or hot-standby formation providing continuous control and monitoring in the event of a server failure.

Initially, more "open" platforms such as Linux were not as widely used due to the highly dynamic development environment and because a SCADA customer that was able to afford the field hardware and devices to be controlled could usually also purchase UNIX or OpenVMS licenses. Today, all major operating systems are used for both master station servers and HMI workstations.

6. Operational philosophy

For some installations, the costs that would result from the control system failing are extremely high. Possibly even lives could be lost. Hardware for some SCADA systems is ruggedized to withstand temperature, vibration, and voltage extremes, but in most critical installations reliability is enhanced by having redundant hardware and communications channels, up to the point of having multiple fully equipped control centres. A failing part can be quickly identified and its functionality automatically taken over by backup hardware. A failed part can often be replaced without interrupting the process. The reliability of such systems can be calculated statistically and is stated as the mean time to failure, which is a variant of mean time between failures. The calculated mean time to failure of such high reliability systems can be on the order of centuries.

7. Communication infrastructure and methods

SCADA systems have traditionally used combinations of radio and direct serial or modem connections to meet communication requirements, although Ethernet and IP over SONET / SDH is also frequently used at large sites such as railways and power stations. The remote management or monitoring function of a SCADA system is often referred to as telemetry.

This has also come under threat with some customers wanting SCADA data to travel over their pre-established corporate networks or to share the network with other applications. The legacy of the early low-bandwidth protocols remains, though. SCADA protocols are designed to be very compact and many are designed to send information to the master station only when the master station polls the RTU. Typical legacy SCADA protocols include Modbus RTU, RP-570, Profibus and Conitel. These communication protocols are all SCADA-vendor specific but are widely adopted and used. Standard protocols are IEC 60870-5-101 or 104, IEC 61850 and DNP3. These communication protocols are standardized and recognizedby all major SCADA vendors. Many of these protocols now contain extensions to operate over TCP/IP. It is good security engineering practice to avoid connecting SCADA systems to the Internet so the attack surface is reduced.

RTUs and other automatic controller devices were being developed before the advent of industry wide standards for interoperability. The result is that developers and their management created a multitude of control protocols. Among the larger vendors, there was also the incentive to create their own protocol to "lock in" their customer base. A list of automation protocols is being compiled here.

Recently, OLE for Process Control (OPC) has become a widely accepted solution for intercommunicating different hardware and software, allowing communication even between devices originally not intended to be part of an industrial network.

14.12 Programmable logic controller (PLC)

A **programmable logic controller** (PLC) or **programmable controller** is a digital computer used for automation of electromechanical processes, such as control of machinery on factory assembly lines, control of amusement rides, or control of lighting fixtures. PLCs are used in many different industries and machines such as packaging and semiconductor machines. Unlike general-purpose computers, the PLC is designed for multiple inputs and output arrangements, extended temperature ranges, immunity to electrical noise, and resistance to vibration and impact. Programs to control machine operation are typically stored in battery-backed or non-volatile memory. A PLC is an example of a real time system since output results must be produced in response to input conditions within a bounded time, otherwise unintended operation will result.

Control panel with PLC (grey elements in the center). The unit consists of separate elements, from left to right; power supply, controller, relay units for in- and output

The main difference from other computers is that PLCs are armored for severe conditions (dust, moisture, heat, cold, etc) and have the facility for extensive input/output (I/O) arrangements. These connect the PLC to sensors and actuators. PLCs read limit switches, analog process variables (such as temperature and pressure), and the positions of complex positioning systems. Some even use machine vision. On the actuator side, PLCs operate electric motors, pneumatic or hydraulic cylinders, magnetic relays or solenoids, or analog outputs. The input/output arrangements may be built into a simple PLC, or the PLC may have external I/O modules attached to a computer network that plugs into the PLC.

1. System scale

A small PLC will have a fixed number of connections built in for inputs and outputs. Typically, expansions are available if the base model does not have enough I/O.

Modular PLCs have a chassis (also called a rack) into which are placed modules with different functions. The processor and selection of I/O modules is customised for the particular application. Several racks can be administered by a single processor, and may have thousands of inputs and outputs. A special high speed serial I/O link is used so that racks can be distributed away from the processor, reducing the wiring costs for large plants.

2. User interface

PLCs may need to interact with people for the purpose of configuration, alarm reporting or everyday control.

A Human-Machine Interface (HMI) is employed for this purpose. HMIs are also referred to as MMIs (Man Machine Interface) and GUI (Graphical User Interface).

A simple system may use buttons and lights to interact with the user. Text displays are available as well as graphical touch screens. More complex systems use a programming and monitoring software installed on a computer, with the PLC connected via a communication interface..

3. Communications

PLCs have built in communications ports usually 9-Pin RS232, and optionally for RS485 and Ethernet. Modbus or DF1 is usually included as one of the communications protocols. Others' options include various fieldbuses suchas DeviceNet or Profibus. Other communications protocols that may be used are listed in the List of automation protocols.

Most modern PLCs can communicate over a network to some other system, such as a computer running a SCADA (Supervisory Control And Data Acquisition) system or web browser.

PLCs used in larger I/O systems may have peer-to-peer (P2P) communication between processors. This allows separate parts of a complex process to have individual control while allowing the subsystems to co-ordinate over the communication link. These communication links are also often used for HMI (Human-Machine Interface) devices such as keypads or PC-type workstations. Some of today's PLCs can communicate over a wide range of media including RS-485, Coaxial, and even Ethernet for I/O control at network speeds up to 100 Mbit/s.

4. PLC compared with other control systems

PLCs are well-adapted to a range of automation tasks. These are typically industrial processes in manufacturing where the cost of developing and maintaining the automation system is high relative to the total cost of the automation, and where changes to the system would be expected during its operational life. PLCs contain input and output devices compatible with industrial pilot devices and controls; little electrical design is required, and the design problem centers on expressing the desired sequence of operations in ladder logic (or function chart) notation. PLC applications are typically highly customized systems so the cost of a packaged PLC is low compared to the cost of a specific custom-built controller design. On the other hand, in the case of mass-produced goods, customized control systems are economic due to the lower cost of the components, which can be optimally chosen instead of a "generic" solution, and where the non-recurring engineering charges are spread over thousands or millions of units.

For high volume or very simple fixed automation tasks, different techniques are used. For example, a consumer dishwasher would be controlled by an electromechanical cam timer costing only a few dollars in production quantities.

A microcontroller-based design would be appropriate where hundreds or thousands of units will be produced and so the development cost (design of power supplies and input/output hardware) can be spread over many sales, and where the end-user would not need to alter the control. Automotive applications are an example; millions of units are built each year, and very few end-users alter the programming of these controllers. However, some specialty vehicles such as transit busses economically use PLCs instead of custom-designed controls, because the volumes are low and the development cost would be uneconomic.

Very complex process control, such as used in the chemical industry, may require algorithms and performance beyond the capability of even high-performance PLCs. Very high-speed or precision controls may also require customized solutions; for example, aircraft flight controls.

Programmable controllers are widely used in motion control, positioning control and torque control. Some manufacturers produce motion control units to be integrated with PLC so that G-code (involving a CNC machine) can be used to instruct machine movements.[1]

PLCs may include logic for single-variable feedback analog control loop, a "proportional, integral, derivative" or "PID controller." A PID loop could be used to control the temperature of a manufacturing process, for example. Historically PLCs were usually configured with only a few analog control loops; where processes required hundreds or thousands of loops, a distributed control system (DCS) would instead be used. However, as PLCs have become more powerful, the boundary between DCS and PLC applications has become less clear-cut.

PLCs have similar functionality as Remote Terminal Units. An RTU, however, usually does not support control algorithms or control loops. As hardware rapidly becomes more powerful and cheaper, RTUs, PLCs and DCSs are increasingly beginning to overlap in responsibilities, and many vendors sell RTUs with PLC-like features and vice versa. The industry has standardized on the IEC 61131-3 functional block language for creating programs to run on RTUs and PLCs, although nearly all vendors also offer proprietary alternatives and associated development environments.

Index

A

B

C

D

E

F

G